D0846973

The CALVIN INSTITUTE OF CHRISTIAN WORSHIP LITURGICAL STUDIES Series, edited by John D. Witvliet, is designed to promote reflection on the history, theology, and practice of Christian worship and to stimulate worship renewal in Christian congregations. Contributions include writings by pastoral worship leaders from a wide range of communities and scholars from a wide range of disciplines. The ultimate goal of these contributions is to nurture worship practices that are spiritually vital and theologically rooted.

PUBLISHED

The Pastor as Minor Poet
M. Craig Barnes

Touching the Altar: The Old Testament and Christian Worship
Carol M. Bechtel, Editor

Resonant Witness: Conversations between Music and Theology
Jeremy S. Begbie and Steven R. Guthrie, Editors

God Against Religion: Rethinking Christian Theology through Worship
Matthew Myer Boulton

By the Vision of Another World: Worship in American History
James D. Bratt, Editor

Inclusive yet Discerning: Navigating Worship Artfully
Frank Burch Brown

What Language Shall I Borrow? The Bible and Christian Worship
Ronald P. Byars

A Primer on Worship
William Dyrness

Christian Worship Worldwide: Expanding Horizons, Deepening Practices
Charles E. Farhadian

Dwelling with Philippians: A Conversation with Scripture through Image and Word
Elizabeth Steele Halstead, Paul Detterman, Joyce Borger, and John D. Witvliet

Gather into One: Praying and Singing Globally
C. Michael Hawn

The Substance of Things Seen: Art, Faith, and the Christian Community
Robin M. Jensen

Our Worship
Abraham Kuyper, Edited by Harry Boonstra

Wonderful Words of Life:
Hymns in American Protestant History and Theology
Richard J. Mouw and Mark A. Noll, Editors

Discerning the Spirits:
A Guide to Thinking about Christian Worship Today
Cornelius Plantinga Jr. and Sue A. Rozeboom

Voicing God's Psalms
Calvin Seerveld

My Only Comfort: Death, Deliverance, and Discipleship
in the Music of Bach
Calvin R. Stapert

A New Song for an Old World: Musical Thought in the Early Church
Calvin R. Stapert

An Architecture of Immanence: Architecture for Worship and Ministry Today
Mark A. Torgerson

A More Profound Alleluia: Theology and Worship in Harmony
Leanne Van Dyk, Editor

Christian Worship in Reformed Churches Past and Present
Lukas Vischer, Editor

We Have Seen His Glory: A Vision of Kingdom Worship
Ben Witherington III

*The Biblical Psalms in Christian Worship:
A Brief Introduction and Guide to Resources*
John D. Witvliet

By the Vision of Another World

Worship in American History

Edited by

James D. Bratt

WILLIAM B. EERDMANS PUBLISHING COMPANY

GRAND RAPIDS, MICHIGAN / CAMBRIDGE, U.K.

© 2012 James D. Bratt
All rights reserved

Published 2012 by
Wm. B. Eerdmans Publishing Co.
2140 Oak Industrial Drive N.E., Grand Rapids, Michigan 49505 /
P.O. Box 163, Cambridge CB3 9PU U.K.

Printed in the United States of America

18 17 16 15 14 13 12   7 6 5 4 3 2 1

Library of Congress Cataloging-in-Publication Data

By the vision of another world: worship in American history /
    edited by James D. Bratt.
        p.   cm.   — (The Calvin Institute of Christian Worship Liturgical Studies)
    Includes index.
    ISBN 978-0-8028-6710-0 (pbk.: alk. paper)
    1. Worship — History.   2. United States — Church history.
    I. Bratt, James D., 1949-

    BV8.B9   2012
    277.3 — dc23

                                    2011030941

www.eerdmans.com

Contents

Contents

COMMENTARIES

Introduction: Transmitting Other Worlds

James D. Bratt

"The vistas it opens and the mysteries it propounds are another world to live in," Harvard philosopher George Santayana once said of religion; in fact, "another world to live in — whether we expect ever to pass wholly into it or no — is what we mean by having a religion."[1] A good number of his contemporaries (Santayana was writing in 1906) thought that "otherworldliness" was precisely the problem with religion in the industrializing, scientific order of their times. The seven historical case studies in this volume, by contrast, would indicate that Santayana was right: a vision of some "other world" can and does exert powerful influence on the more immediate domain of everyday experience. This book aims to show how ritual (in these cases, Christian worship) serves as the key mechanism by which that other world comes to be "lived in" — that is, comes to be communicated to, inhabited by, and thus to shed its influence abroad through the lives of its believers. No doubt there are other mechanisms at work in this complex transmission, but religious ritual is probably the most central; it is certainly the most recurrent and persistent. The book thus aims to commend, to encourage, and to exemplify the study of worship practices to historians interested in American religion.

At the same time, as a set of *historical* studies this volume seeks to commend the value of history to students of ritual. To take just the intentionally Christian side of that field, the guild of liturgical studies has flourished over the last thirty years as the liturgical mandates of the Second Vatican Council settled deep down in the tissues of Roman Catholic parishes,

---

1. George Santayana, *The Life of Reason; or, The Phases of Human Progress,* vol. 3: *Reason in Religion* (New York: Charles Scribner's Sons, 1906), p. 6.

as Orthodox congregations came to a new interaction with their North American environment, and as Protestants of all categories engaged in protracted, sometimes bitter, "worship wars." Such catalysts, however, can induce present-mindedness among participants on the one hand and a countervailing search for enduring norms at the roots of tradition on the other. Potentially lost in that oscillation is the middle ground of religious history, where — especially in America — old tradition and new circumstance have been engaged in a dance of innovation and restoration for a very long time. History offers scholars in other disciplines the chance to study change and development up close, to look at the dynamics that ensue when norms are instantiated in the concrete, subject to the pressures of time yet also resilient and shaping responses across time. American religious history has flourished fully as much as have liturgical studies over the past forty years, and this volume offers people in the latter field some exemplary fruits of that harvest. With it comes an invitation for them to go out and gather more, adapting the historian's techniques of fully contextual and developmental inquiry to their own studies.

If historians long pretended to be above questions of the current moment, they no longer do; liturgical scholars never even pretended. That honesty points to a third audience for this volume: the guild of practical theologians who, along with pastors, congregational leaders, and observers professional and amateur, wish to understand and improve the practices of church life, to help a congregation live up to the norms that its particular tradition espouses so that the best of *that* other world is well and truly communicated in the assembly during worship and in the life of the people dispersed during the workweek. The ghost of the old-fashioned historian here arises to warn off the naïve about history's potential on this front. To the bromide that "we have to study history so we don't repeat its mistakes," that cynic declaims that the only thing we learn from history is that we don't learn from history. More accurately, we can say that history never repeats itself. But it does rhyme, and it is resonances from the past that these seven historical studies offer practitioners in the present. Microhistories such as these excel in capturing fine detail and complexity, at best provoking in present-day observers the shock of recognition, at least providing analogues to current situations.

To give readers as wide an array of objects as possible to begin such contemplations, the essays here dig in across a broad span of time, place, ethnicity, and denomination in the history of American Christianity. The volume begins with sixteenth-century Puritans in England and concludes with Catholics in the aftermath of Vatican II. In between it stops off to watch the spread of Methodism in the upper South in the new American republic, to observe Tejano Catholics worshiping to keep their worlds together in the wake of Texas's secession from Mexico, and to hear how African-American Baptists coped with the disappointments of post-Reconstruction Georgia. In the twentieth century it follows the movement for the renewal of Catholic liturgy and social thought from its origins in the mid-century heartland to the aftermath of its triumph in late-century cities, while on the Protestant side it looks at the transit of political leadership from one type of Calvinists to another in an upper-Midwest city. On the shelf of liturgies it offers everything from ecstatic revivalism, white and black, to high-church processional with professional choir, from tobacco masses in Kentucky to the Genevan Psalter in West Michigan over to street festivals in San Antonio. Additional cases could have been multiplied by the score; the ones selected claim no merit of rank or salience but simply offer some representative variety while keeping the book reasonably sized.

Worship, Work, and Worldview

With such a span of cases and with three audiences in mind — religious historians, students of liturgy, and practical theologians — the authors in this volume set out to answer one question: how did *worship, work,* and *worldview* interact among the group they studied? The question forced the authors into the familiar pursuit of tracking how Sunday or feast-day carried over into the workweek, but also to follow traffic in the other direction: to see how the workweek shaped the worship. Behind, around, and between those separate flows, it is further assumed, lies a coherent set of assumptions, beliefs, norms, and hopes that frame all of experienced reality and its interpretation. That is, every community works life via a worldview, something larger than worship, though deeply informed by it; something animating and translating work into meaning, while also being nurtured by it. This approach militates against any simple sacred-secular, ritual-ethical, transcendent-immanent, or similar binary divide. It assumes steady interaction in a coherent matrix, both within the believer and within and among a believing community.

The rejection of binary splits is a commonplace of postmodernist approaches; the assertion of coherent worldview is more classically modernist. This volume rides that divide intentionally, in the interest of greater productive potential. We should therefore briefly revisit some of Santayana's modernist contemporaries to see the classic objections that he, and this volume, had to face; and then look at how the varieties of interaction between worship, work, and worldview are sufficiently illuminating of both the generality and the specificity of American religion to merit further investigations in the scholarly guilds this book has in view.

That some transmission took place from "another world" to this one, and that it did so by means of ritual practice, was a thesis that a good many of Santayana's contemporaries rejected. Set aside religion's atheist critics — most famously, Marx, Freud, and Nietzsche — who regarded religion as a delusory displacement of something more real, an "otherworldly" projection of this-worldly issues. More sympathetic secularists took religious experience seriously, but still regarded the worlds experienced as immanently human. For instance, William James, a founder of modern psychology and Santayana's friend and colleague in Harvard's philosophy department, produced his groundbreaking *Varieties of Religious Experience* just four years before Santayana published his dictum on religion in *The Life of Reason*. Reviewing a fascinating array of subjects over hundreds of pages, the *Varieties* in the last half of its last chapter finally undertakes some consideration as to whether the object with which the subjects *thought* they were engaged — namely, a supernatural being whose transcendence had one way or another become available to them — was real. James allowed the shadow of that possibility, but found the internal dynamics of religious appropriation to be far more interesting and potent. And though ritualized behavior appears all through the *Varieties,* it gets little of James's attention compared to the quest for personal integrity. Perhaps the two under-emphases had something to do with each other.

Self-styled progressives within religious bodies in Santayana's time were leery of otherworldliness too. These included the social-gospel and modernist parties in American Protestantism and to a lesser extent modernists and some "Americanists" in the Catholic house. Typically these critics saw transcendent and immanent on the one hand and ritual and ethics on the other as involved in zero-sum games, with one element in each pair necessarily winning at the expense of the other. The progressives were not only partisans of the latter side in each contest, they believed the two games to be interlocked. Thus, both to save religion and to improve the world, "mere" ritual had to make way for ethical power, while — aiding and aided by that process — any putative other world ought to be dissolved into this one with little remainder. Over time this line of thought gained particular ascendancy among scholars of African-American religion, where ritual observances, otherworldly language, and daily disenfranchisement were all at their most intense. That those three were not only simultaneous but mutually perpetuating phenomena became conventional wisdom, proof positive of the problem of traditional religion in the eyes of its critics both within and without the household of faith.

It is noteworthy, then, to see how highly Santayana esteemed ritual above dogma in religious life. He particularly disparaged the ambience around him at Harvard as the terminally rationalized and ethicized residue of an already ritually impoverished English Puritan faith. Retaining his Spanish Catholic sensibility even after leaving behind Christian belief, Santayana was profoundly suspicious of the Protestant project in either its secularized or dogmatic forms. *The Life of Reason* set forth the type of existence to which Santayana thought the human race (at least its critical, self-reflective members) was fated, but he deemed that life tolerable, indeed understandable, only with deep appreciation of myth, symbol, and ritual.

The essays in this volume all confirm Santayana's dictum about other worlds, even if they trade his skeptical tone of deracinated fate for the possibilities of creative freedom. We can highlight three of the most striking cases. Harry Stout's diagnosis of New England Puritans explores just the radical reductions of liturgy that would eventually give rise to Santayana's Harvard, but lays out the *ritual* dimensions of Bible reading that made that practice seem for the Puritans to be the last word in transcendent awe. The eternal Word rendered into print had explosive power in this world — indeed, laid the substratum of the American world upon which all else therein has been built, whether in accord or by resistance. As to African-American religion, Paul Harvey demonstrates that it was direct, sometimes ecstatic apprehension of a God and a set of ethical norms that transcended — in fact, directly contradicted — the dictates of Jim Crow that kept hope and human dignity alive for Georgia Baptists a century ago and helped lay the groundwork for the civil-rights movement half a century later. Third, the Catholic visionaries who hoped to renew rural life in the United States between the world wars seized upon the first fruits of Catholic liturgical reform to warrant change both at worship and at work in the name of enduring canons. For them, most explicitly of all the case studies in this volume, time and eternity, earth and heaven, ethics and ritual were decidedly not a zero-sum game but a mutually reinforcing circle.

James D. Bratt

Varieties of Ritual Experience

For current scholars it is not the plausibility but the locations and ritual transmissions of spiritual power that raise the more interesting questions. This volume illustrates the variety of answers that itself feeds that interest. Put another way: granted that there exists a transcendent realm, exactly where does it lie, and how does it get down to us? Furthermore, should that last preposition be "down" or "over" or "into" or something else? And who is the "us"? A group defined by ritual participation, to be sure, but also something before that? Does worship shape or reflect community? To such questions and others like them these essays simply answer "yes." That is to say, historians are not sticklers for consistency, liturgical norms, or theoretical prolegomena. They ride such stories as they find or fashion, confident that the results are sufficiently illuminating for other disciplines to categorize.

Take, for instance, the matter of space, sacred and civil, its intersection with time, and how these are disposed. Ruth Doan shows how, for the many new Methodists who were women and so politically disenfranchised in the early nineteenth century, the promise of liberty that men were so much talking about in the wake of national independence came true first of all in the spiritual realm by means of the creation of new ritual spaces, from which power radiated to rearrange customary domestic space. Timothy Matovina's Tejano Catholics, on the other hand, found themselves dislocated by staying put when civil space was redefined by the political rebellion that created the Republic of Texas. Traditional religious festivals provided a bridge of continuity over that disruption and a font of reconciliation for the Tejano community itself divided by the event. Even more important was the perennial Sunday liturgy that strengthened participants for struggles that had not changed at all under the parlous conditions of quotidian life. Closer to the present, for the Dutch Calvinists in James Bratt's essay, Christian truth was high and lifted up, eternal in the heavenly kingdom of a majestic God; yet it came to them via an ancestral liturgy that spanned the Atlantic Ocean from the "old country" to the new. After they had settled down and began to acquire political power in the new land, their worship opened up to more ecumenical and global forms — a response to new responsibilities. The more venerable type of Calvinists they displaced in local politics, heirs of New England Puritanism, had earlier in the twentieth century moved up the liturgical ladder as they returned a succession of parishioners to the U.S. Senate and federal bench, only eventually to lose sway by moving their church from urban to suburban space.

All of the communities studied in this volume found "this world" not to be so self-evident, and found clearer definition of and direction in it by reference to a transcendent frame of ethics, aesthetics, or being that came alive, and came to be lived in, via worship. But people concerned with present-day congregational life might wonder what lessons these cases might provide for their own situations. Unfortunately, besides the dictum that history rhymes but never repeats, the only infallible rule might be the law of unintended consequences. That has been manifest nowhere more dramatically than in Roman Catholic parishes across the United States in the wake of the Second Vatican Council. Leslie Tentler's poignant essay, mixing personal memoir and clergy interviews with more detached history, shows how a compelling world was lost when it was hoped that a brighter future would be gained. That this occurred at the behest of people better educated than ever in, as well as deeply committed to, the faith must give scholar-educators in any discipline pause. That it occurred when the traditional Latin Mass gave way to the liturgy "of the people," only to see fewer people actually show up for worship, might attest to the need for manifestly otherworldly forms to convey the "other world" with conviction. Or maybe not. Maybe, as Professor Tentler muses, the emptying out would have occurred anyway. Maybe the old as well as the new liturgy would not have carried conviction. For the third rule of history is ambiguity. History notoriously claims only the comprehension afforded by hindsight, but if things had turned out differently in case x, y, or z, the historian's craft would make that too seem to have been inevitable. It never is inevitable, as that wise Old Testament historian discovered: time and chance happen to us all.

It was not predictable, nor certainly was it their desire, that the Puritans' fixation on words would one day make belief more difficult. It was perhaps inevitable but certainly not desired that vernacular Methodism would bequeath ritual instability to future generations, pitting holiness zealots against high-church acolytes in the ranks, while Millerites departed by one door and Spiritualists by another. The dramatic otherworldliness of African-American Baptists *could* leave the impression of acquiescing to Jim Crow. But we should also recall that intentions sometimes held. Liturgical change in Grand Rapids congregations did work to galvanize successive generations in loyalty and conviction, and Tejano Catholics maintained vibrant communities year in and year out, whatever the challenges of the political or meteorological weather. Sometimes liturgical negotiations worked out better than anyone could have realistically hoped. When Afro-Baptist leaders acquiesced to common-folk pleas that traditional elements be blended into "respectable" churches, the numbers at worship multiplied and found new vitality in old forms. Even more this inadvertently built a musical bridge over to the white world on the other side of segregation, and the traffic that bridge bore helped bring down the separating wall.

Historical case studies can only show different strategies people follow in living by the vision of another world in the full ambience of the present. They can show the benefits and costs of magnifying or lessening the contrast between the two, and trace the shifting circumstances by which the worlds themselves change, destabilize, even return. Like literature, history can only offer stories of the complexly human as most of what we know about the present, and all we know of the future. It asks that readers be careful, critical, and compassionate, and then proceed as best they can to bring down to earth a better world to live in.

ESSAYS

Liturgy, Literacy, and Worship in Puritan Anglo-America, 1560-1670

Harry S. Stout

Although my particular focus in this essay will be on Anglo-American Puritan liturgy in the seventeenth century, it is important to see this movement as the outgrowth of a profound and often rancorous set of sixteenth- and seventeenth-century debates that erupted between the state Church of England, supported by the Crown and Parliament, and the dissenting counterculture of Puritanism, whose seedbed was Geneva and the English universities, especially Cambridge University. In significant ways these two battling traditions would shape the evolution of churches and congregations in early America. Members of the Church of England would be especially strong in the Chesapeake and to a lesser extent New York, while Puritans would be especially strong in New England. Both functioned effectively in their regions as "established" churches which enjoyed the support and coercive energies of their governments. Puritan "dissenters" and Anglican "establishmentarians" stood as the ecclesiastical paradigm alongside which other traditions and movements understood themselves and their distinctives. As case studies they are indispensable for understanding the subsequent evolution of liturgical practice in American congregations.

In exploring Puritan liturgy and worship, in England and New England, it is important to understand how decisively worship shaped all of Puritan life including church, state, economy, schools, and families. Far from being incidental or irrelevant to the Puritans' revolutionary ideology, a text-based liturgy and worship served as the mobilizing trigger and master organizer of the Puritan state.

Nowhere were Puritans in England and New England more radical and unique than in their worship and liturgy. Their lack of a printed liturgy, together with a "plain style" rhetoric in preaching, prompted Anglican critics to recoil in horror at the theological betrayal they witnessed. Far from being more "pure," these Puritans appeared to established churchmen to be just the opposite: sacrilegious and even profane. In a sermon preached during the Commonwealth period when English Puritans executed their king and established a "holy Commonwealth" under Oliver Cromwell, Bishop Jeremy Taylor had occasion to remark on the "profaneness" of Puritans who "neglect the exterior part of Religion: and this is so vile a crime, that hypocrisie while it is undiscovered is not so much mischeveous as open profaneness, or a neglect and contempt of external religion."[1] Although the Puritan was many things, the Anglican sense of nonconformity-as-profane is difficult for the historian to understand. Judged by their words and actions — to say nothing of later stereotypes — the Puritans appear to be anything but profane. The voluminous literature on Puritanism habitually fastens on their intense inner spirituality expressed among other places in the new literary genre of the spiritual autobiography; an unprecedented degree of lay involvement and theological sophistication; an almost obsessive attention to Sabbath-keeping and sermon attendance; a proclivity for extemporaneous "heartfelt" prayer; and an unflinching loyalty to *sola Scriptura* as the only rule of faith and life.[2] Their very title "Puritan" addressed the fervent religious faith which was their most distinctive quality.

Yet at the same time that historians have given the Puritans high marks for piety, they have recognized that it was a piety rooted in far different impulses than that which drove earlier religious movements. If the Puritans were zealous it was a zeal marked by liturgical iconoclasm as much as spiritual renewal; and if they were religious it was a type of religiosity that was self-evidently novel and revolutionary in implication. As Bishop Taylor's complaint suggests, the seventeenth-century sense of profane had less to do with atheistic beliefs and a godless lifestyle than with attitudes toward the "external" forms of rituals and worship. And on this

---

1. Jeremy Taylor, *The Whole Works of the Right Rev. Jeremy Taylor, D.D.*, R. Heber, ed. (1863; reprinted, New York: Georg Olms Verlag, 1970), 4:52.

2. Classic expositions of these themes can be found in William Haller, *The Rise of Puritanism* (New York: Columbia University Press, 1938); M. M. Knappen, *Tudor Puritanism* (Chicago: University of Chicago Press, 1939); Patrick Collinson, *The Elizabethan Puritan Movement* (Los Angeles: University of California Press, 1967); and Perry Miller, *The New England Mind: The Seventeenth Century* (New York: Macmillan, 1939). More recently, see Peter Lake, *Moderate Puritans and the Elizabethan Church* (Cambridge: Cambridge University Press, 2004), and Bryan D. Spinks, *Freedom or Order? The Eucharistic Liturgy in English Congregationalism, 1645-1980* (Allison Park, Pa.: Pickwick Publications, 1984).

level his accusation is not so misplaced. Puritans *did* run roughshod over liturgical conventions that had governed Christian worship for millennia and, in that fact alone, did more to pave the way for their revolutionary society than any other cause.

When Puritan worship is examined in the anthropological categories of ritual and belief, the Anglican charge carries with it a fundamental insight into the nature of Puritanism which has largely been ignored by historians. Indeed, Taylor's sense of the profane residing in attitudes toward ritual forms coincides with a broad body of contemporary anthropological literature that distinguishes ("sacred") traditional cultures from ("profane") modern cultures primarily in their contrasting attitudes toward ritual, tradition, and social authority. At some point in the history of Western culture the faith in inherited ritual forms disappeared and was replaced by a "modern" religious-like faith in what Max Weber first termed "legal-rational" modes of organizing society and supplying cultural meaning. "Moderns" picture society as a social contract between consenting autonomous individuals. The official bond of society is content not form, written constitutions eternally preserved in print. Rituals such as presidential inaugurations, royal coronations, or military parades are perceived as a mere embellishment of political realities.[3]

While very successful in pointing out the chasm separating traditional cultures from modern, anthropologists are less successful in delineating how that transformation took place. Where are the fault-lines separating traditional from modern? And what might liturgy and worship have to do with them? Before the modern faith in reason-over-ritual could triumph, the older faith in traditional institutions upheld by ceremonial forms had to be undermined.[4] This, I would argue, is precisely what Puritans

3. See, for example, E. J. Hobsbawm, *Primitive Rebels: Studies in Archaic Forms of Social Movements in the Nineteenth and Twentieth Centuries* (New York: Oxford University Press, 1959), p. 150. Mary Douglas describes modern attitudes toward religious ritual in terms of the belief that "a rational, verbally explicit, personal commitment to God is self-evidently more evolved and better than its alleged contrary, formal, ritualistic conformity" in *Natural Symbols: Explorations in Cosmology* (New York: Pantheon Press, 1970), p. 4. Of course the faith in reason-over-ritual is its own kind of ritual. See Clifford Geertz, "Centers, Kings, and Charisma: Reflections on the Symbolics of Power," in *Culture and Its Creators: Essays in Honor of Edward Shils,* Joseph Ben-David and T. N. Clark, eds. (Chicago: University of Chicago Press, 1977), pp. 150-71.

4. Max Weber, *The Theory of Social and Economic Organization* (1947; reprinted, New York: Macmillan, 1974), and *The Protestant Ethic and the Spirit of Capitalism* (1930; reprinted, New York: Scribner's, 1958).

achieved in their worship and it spilled over into all other walks of life in ways that are now recognizably "modern" and "ideological." While notable scholars like Max Weber and Michael Walzer have discussed the Puritans' modernity in terms of capitalism and political ideology, they failed to identify the fountainhead of this revolution in Puritan worship.[5] In the following pages I will suggest that Puritanism represented a critical transition or fault-line that unintentionally eroded faith in the traditional sacred cosmos and paved the way for a modern society bound together by ideological consensus rather than inherited ceremonial forms. Despite their intense religiosity the Puritans inadvertently paved the way for new secular bases of order by calling into question and condemning traditional notions that things are the way they are because they have always been that way. The argument set forth in this essay is necessarily abstract in that it fastens on only one dimension (worship) of Puritan religious life. It is *not* meant to imply that Puritans were modern or, for that matter, that Anglicans were traditional. In terms of their attachment to a view of the universe that was essentially static and religious the Puritans remained close to the medieval world which spawned them. But in their attitudes toward traditional ceremonies and nonverbal ritual they shared more with modern people than with their medieval forebears. They were (again in Weber's terminology) a "transitional" or "charismatic" movement which served as a bridge between the old and the new, the traditional and the modern.

The secularizing potential of Puritanism is perhaps most apparent in their hostile attitudes toward existing forms of worship. And here we must be sensitive not only to *how* their attitudes diverged from that which preceded them in the Christian tradition, but also *why* they differed so dramatically. Political or economic explanations are not in themselves sufficient explanations. They miss internal cultural sources that are to be discovered primarily on the level of language and communications.[6] Though notoriously difficult to define in sociological categories, the least that can be said of the Puritans who would inaugurate the godly Com-

---

5. Weber, *The Protestant Ethic and the Spirit of Capitalism,* and Michael Walzer, *The Revolution of the Saints: A Study in the Origins of Radical Politics* (Cambridge: Harvard University Press, 1982).

6. For applications of the linguistic perspective, see Boyd Berry, *Process of Speech: Puritan Religious Writing and Paradise Lost* (Baltimore: Johns Hopkins University Press, 1976), and Paul Christianson, *Reformers and Babylon: English Apocalyptic Visions from the Reformation to the Eve of the Civil War* (Toronto: University of Toronto Press, 1978).

monwealth and settle the New World is that they were almost universally literate.[7] They were the first English-speaking movement to be legitimately characterized as a "people of the Book" and, as such, were clearly set apart from traditional, "aural" cultures. Is there a connection between print, literacy, and worship that can help us to understand the destructive attitudes toward ritual and ceremony?

In his introduction to a collection of essays on the history of Jewish and Christian faith communities, historian John Van Engen urges scholars of religion to consider the primary media of communications in different faith communities as a way of understanding the particularities of various religious groups. In particular he focuses on literacy: "What of the difference between the literate and the nonliterate, manuscript culture and print culture? Did practices and materials appeal to the eye, as in images, stained glass windows, and icons? Or to the ear, as in sung prayers, preached sermons, and hymns? Or to the mind by way of printed instructions, catechisms, devotional books?"[8]

The questions Van Engen raises come to the very core of what made Puritans unique and modern. Literacy mattered. And it mattered decisively. Puritans emerged as the first English-speaking faith community to employ the "tools" of literacy to construct entirely new conceptions of religion and right living. Liturgy, in Van Engen's terms, "formed" a particular "practice" not only on Sunday, but through all aspects of life.

I

Before the Puritans, Christian worship and liturgy was necessarily "aural" and non-literate. In its broadest sense liturgy means simply "service" to God. It signifies the external forms through which public worship is enacted. For traditional religious communities public worship constituted the primary ritual of solidarity that grounded religion beneath the realm

7. In New England, historian Kenneth Lockridge demonstrates that male literacy rates approached universality and women were close. See Lockridge's *Literacy in Colonial New England: An Enquiry into the Social Context of Literacy in the Early Modern West* (New York: Norton, 1974), pp. 72-101. See also William Gilmore-Lehne, *Reading Becomes a Necessity of Life: Material and Cultural Life in Rural New England, 1780-1835* (Knoxville: University of Tennessee Press, 1989).

8. John Van Engen, ed., *Educating People of Faith: Exploring the History of Jewish and Christian Communities* (Grand Rapids: Eerdmans, 2004), p. 26.

of speculative ideas and into the arena of experience and group participation. The recognition that Christian worship existed prior to doctrine led the liturgicologist R. P. C. Hanson to argue that "when we trace the development of patristic literature we discover something of how the intellectuals thought. But when we trace the development of Christian worship we are seeing theology at its grass-roots, theology from the inside, the theology of the ordinary man."[9] Like the coronation of a king or the invocation of parliament, the forms and settings of religious worship are filled with cultural messages that the historian needs to interpret.

Besides the theological significance of liturgy and worship as prior to and more foundational to faith than ideas and "doctrines," there is also a powerful ritual significance to liturgy that was richly developed in the classic work of historian of religion Mircea Eliade. Although primarily concerned with pre-literate or non-literate religious communities, Eliade provides a theoretical focus that is broad enough to include an analysis of Christian worship in the Puritan era.[10] Eliade insisted that ritual cannot be understood as epiphenomenal, for it is an irreducible element of religion that must be explained in its own terms. Amassing evidence from a broad range of religious traditions across time and space, Eliade refuted the assumption that culture was originally secular and that only in the course of time were mundane objects consecrated to the sacred inventions of man. This (modern) assumption actually reverses the historical sequence, for in all traditional cultures nature was perceived as a bearer of the sacred. Occasional and regular "hierophanies" manifested the holy in a direct, visible manner. Natural objects were worshiped, Eliade argued, "precisely because they [were] hierophanies, because they show[ed] something that is no longer stone or tree but the sacred."[11] Because persons can communicate and understand the unknown only in terms of the known, they regarded the natural rhythms of work and nature as revealing a supernatural meaning higher than their natural sense.

In traditional cultures the categories of space and time are neither linear nor uniform. To protect themselves from a hostile environment, traditional societies lived as close as they could to special, sacred places. Profane space assumed meaning only when oriented around the absolute point of depar-

---

9. J. Danielous, A. H. Couratin, and John Kent, *Historical Theology* (Baltimore: Penguin, 1969), p. 131.

10. See especially Mircea Eliade, *The Sacred and the Profane: The Nature of Religion* (New York: Harcourt, Brace & World, 1957).

11. Eliade, *The Sacred and the Profane*, p. 12.

ture at the "center of the universe": "religious man's desire to live in the sacred is in fact equivalent to his desire to take up his abode in objective reality, not to let himself be paralyzed by the never-ceasing relativity of purely subjective experiences, to live in a real and effective world, not in an illusion."[12] Sacred time, moreover, is not linear but cyclical; it is past events ritually made present. The notion of unilinear mechanical or digital time stands in stark contrast to sacred time which, "by its very nature . . . is reversible in the sense that, properly speaking, it is primordial mythical time made present. Every religious festival, any liturgical time, represents the reactualization of a sacred event that took place in a mythical past. . . ."[13] Typically the solar year provided the cycles for ritual celebrations and renewal.[14] By entering into sacred space and time traditional societies came into contact with the source of life and, in so doing, gained some measure of control over their lives.

In such a world, ceremony and ritual are more important than any other human activities. Religious rites are stereotyped and highly coded channels of communication through which the community of faith enters sacred time and space.[15] They constitute the primary forms through which reality is ultimately perceived. As Emile Durkheim first suggested, ritual celebrations create and sustain community. Without them society ceases to exist.[16]

II

Eliade recognized both continuities and discontinuities when applying the broad comparative framework of myth and ritual to the evolution of

12. Eliade, *The Sacred and the Profane,* p. 28. This spatial orientation is not limited to ancient times. In twenty-first-century New York, for example, Haitian immigrants remain tied to their traditional Vodou spirits by bringing beads, icons, and bits of soil from Haiti into their urban high-rise apartments. See Karen McCarthy Brown, "Staying Grounded in a High-Rise Building: Ecological Dissonance and Ritual Accommodation in Haitian Vodou," in *Gods of the City: Religion and the American Urban Landscape,* Robert Orsi, ed. (Bloomington: University of Indiana Press, 1999), pp. 79-102.

13. Eliade, *The Sacred and the Profane,* pp. 68-69.

14. Louis Bouyer, *Rite and Man: Natural Sacredness and Christian Liturgy* (Notre Dame: University of Notre Dame Press, 1967), p. 190.

15. Foundational discussions of ritual and communications can be found in Anthony F. C. Wallace, *Religion: An Anthropological View* (New York: Random House, 1966), and Douglas, *Natural Symbols,* pp. 9, 33.

16. Emile Durkheim, *The Elementary Forms of Religious Life: A Study in Religious Sociology* (New York: Thomas Crowell, 1915).

Christian worship. What made Christianity so innovative was the existence of the God-man Jesus Christ living in historical space and time. Nature was no longer the sole or primary bearer of the sacred, and the faith did not rely on myths from primordial time, *ab origine,* to sanctify existence. The "supreme theophany" of Jesus Christ meant that history surpassed nature as the primary bearer of the sacred and that myths would rely on Christ's spoken words (the "gospel") witnessed to and recorded by contemporary apostles.

The Christians' unequivocal appeal to their one true God created what H. Richard Niebuhr termed the "enduring problem" of reconciling the exclusive claim of Christianity with a "pagan" civilization attuned to universal natural symbols.[17] For the early church the primary problem became reconciling the unique historical event of Jesus Christ with long-familiar natural hierophanies. In dealing with primitive people who instinctively perceived reality through ritual forms the church could only communicate its faith in kind. Christian missionaries practiced a liturgical syncretism that incorporated pagan symbols and rituals into the Christian message. Peasant images and festivals were retained and their meaning was altered to fit the Christian framework.[18] To communicate its message the Catholic Church relied heavily upon highly visual imagery and the sacraments. Because there were neither vernacular Bibles nor literate readers, worship was centered around action and ceremony rather than sacred vernacular texts and doctrinal comprehension.

The implications of mystery and natural symbolism for worship were not obvious. Pagan rites and rituals, sacred calendars, and vestments were not discarded but instead retained as symbols that actively manifested the "saving mystery" of the Christ event. Daniel Sullivan described the relationship of Catholic Christianity with natural symbols as one of unification: "In the new revelation the old cosmic cycle is broken, and a new symbolic dimension is disclosed: God reveals Himself in the singular, historic event as well as in the universal cosmic cycles and the historic revelation gives to the cosmic symbolism itself an inner meaning which it did not have before; the cosmic itself is brought into line with the historic."[19] Because natural symbols and non-verbal gestures were believed to be

17. H. Richard Niebuhr, *Christ and Culture* (New York: Harper & Row, 1951), pp. 1-44.

18. Mircea Eliade, *Images and Symbols: Studies in Religious Symbolism* (New York: Sheed & Ward, 1961), p. 175.

19. Daniel Sullivan, "Symbolism in Catholic Worship," in *Religious Symbolism,* F. Ernest Johnson, ed. (1955; reprinted, Port Washington, N.Y.: Kennikat, 1969), p. 48.

meaning-bearing just as words were, worship was highly ceremonial. The church itself was the indispensable sacrament and the external forms of worship were as intrinsically sacred and meaningful as the spoken proclamation. The performance of ritual actions within the church became the necessary precondition to salvation.

As did other religious cultures, Catholic Christianity identified sacred spaces and sacred times. God made himself specially present within the sacred space of the cathedral. As Eliade observes, "the Christian basilica and, later, the cathedral take over and continue all these [natural] symbolisms. . . . The interior of the church is the universe; the altar is paradise which lay in the East. . . . The West, on the contrary, is the realm of darkness."[20] Similarly, the sacred time of the church was cyclically marked off around a sacred liturgical calendar that commemorated signal events in the history of the church. Within the sacred space of the church and the sacred time of worship God made himself specially available to those who worshiped him.

This "traditional" frame of mind valued external forms and settings and believed them to be specially instituted channels of grace. By the third century Christian worship centered on the "Eucharist" or "Thanksgiving" of the Lord's Supper. Within the sacred space of the church the altar became central because it contained the special abode of the risen Christ. Catholic worship took its inspiration from the mystery of Incarnation, which revealed that there was no inherent contradiction between the natural and the sacred. In the Eucharist the Christ was once again made ritually present as he sacrificed himself anew in a mysterious way for the members of his body. Louis Bouyer recognizes how central the Eucharist became in the Catholic Church: "the sacred time *par excellence* for Christianity is the time of the celebration of the Eucharist, just as sacred space . . . is the place of its celebration."[21]

The mystery and ritual that surrounded the Eucharist came to inform all of Catholic worship. James Hastings Nichols explains how: "The sacramental act [of the Eucharist] was in itself propitiatory, because in some sense the body and blood of Christ was sacrificed. Thereby the door was opened to admit again the whole apparatus of temple, priests, altars, sacrifices which had passed with the old Jewish dispensation. . . . Thereafter a 'special priesthood' was needed to make the cultic approaches to a God

---

20. Eliade, *The Sacred and the Profane*, p. 61.
21. Bouyer, *Rite and Man*, p. 204.

imperfectly reconciled, it appeared, by the Cross."[22] Nichols's insight, while valid, is written from a modern, Protestant perspective. In his classic book, *The Decline of Magic,* Keith Thomas recognizes the centrality of the Eucharist and ceremony in its own context:

> Today we think of religion as a belief, rather than a practice, as definable in terms of creeds rather than in modes of behavior. But such a description would have fitted the popular Catholicism of the Middle Ages little better than it fits many other primitive religions. A medieval peasant's knowledge of Biblical history or Church doctrine was, so far as one can tell, extremely slight. The Church was important to him not because of its formalized code of belief, but because its rites were an essential accompaniment to the important events in his own life — birth, marriage, and death. . . . Religion was a ritual method of living, not a set of dogmas.[23]

As Thomas suggests, the forms and rituals of the early church took precedence over theological belief. It could not be otherwise in an aural culture where there was no typographic content to be analyzed and reflected upon. The Catholic sense of the sacred residing in ritual objects, particularly the Eucharistic elements, was so pervasive that special cares were taken to avoid profanation. Celebration in one kind (i.e., only the bread or wafer, not the wine) was not practiced out of doctrinal conviction, but out of a devout fear of profaning the elements. To eliminate the natural forms and symbols of worship, or to deny their sacred efficacy, would be to shut off primary approaches to the sacred that God himself had instituted when he formed the Christian church.

In its repudiation of the Catholic Church, the Protestant Reformation dealt a mortal blow to the prevailing economy of grace. Unlike the medieval church, Protestantism began on the level of belief rather than ritual. Faithfulness in doctrine replaced ritual performance as the primary "mark" of the Christian. As Francis Clark recognizes, "for the Catholic Church it was not the attack on the Papacy that was the most fateful event which happened in the Reformation, but the emptying out from her Mysteries of the objective source of power."[24] The doctrine of justification by

---

22. James Hastings Nichols, *Corporate Worship in the Reformed Tradition* (Philadelphia: Fortress, 1968), p. 25.

23. Keith Thomas, *The Decline of Magic* (New York: Scribner's, 1971), p. 76.

24. Francis Clark, S.J., *Eucharistic Sacrifice and the Reformation* (Oxford: Oxford University Press, 1967), p. 107.

faith alone meant that rituals, ceremonies, and external forms were no longer efficacious in abstraction; they could no longer *do* anything without the prior gift of grace.

Although the Reformers "emptied out" the church's power of sacramental grace, they did not immediately and entirely destroy the prevailing forms and rituals of Christian worship. Worship is among the most conservative of social institutions and is not easily uprooted. Despite the removal of shrines and images, the Protestants retained familiar forms. Rather than destroy forms, Protestants (like Catholics earlier) took the existing structure of worship and reinterpreted its meaning with the framework of justification by faith. The Protestant liturgy itself was adapted from the Latin Mass. Reformation leaders never intended to do away with the liturgy, but only to present a common, vernacular service for clergy and laity alike. Although later Puritans would label printed Protestant liturgies a "popish dreg," it is important to remember that the common liturgy was Reformation document and Protestant innovation.

In creating a Protestant liturgy Martin Luther retained the existing outward forms and ceremonies of worship as long as they were not specifically prohibited by Scripture. His *Formula Missae* was published in 1523 and adhered closely to the order of the Latin Mass, eliminating only the obvious references to the Eucharist as merit or sacrifice. Because simple lay people had no knowledge of Latin, Luther provided a vernacular *Deutsche Messe* in 1525 which, like its Latin predecessor, insisted that the Protestant Church could not survive without the spiritual food and water of "external rites," even if they did not automatically *(ex opere operato)* "commend us to God."[25] In no uncertain terms Luther insisted that "it is not now, nor has it ever been in our mind to abolish entirely the whole formal cultus of God, but to cleanse that which is in use. . . ."[26] Purification, not elimination, was the original goal of Protestant liturgy.

In large measure Anglican worship was modeled after the Lutheran liturgy. The Elizabethan *Book of Common Prayer*, like Luther's liturgy, took both Scripture and tradition as criteria for worship.[27] The rationale for liturgy and worship can be found in the prayer book's introductory statement, "On Ceremonies," where we learn that the Anglican Church held

25. Martin Luther, *Formula Missae*, reprinted in *Liturgies of the Western World*, Bard Thompson, ed. (New York: Meridian, 1961), p. 114.

26. Luther, *Formula Missae*, p. 107.

27. See Horton Davies, *Worship and Theology in England* (Princeton: Princeton University Press, 1967), vol. 2.

strictly to the holiness of a fixed liturgy which was "apt to stir up the dull mind of man to remembrance of his duty to God by some notable and special signification. . . ."[28]

The organization of the Anglican liturgy corresponded closely to the Missal, Processional, and Manual of the Mass. Only the Canon was drastically altered to avoid doctrinal intimations of transubstantiation. The sacraments of extreme unction, ordination, confirmation, marriage, and absolution were retained as sacred rites and ordinances of the church.[29] The daily offices of matins and evensong are unique in Protestantism, in that they offered a daily prayer liturgy for the church whose doors were open seven days a week. Worship readings were read without explication and were largely modeled after the medieval lectionary, differing in the elimination of extrabiblical selections. The collects themselves were translated by Archbishop Canmer from the Latin Missal into the English vernacular.[30]

When they went to church, Anglican worshipers entered a separate world of sacred time and space surrounded by consecrated objects and striking visual images much in keeping with the sacred world of medieval Christianity. Sacred time was retained in the Anglican liturgy with an abbreviated calendar that interpreted the cyclical seasons within the sovereign plan of redemption. Signal activities and persons in the history of the church formed the "red letter" days around which worship was ordered. As in Catholicism, the exterior of the church was modeled after the basilica and cathedral and the design of the Latin cross was retained as a symbol of the passion of Christ. The only stained glass windows or statuaries that were removed were those which directly suggested the intercession of the saints. To accommodate the central act of worship in the Eucharist the interior of the church was clearly divided between the nave of popular assembly and the chancel which housed the altar. Archbishop William Laud left little doubt about his liturgical preference: "I say greatest, yea greater than the pulpit; for there it is *Hoc est corpus meum*, 'This is My Body.' . . ."[31] Similarly, Jeremy Taylor asserted that "the summe is this. Where God is present, there he is to be worshiped, and so according to the degree of his presence. He is specially present in Holy places, as Temples, Churches, Altars, for that being the place of the greatest Sanctity, there ought to be the

28. John E. Booty, ed., *The Book of Common Prayer, 1559: The Elizabethan Prayer Book* (Charlottesville: University of Virginia Press, 1976), p. 19.

29. Booty, ed., *The Book of Common Prayer, 1559*, pp. 48-67.

30. Booty, ed., *The Book of Common Prayer, 1559*, pp. 77-246.

31. Quoted in Davies, *Worship and Theology in England*, 2:13.

expression of the greatest devotion."[32] By Laudian fiat the altar was placed in the east and covered with silk and scented candles upon which the ornate chalice rested.[33] To avoid profaning the altar Laud insisted that it be "railed" to avoid human contact.

The candles, processions, cherubim, and commemorated saints in Anglican churches constituted an integral part of worship. They were intended to convey a deep sense of the numinous and of the historical continuity of the Christian church uniting with the heavenly angels in liturgical unison. For the same reason the liturgy retained a broad variety of gestures, cadences, ceremonies, pageantry, and vestments designed to stir up in the worshipers a sense of the majesty of Christ. The specified position for receiving the Eucharist was kneeling, as befitting the King of Kings. In the sacrament of marriage the special relationship of man and woman was symbolized by the ring, and, in birth, children were baptized with the sign of the cross.[34] The vestments themselves switched with the seasons and with the nature of worship. The surplice was deemed sufficient for matins and evensong, while the celebration of the Eucharist required the alb, tunicle, and cope. Although gestures, like ceremony, were theologically *adiaphora*, they were socially and liturgically necessary. To destroy all ritual contact with the historic church of Christ would be to introduce innovation and disorder.

III

In accounting for the Puritan repudiation of Anglican worship many historians have pointed to the Reformed tradition of worship formulated most completely by John Calvin. For those Marian exiles who would form the nucleus of the Puritan movement Calvin's liturgy was binding. The Genevan liturgy was translated almost verbatim into the English-language *Geneva Service Book*.[35] The early Puritans believed, with Calvin, that "all who introduce newly invented methods of worshiping God really worship

32. Taylor, *The Whole Works*, 5:325-26.

33. Davies, *Worship and Theology in England*, 2:337.

34. Booty, ed., *The Book of Common Prayer, 1559*, p. 275.

35. William D. Maxwell, ed., *The Liturgical Portions of the Genevan Service Book* (London: Oliver & Boyd, 1931). The Calvinist background to the liturgy is described in William Whittingham, *A Brief Discourse of the Troubles at Frankfurt, 1554-1558* (1846; reprinted, London: Arber, 1907).

and adore the creatures of their own distempered imaginations."[36] And, like Calvin, the early Puritans shared a sense of the real spiritual presence of the risen Christ in the Eucharist and considered Zwingli's simple memorialism "almost prophane."[37] The early Puritans never objected to prayer books per se, and they could not conceive of worship without a set liturgy of confession, prayer, praise, proclamation, and sacrament.

The Calvinist influence on Puritan worship did not last. Although in terms of doctrine the seventeenth-century Puritans became "new and more narrowly dogmatic Calvinists," in terms of worship they were separating themselves from Geneva. By the time of Elizabeth the Puritans were moving toward what historian Bryan Sinks labels a "liturgical anarchy."[38] How shall we explain this radical liturgical shift? Economics, politics, and Reformed theology are not in themselves sufficient to account for the rapid spread of seventeenth-century non-liturgical Puritanism. Between the Marian exiles in Geneva and the Elizabethan Puritan movement lay a signal *literary* innovation that would destroy Protestant notions of common prayer and foster in their place a vicious anti-liturgical attitude which, to the Reformers, would have seemed almost blasphemous. That innovation was the "Geneva Bible."[39]

The Protestant principle of *sola Scriptura* had existed in principle for a long time. But the church could not be organized solely around Scrip-

36. John Calvin, *Institutes of the Christian Religion* (Grand Rapids: Eerdmans, 1953), I:4:3.

37. Bryan D. Spinks, *From the Lord and "the Best Reformed Churches": A Study of the Eucharistic Liturgy in the English Puritan and Separatist Traditions, 1550-1633* (Rome: C.L.V.-Edizioni Liturgiche, 1984), p. 25. See also Williston Walker, "The Genesis of the Common Form of Public Worship in our Non-Liturgical Churches," *Papers of the American Society of Church History*, 2nd Ser., 1 (1913): 81-93.

38. Spinks, *From the Lord*, p. 25.

39. I have described the production and significance of the Geneva Bible at greater length in my essay "Word and Order in Colonial New England," in *The Bible in America: Essays in Cultural History*, Nathan O. Hatch and Mark A. Noll, eds. (New York: Oxford University Press, 1982), pp. 19-38. Additional information on the Geneva Bible can be found in Hardin Craig, "The Geneva Bible as a Political Document," *Pacific Historical Review* 7 (1938):40-49; Basil Hall, *The Genevan Version of the English Bible* (London: Presbyterian Church of England, 1957); Lewis Lupton, *A History of the Genevan Bible*, 4 vols. (London: privately printed, 1966); Richard Greaves, "Traditionalism and the Seeds of Revolution in the Social Principles of the Geneva Bible," *Sixteenth Century Journal*, 7 (April 1976): 94-109; and the introductory essay in Lloyd E. Berry, ed., *The Geneva Bible: A Facsimile of the 1560 Edition* (Madison: University of Wisconsin Press, 1969), pp. 1-28 (hereafter cited as *The Geneva Bible*).

ture until it had a literate congregation with access to their own vernacular Bibles, and these Bibles did not exist until the Marian exile William Whittingham and his Genevan colleagues produced the first widely accessible edition in the language of common English readers. Along with the Genevan liturgy the English exiles produced a Bible that would become the hallmark of English Puritanism. The translation was completed in 1560 and copies were almost immediately available in a single-volume, Roman-type edition. The phraseology is rich in the common idiom of the day and resonates with meanings sure to impress the literate but untutored mind. The Geneva Bible's destination was never the parish but the household. It was to go through seventy entire editions and thirty editions of the New Testament and psalms in the reign of Elizabeth. By the time Puritanism had grown powerful enough to execute Charles I and establish the Commonwealth, the Geneva Bible had gone through over 160 editions.[40] It was the Bible of Shakespeare and Spenser; its marginal commentaries informed the theology of *Paradise Lost*. When Oliver Cromwell's New Model Army embarked on its sacred crusade every soldier was assigned a "Soldier's Pocket-Bible" filled with selections from the Genevan translation.[41]

Despite the fact that the "Bishop's Bible" was sanctioned by ecclesiastical authority for use in public worship, the Geneva Bible circumvented official channels and found its way into common dwellings throughout the realm, wherever there were literate readers. While the number of literate Englishmen was extremely low, a disproportionate number were drawn to the Geneva Bible and the community that formed around it. Within a generation it had outstripped all other versions in circulation and came to stand as the unchallenged emblem of dissenting popular piety in the English realm.[42] Biblical scholar F. F. Bruce points out that the Genevan version "became the household Bible of English-speaking Protestants . . . its

---

40. Distribution figures can be found in Charles Eason, *The Genevan Bible: Notes on its Production and Distribution* (Dublin: Eason & Sons, 1937).

41. *The Soldier's Pocket-Bible: Issued for the Use of the Army of Oliver Cromwell, A.D. 1643* (reprinted, New York: American Bible Society, 1862). For discussions of the "ideological" character of the New Model Army, see Boyd M. Berry, *Process of Speech: Puritan Religious Writing and Paradise Lost* (Baltimore: Johns Hopkins University Press, 1976), pp. 170-75, and Michael Walzer, *The Revolution of the Saints: A Study in the Origins of Radical Politics* (Cambridge: Harvard University Press, 1965), pp. 268-99.

42. See Charles Eason, *The Genevan Bible: Notes on its Production and Distribution* (Dublin: Eason & Son, Ltd., 1937).

excellence as a translation was acknowledged even by those who disagreed with the theology of the translators."[43] When presented with their own copies of the Geneva Bible, common English readers encountered a document that was directed to their convenience and comprehension in every way. Physically, the translation was issued in a relatively inexpensive single-volume, Roman-type edition that was conveniently organized into sentence units of "verses" and "chapters." Substantively, they enjoyed a "plainly rendered" translation expressed in the language of their own idiomatic speech. As the Bible's preface to the reader made plain, the translation was not aimed at learned scholars but at common readers throughout the realm. Textual decisions were governed by the needs of "simple readers" to understand the "hard places" of Scripture. Like the "plain style" sermons that flowed from it, the translation was devoid of circumlocutions and Latinisms that would only distract the reader from a text "which is the light to our paths, the keye of the kingdome of heaven, our comfort in affliction, our shielde and sworde against Satan, the schoole of all wisdome, the glasse wherein we beholde God's face, the testimonie of his favour, and the only food and nourishment of our soules." The Geneva Bible was, in brief, the first English translation that could legitimately be characterized as a people's Bible.

To enhance the bible's popular intelligibility the translators included a massive body of marginal commentary, which was drawn largely from Calvin's commentaries.[44] In all, the commentary exceeded 300,000 words in length and constituted, in effect, a self-contained theological library for common readers. Aside from the bible itself, the Genevan commentary was the only literary product all people shared in common and it exerted a far more direct influence on the popular religious imagination than the less widely circulated sermons, devotionals, and spiritual autobiographies. The physical linkage of text and commentary on every page gave added weight to the notes and conveyed the appearance of a direct extension of sacred writ. When we view the contents of these notes and biblical texts we are observing the symbolic universe of popular piety and worship at its most direct and formative level.

Official injunctions against the Geneva Bible only increased the desire

---

43. F. F. Bruce, *The English Bible: A History of Translations from the Earliest English Versions to the New English Bible* (New York: Oxford University Press, 1970), pp. 86-92.

44. S. L. Greenslade, ed., *The Cambridge History of the Bible* (Cambridge: Cambridge University Press, 1963), 3:158-59.

of the people to read and discuss the new book that their parents had never even seen, let alone been able to read. And the annotated Bible, in turn, whetted their appetite for a more systematic exposition of the Word. Neither the prayer liturgy nor the richly ceremonial Eucharist gave these Bible readers the answers to the "reflective" questions raised by the printed Word. Puritan congregational members, contemptuous of a non-teaching priesthood, compared the established church to stained glass windows: they were ornate and beautiful, but ultimately distorted the true rays of God's revelation to man. Increasingly the cry went out for preachers who could interpret this book of God in a way that they could understand and follow. They asked (as reading always encourages one to ask) for someone who could explain the intellectual meaning of what they were reading; for someone who could explain the doctrine of their faith.

The group of Puritan preachers spread rapidly in university chapels, public assemblies, and privately funded lectureships.[45] They depended exclusively on their ability to persuade. Their basis of support was ideological not traditional, and they could succeed only so long as they could maintain the loyalty of their audience.[46] Beyond everything else, the Puritan leaders were public teachers who cast their message around an expository interpretation of the printed vernacular Word. There was not a pure theologian or formal logician in the lot of them. What made their message socially significant was not the coherence of their theology, but the *communication* of that coherence, frail and piecemeal as it was, to an increasingly literate public demanding information, explanations, and a personal sense of significance that traditional customs and institutions were not equipped or inclined to provide.

It is impossible to understand the anti-liturgical shift in Puritanism without also recognizing the rise in literacy. James Hastings Nichols points out that

> The Puritan movement was associated with a sociological development of some significance, the rise of a literate middle class laity. In contrast

45. On the growth of Puritan Lectureships, see Paul S. Seaver, *The Puritan Lectureships: The Politics of Religious Dissent* (Stanford: Stanford University Press, 1970), and C. Hill, *Society and Puritanism in Pre-Revolutionary England* (Oxford: Oxford University Press, 1964), pp. 79-97.

46. Walzer, *The Revolution of the Saints*, and Harry S. Stout, *The New England Soul: Preaching and Religious Culture in Colonial New England* (New York: Oxford University Press, 1986).

to the sixteenth century situation, most members of the Puritan congregations apparently could, and did, read their own Bibles privately, along with a tremendous new devotional literature.[47]

In cultural terms we can see in the Puritans' exclusive orientation around text-based sermons and strict biblicism a fundamental re-ordering of the sensorium from sound to sight, and with that reordering, a cultural transformation from "traditional" to "modern." As anthropologist Jack Goody recognizes:

> In many cases it is "oral" and "literate" that need to be opposed rather than "traditional" and "modern." Awareness of alternatives is clearly more likely to characterize literate societies, where books and libraries give an individual access to knowledge from different cultures and from different ages. . . . But it is not simply the awareness of being exposed to a wider range of influences. . . . It is rather that the *form* in which the alternatives are represented makes one aware of the differences, forces one to consider contradiction, makes one conscious of the rules of argument, forces one to develop such "logic." And the form is determined by the literary or written mode. Why? Because when an utterance is put in writing it can be inspected in much greater detail, in its parts as well as in its setting: in other words, it can be subjected to a quite different type of scrutiny and critique than is possible with purely verbal communication. Speech is no longer tied to an "occasion"; it becomes timeless. Nor is it attached to a person; on paper, it becomes more abstract, more depersonalized. . . . "Traditional" societies are marked not so much by the absence of reflective thinking as by the absence of the proper tools for constructive rumination.[48]

The nearly universal access that Puritan readers would have to the Bible and the highly literate character of its constituency brought about a

---

47. Nichols, *Corporate Worship*, p. 103. Discussions of English literacy can be found in Thomas, *The Decline of Magic*, p. 4; C. S. L. Davies, *Peace, Print, and Protestantism, 1450-1558* (London: Paladin, 1976), pp. 190-91; and John Wilkes, "The Transformation of Dissent: A Review of the Change from Seventeenth to the Eighteenth Centuries," in *The Dissenting Tradition*, C. Robert Cole and Michael E. Moody, eds. (Athens: Ohio University Press, 1975), p. 113.

48. Jack Goody, "Literacy, Criticism, and the Growth of Knowledge," in Ben-David and Clark, eds., *Culture and Its Creators*, pp. 234-35. See also Walter J. Ong, *The Presence of the Word* (New Haven: Yale University Press, 1967).

mode of worship unprecedented in the English-speaking world. Bible readers who were accustomed to having the Word of God presented to them in vernacular propositional sentences could only understand printed liturgies as distorting the "clear light" of Scripture. While poetic cadences and repetitious phrases may have been necessary to an aural culture unable to fix statements in print they were, to Puritan readers, "needless repetitions." Unlike Scripture the *Book of Common Prayer* was a human invention, "an unperfected booke, culled and picked out of that popishe dunghil, the Masse booke full of all abhominations."[49] As such, it had to be utterly discarded. Archbishop Richard Hooker recognized the independent status vernacular Bibles conferred on common readers, together with the implications for traditional worship and social order:

> . . . which opinion once inserted into the minds of the vulgar sort, what it may grow unto God knoweth. This much we see, it hath already made thousands so headstrong in gross and palpable errors, that a man whose capacity will serve him to utter five words in sensible manner blusheth not in any doubt concerning matter of Scripture to think his own bare *yea* as good as the *nay* of all the wise, grace, and learned judgements that are in the whole world: which insolency must be repressed, or it will be the very bane of Christian religion.[50]

IV

Puritan worship was characterized by an unprecedented emphasis on Bible reading and systematic exposition of doctrinal meaning. As Perry Miller and others have demonstrated, there was a conscious intent in Puritan sermons to reduce everything to an intellectual meaning.[51] This inevitably suppressed the mystery and ritual that characterized Christian worship for centuries. From the premises that God's Word was limited to Scripture and that Scripture was intended to be read by those who under-

49. "The Second Admonition to Parliament," in *Puritan Manifestoes: A Study of the Origin of the Puritan Revolt,* W. H. Frere and C. E. Douglas, eds.(London: S.P.C.K., 1954), p. 21.

50. Richard Hooker, *Of the Laws of Ecclesiastical Polity* (New York: St. Martin's, 1975), p. 178.

51. See especially Perry Miller, *The New England Mind: The Seventeenth Century* (New York: Macmillan, 1939).

stood logic — that it was, in effect, a divine textbook — Puritan preachers honed the art of homiletics or sacred oratory into a science as precise as the humanists' science of rhetoric. Their sermons evidenced a distinctive "plain style" rhetoric that diagrammed the logical structure of Scripture with geometric precision.[52] In what was to become a binding literary form that Puritans never deserted, the plain style sermons overwhelmed the listener with a series of interrelated propositional statements all logically ordered (we should say "by the numbers") and arranged in such a way that literate people were taught a new way of knowing; a way of knowing that answered the questions they were raising. The method was so effective that, with practice, the devout laity could master it for themselves and proceed to "open up" the doctrinal meaning of their own Bibles. Even more important, the ministers themselves would no longer have to rely on homilies or printed sermons that they read or paraphrased. They could generate their own sermons.

The Puritan liturgy was formally codified by the Westminster Assembly in 1644. At first glance it is apparent that the *Westminster Directory* of worship, as it was titled, was no liturgy at all in the traditional sense of the term. It was merely a "directory" for ministers only. The directory was intended to be only a rough guide to worship. It mandated extemporaneous prayers and praise, which became "party Badges" that immediately distinguished Anglican from Puritan worship.[53] Fixed sermons in the form of homilies were regarded as no true sermons at all; like fixed prayers, they were eliminated from worship. But the distinctively plain, vernacular sermons, lacking in any classical allusions or ancient languages, dominated all parts of worship. From the marginal commentaries of the Geneva Bible the readers learned that the minister's spoken word was God's word and that "he that condemneth God's ministers condemneth God himself."[54] Even the closing prayer, according to the *Westminster Directory,* should sum up the major "heads" of the sermon. Because the intellectual meaning of Scripture was so central to Puritanism there could be no unexplained reading of Scripture verses. In place of the Anglican pericopes the *Directory* insisted that every worship

---

52. Puritan methods of biblical analysis and preaching were derived chiefly from the French logician Peter Ramus. For a thorough discussion of Ramus's rhetoric, see Walter J. Ong, *Ramus: Method and the Decay of Dialogue from the Art of Discourse to the Art of Reason* (Cambridge: Harvard University Press, 1958), and Miller, *The New England Mind,* pp. 111-364.

53. Davies, *Worship and Theology,* 2:189.

54. *The Geneva Bible,* p. 32.

service include readings of a full chapter from each Testament with exposition of doctrinal meaning.[55] Scripture reading, like prayer, became an abbreviated sermon.

Sacred space as conventionally understood with reference to special places of inherent holiness ceased to exist in Puritan worship. The church of Christ was invisible and the meeting house was a strategically located place of convenience where the faithful might gather together and hear the proclamation of the Word. In New England, the meeting houses were, as their title indicates, *houses* set aside for public worship; they claimed no sacred significance. The interior of the meeting house was not designed to stir up the imagination but to serve the functional criteria of enhancing the lecture of the sermon. The pulpit dominated the interior much as a lectern orients a classroom.[56] There were no stained glass windows, statuaries, or consecrated objects designed to impart a sacred significance.

In like manner, sacred time lost its earlier significance in Puritan worship. Horton Davies argues that "the single most notable characteristic of the Puritan calendar was its iconoclasm."[57] The sacred calendar of the *Book of Common Prayer* was entirely rejected, and with it the notion of holy days around which profane time revolved. In place of the calendrical system of festivals and Holy Days, the Puritans insisted on observing only the weekly Sabbath — a special, regular day marked off in modern mechanical time.[58] The Sabbath assumed central significance to the Puritan not as a sacred time instituted by the force of tradition, but as a commandment, upon which hinged the whole keeping of the written law. The Sabbath was given man for the sake of sanctification. The Puritans clearly separated ritual from sanctification and insisted that "the whole keeping of the Lawe standeth in the true use of the Sabbath, which is to cease our workes and to obey the will of God."[59]

The sacramental theology and practice of the Puritans stood in sharp

55. Nichols, *Corporate Worship*, p. 101.

56. See Ola E. Winslow, *Meetinghouse Hill, 1630-1783* (New York: Macmillan, 1952), and Peter Benes and Phillip Zimmermen, *New England Meeting House and Church, 1630-1850: A Loan Exhibition at the Currier Gallery of Art, Manchester, New Hampshire* (Boston: Boston University, 1979).

57. Davies, *Worship and Theology*, 2:240.

58. On the modern qualities of Puritan sabbatarianism, see Hill, *Society and Puritanism*, p. 209.

59. *The Geneva Bible*, p. 41.

contrast to previous modes of Protestant worship. In looking at the incidence and explanation of biblical types and symbols readers learned that they were simply signs with no inherent efficacy. Only sacraments specifically instituted by Christ had any sacred significance. The sacraments themselves were stripped of their centrality to an extent unprecedented in the Reformed tradition. From the Geneva Bible's notation on the Old Testament Passover Lamb readers learned that "the lambe was not the Passover, but signified it: as sacraments are not the thing itself, which thei do represent, but signifies it."[60]

Puritans did not recognize the altar as the special throne of the living Christ. The *Westminster Directory* insisted that the Lord's Supper be preceded by a sermon in which the meaning of the sacraments would be given out in plain language. Increasingly the intellectual meaning and not the ritual action became central. The Eucharist became a symbolic abstraction of a sort that could only exist in typographic cultures conditioned to make clear-cut distinctions between form and content. Such distinctions drove the Puritans to insist that the sacramental sign not be confused with what is signified. Confusing the sign with the savior was, at best, ignorance, and at worst, idolatry, and from the commentary on Exodus the Puritans learned "not onely not to worship idols, but to destroye them."[61]

In worship services the weekly celebration of the Eucharist was replaced by occasional celebrations and weekly sermons. Calvin's complex concept of the mysterious presence of the Holy Spirit as a "seal" to the promise of salvation could not be easily communicated to lay theologians, so the Eucharist tended to become represented as a special mnemonic. Not only was the *ex opere operato* of the Eucharist denied, but the *operato* itself became subordinate to the doctrine proclaimed from the pulpit. The "sign" of the sacrament had to "speak" in so many words, and the speech act dominated the sacramental act. Horton Davies argues that William Ames's Eucharistic theology subtly departed from that of Calvin: "Ames is clearly in the tradition of Calvin, but the logical rigour of his definitions, the consecutive march of his propositions like soldiers, and the general take-it or leave-it attitude, indicate that we are in a different atmosphere. In it Calvin's sense of awe, [his] humble recognition of mystery and sheer gratitude, have disappeared."[62]

---

60. *The Geneva Bible,* p. 29.
61. *The Geneva Bible,* p. 35.
62. Davies, *Worship and Theology,* 2:314.

In the final analysis neither natural objects nor non-verbal rituals appeared in Puritan worship. Verbal communication was considered the only valid mode of communication; it cut through meaningless forms to the pure content of Scripture. Ceremonies that once imparted an awe-inspiring experience of the *mysterium tremendum* came to stand between the Puritan and the plain sense of God's Word. Their reverence for ordinary language and plain style issued in nothing less than a new conception of language itself that challenged the existing "neo-classical" oratory of the Anglican divines. The Puritans' "Second Admonition to Parliament" was ruthlessly direct in its attack on Anglican speech. They preach, the writers of the Second Admonition asserted, "as ignorant Asses, loitering and idell bellyed Epicures . . . that thincke all the grace of preaching lieth in affected eloquence, in fonde fables to make their hearers laughe, or in ostentation of learning of their Latine, their Greke, their Hebru tongue, and of their great reading of antiquities: when God knoweth, moste of them have little further matter then is in the infinite volumes of common places. . . ."[63] Words could not be selected for the sake of art; they were instruments to be used functionally in the conveyance of simple propositional truth. Without intending to create a new aesthetic standard, this method of plain speech anticipated the "realistic" prose which was to characterize both scientific discourse and the literary novel in the eighteenth century.[64] Such consequences were unintended. Like everything else, Puritan speech derived from a direct imitation of the vernacular Bible.

Puritans insisted that their iconoclasm was in the interests of godly living and, on the level of conscious intent, this is no doubt true. Yet, as we have seen, Puritanism is as important for its consequences as its origins. When the religious fervor waned there was no longer an inherited tradition to instinctively fall back on. The traditional center of the universe had disappeared, and with it the stability engendered by sacred fiat. As Leonard Trinterud explains:

> Once the idea of the King in politics, or the creed, the order, or the liturgy in theology had been eliminated there was no longer any "given" or "established" form or norm in society. Recurrent or even perpetual revolution was possible, for mutual agreement of the majority of people

63. "The Second Admonition to Parliament," pp. 109-10.

64. Ian Watt, *The Rise of the Novel: Studies in Defoe, Richardson, and Fielding* (Berkeley: University of California Press, 1957), pp. 9-35.

provided no check upon the number of times that the people might change their minds in politics, in doctrine, in order, or in liturgy.[65]

A radicalized worship invariably spilled over into the week, sacralizing a revolutionary new community — a community of "Saints" who were modern and revolutionary. It furthered a radical (Weberian) "work ethic" by channeling sermon-generated anxieties into strivings for success in the material world. And it transformed worldviews by placing a premium on literacy and education. Without intending it, the way was cleared for new principles of order and alternative mythologies of legitimation which could dispense with the sacred altogether.

Conclusion

Seventeenth-century New England congregations replicated the liturgical world of their English forbearers exactly. And more than them they had the flexibility to bring their world of worship directly into their communities by reconfiguring every institution according to biblical writ. In the "Puritan Experiment," there would be no adiaphora; if there was not a specific biblical injunction the practice was discontinued. Every aspect of life would be grounded in particular biblical texts designed deliberately to stifle all creativity or tradition, in order to enact a "Bible Commonwealth." The Lord's Supper was administered occasionally, but sermons dominated the life of the faithful twice on Sundays. Sacraments were reduced to Baptism and the Lord's Supper. Marriage was no longer a sacrament (there were no biblical proof texts for it), and it wasn't even sacred. Rather marriage was a civil ceremony administered by the courts.[66]

Clearly for a learned clergy to endure in a New World "wilderness," and for reading audiences to proliferate, education would be critical in the Puritan colonies. As preaching and worship seeped into every institution of society, schools were created everywhere to ensure that the "old deluder Satan" would not be able to rule by rendering congregations illiterate. At the top, Harvard College, and later Yale College, were founded exactly on the model of the Oxbridge universities where first generation

65. Leonard J. Trinterud, "The Origins of Puritanism," *Church History* 20 (1951): 49.

66. For a good overview of Puritan institution building, see Francis Bremer, *The Puritan Experiment: New England Society from Bradford to Edwards* (Hanover, N.H.: University Press of New England, 1995).

English Puritans trained. The curriculum would be thoroughly classical, with the added innovation that every graduate would have to master Greek and Hebrew.[67] This, of course, was to ensure that the Scriptures would continue to be studied in their original tongues as well as the people's vernacular.

To a remarkable degree New England Puritans succeeded in creating and perpetuating their worshipful communities throughout the seventeenth century and well into the eighteenth.[68] The Geneva Bible would be replaced by the new "Authorized" or "King James" translation in the first generation, but the liturgy and plain style rhetoric of worship remained unchanged. In a New World environment where social stability barely existed in Spanish, French, or English colonies, and where revolution and conflict were endemic, the perpetuation of a Bible Commonwealth may have been the Puritans' greatest achievement.[69] And that achievement, in turn, owed more to worship than to any other religious or cultural force.

---

67. Still useful is Samuel Eliot Morison, *The Founding of Harvard College* (Cambridge: Harvard University Press, 1935).

68. See Stout, *The New England Soul.*

69. See T. H. Breen and Stephen Foster, "The Puritans' Greatest Achievement: A Study of Social Cohesion in Seventeenth-Century Massachusetts," *Journal of American History* 60 (1973): 5-22.

Worship, Experience, and the Creation of Methodist Place

Ruth Alden Doan

As the Methodist movement emerged on both sides of the Atlantic in the eighteenth century, people discovered new ways of experiencing their religious lives. Introduced to Methodism through both common and distinctive modes of worship — preaching, class meetings, solitary worship, quarterly meetings, love feasts, camp meetings — new adherents discovered in worship guidelines for what was essential in Methodism, for how to live a good life, for how to build a good society, and for finding their place both literally and figuratively. Because Methodism was so new and because of the nature of its central experiences, followers of the new movement did not always find a single path to the good life and the good society; rather, through their own behavior they proposed a diverse set of the directions that Methodist life might follow. Open opportunities for imagining and creating new spiritual and social worlds appeared in the context of physical spaces that Methodists experienced as locations open to meaning. When Methodists worshiped together, they created "none other than the house of God" and "the gate of heaven."[1]

The Methodist movement emerged in eighteenth-century England out of the work of Anglican preacher John Wesley who, in classic Protestant tradition, sought to reform his church rather than form a new one. Wesley touched many who sought new experience and new discipline in their religious and social lives. A long spiritual struggle came to a climax in a touchstone of Methodist experience, Wesley's own moment at Aldersgate, when he felt his "heart strangely warmed." For Wesley himself,

---

1. Thomas Rankin in *The Journal and Letters of Francis Asbury*, Elmer T. Clark et al., eds. (Nashville: Abingdon Press, 1958), 1:221.

however, the disciplined group may have defined his movement as much as did religious experience. Wesley invented the class meeting — a group of believers gathered to watch over one another's spiritual development — as the characteristic "methodistical" structure.[2] Within the class meeting, a Methodist found spiritual brothers or sisters who upheld rigorous standards of devotion and behavior. Although members of a class meeting might discuss belief, the meeting centered on holding them to a narrow spiritual and moral path. Thus Methodism reverberated through the Atlantic world as a movement of experience, piety, and discipline.[3]

The seeds of Methodism came to America with Wesley himself, when he visited Georgia in the 1730s, but the Methodist movement took off on the western side of the Atlantic with the arrival of Methodist preachers from the 1760s on. The movement first took hold in the Chesapeake region and spread both north and south from there. Thus, at the moment when the revolutionary era gave way to the early republic, Methodism was a movement rooted in Chesapeake society but given impetus by the opening moment that came with independence.[4]

As Donald G. Mathews has emphasized, early American Methodism was in its essence a liminal community that broke through out of religious experience.[5] That is, definitions of proper belief, behavior, social relation-

2. English Methodists organized both into class meetings and into bands — a body modeled after Moravian forms — but only the class meeting survived into later American Methodism, perhaps because the American class meeting subsumed the functions of both class and band.

3. On Wesley, see Frederick Dreyer, "A 'Religious Society Under Heaven': John Wesley and the Identity of Methodism," *Journal of British Studies* 25, no. 1 (January 1986): 62-83; Anthony Armstrong, *The Church of England, the Methodists, and Society* (Totowa, N.J.: Rowman and Littlefield, 1973); Albert C. Outler, ed., *John Wesley* (Oxford: Oxford University Press, 1964); Henry D. Rack, *Reasonable Enthusiast: John Wesley and the Rise of Methodism* (Philadelphia: Trinity Press International, 1989); Stanley Edward Ayling, *John Wesley* (Nashville: Abingdon Press, 1979). On English class meetings, see David Lowes Watson, *The Early Methodist Class Meeting: Its Origins and Significance* (Eugene, Ore.: Wipf and Stock, 1985).

4. William Henry Williams, *The Garden of American Methodism: The Delmarva Peninsula, 1769-1820* (Wilmington, Del.: Scholarly Resources, 1984).

5. Donald G. Mathews, *Religion in the Old South* (Chicago: University of Chicago Press, 1977); Mathews, "Evangelical America: The Methodist Ideology," in *Perspectives on American Methodism: Interpretive Essays*, Russell E. Richey, Kenneth E. Rowe, and Jean Miller Schmidt, eds. (Nashville: Abingdon Press, Kingswood Books, 1993), pp. 17-30; Mathews, "Women and the Spirit," paper in the possession of the author; Mathews, "Francis Asbury and Women in the Spirit," paper delivered at the Society for Historians of the Early American Republic. (Mathews's understanding of liminality derives, in turn, from Victor Turner, "Betwixt and

ships, and social spaces emerged through the open door of religious experience that made it possible for believers to reconceive their lives and futures. The one thing that Methodists could agree on was the centrality of that experience. Within that furnace, believers forged notions of the world and the future. As a result, there was no single definition of the moral life, proper authority, or social space within Methodism.

The moment of possibility of early Methodism found reinforcement in the revolutionary moment more broadly. Historian Gordon S. Wood argues that the hierarchical structures of the Old World had crumbled in the context of the New. By the late eighteenth century, opportunities for building horizontal rather than vertical relationships — for inventing communities based in the world of the new republic — opened for Americans in all walks of life.[6] Nathan O. Hatch argues that the post-revolutionary era was perhaps an even more opening and transformative time for popular Christianity in the United States, including but extending well beyond Methodism.[7]

Snapshots of worship illuminate the transformation. Historian Rhys

---

Between: The Liminal Period in Rites de Passage," in *Symposium on New Approaches to the Study of Religion: Proceedings of the 1964 Annual Spring Meeting of the American Ethnological Society,* J. Helm, ed. [Seattle: American Ethnological Society, 1964], pp. 4-20; Turner, *The Ritual Process: Structure and Anti-Structure* [Chicago: Aldine, 1969]; and Turner, *Dramas, Fields, and Metaphors: Symbolic Action in Human Society* [Ithaca: Cornell University Press, 1974].) Other works on early Methodism that have had a significant influence on this essay include Russell E. Richey, *Early American Methodism* (Bloomington: Indiana University Press, 1998); John H. Wigger, *Taking Heaven By Storm: Methodism and the Rise of Popular Christianity in America* (Urbana: University of Illinois Press, 2001); Cynthia Lynn Lyerly, *Methodism and the Southern Mind, 1770-1810* (New York: Oxford University Press, 1998); Christine Heyrman, *Southern Cross: The Beginnings of the Bible Belt* (New York: Alfred A. Knopf, 1997); Ann Taves, *Fits, Trances, and Visions: Experiencing Religion and Explaining Experience from Wesley to James* (Princeton: Princeton University Press, 1999). On a later period, see also A. Gregory Schneider, *The Way of the Cross Leads Home: The Domestication of American Methodism* (Bloomington: Indiana University Press, 1993). Careful studies of worship in the Methodist tradition that have been very helpful in the preparation of this essay are Karen B. Westerfield Tucker, *American Methodist Worship* (New York: Oxford University Press, 2001), and Lester Ruth, *A Little Heaven Below: Worship at Early Methodist Quarterly Meetings* (Nashville: Abingdon Press, 2000).

6. Gordon S. Wood, *The Radicalism of the American Revolution* (New York: Vintage, 1993).

7. Nathan O. Hatch, *The Democratization of American Christianity* (New Haven: Yale University Press, 1989). On the social origins of Methodism, see also Michael J. Crawford, "Origins of the Eighteenth-Century Evangelical Revival: England and New England Compared," *Journal of British Studies* 26, no. 4 (October 1987): 361-97.

Isaac found in Virginia tutor Philip Vickers Fithian the ideal commentator on the place of Anglican worship in the old order in the Chesapeake. Fithian wrote in his journal:

> I observe it is a general custom on Sundays here, with Gentlemen to invite one another home to dine, after Church; and to consult about, & determine their common business, either before or after Service — It is not the custom for Gentlemen to go into Church til Service is beginning, when they enter in a Body, in the same manner as they come out; I have known the Clerk to come out and call them in to prayers. — They stay also after the Service is over, usually as long, sometimes longer, than the Parson was preaching.[8]

Squeezing the sermon in between the important social business of the gentry was not so difficult since, as Fithian noted elsewhere, sermons tended to run no longer than fifteen minutes.[9] Nor was social status erased even in those few minutes: Anglican churches continued in the eighteenth century to seat the congregation by status, with the most eminent in front. Colonists added to this tradition the physical and visual distinction between free and slave by putting such slaves as came to worship in the balcony or gallery, in the back of the church, or outdoors. Nor did Fithian find the preaching inspiring; the Reverend Mr. Smith, he commented in one Sunday entry, was as "Cold as his Subject."[10]

At the very moment when Fithian was commenting upon the culture of Virginia Anglicanism, the Methodist movement was beginning to burn through that Chesapeake region. Soon it extended outward to, among other places, the Pennsylvania home of Henry Boehm. Boehm's account of a quarterly meeting stands in vivid contrast to Fithian's account:

> The meeting began on Saturday, and while the presiding elder [Thomas Ware] was praying the Holy Ghost filled the house where they had assembled. The work of revival commenced, and such were the cries of

8. Philip Vickers Fithian, *Journal and Letters of Philip Vickers Fithian, 1773-1774: A Plantation Tutor of the Old Dominion*, Hunter Dickinson Farish, ed. (Williamsburg, Va.: Colonial Williamsburg, Inc., 1943), pp. 57-58; Rhys Isaac, "Evangelical Revolt: The Nature of the Baptists' Challenge to the Gentry in Virginia, 1765 to 1775," *William and Mary Quarterly* 31 (July 1974): 345-68; Isaac, *The Transformation of Virginia, 1740-1790* (Chapel Hill: University of North Carolina Press, 1982).

9. Fithian, *Journal*, pp. 74 and 104.

10. Fithian, *Journal*, p. 104.

distress, the prayers for mercy heard all over the house, in the gallery as well as the lower part, that it was impossible for Mr. Ware to preach. He came down from the pulpit, and the brethren went to the penitent ones, as they found them in different parts of the house, and pointed them to Jesus, and prayed with them. They were assembled in different groups praying for the broken-hearted, and one after another found redemption in the blood of the Lamb. It was impossible to close the meeting, so it continued all day and most of the night. Sunday morning came, and they attempted to hold a regular love-feast, but all in vain. The cries of mourners, the prayers for mercy, and shout after shout as one after another passed from death unto life, made it impossible to proceed.[11]

Methodist worship was not orderly, cold, or short. Preachers moved from their elevated positions to mingle with the congregation. Voices arose from every corner of the meeting to signify that the Holy Ghost had come down to fill the individual, the congregation, and the house.

Evidence from numbers alone shows the extraordinary success of Methodists in early America. John Wigger opens his account of early Methodism with a summary of the "virtual miracle of growth" that took the movement from perhaps not even 1000 adherents in 1770 to 250,000 in 1820.[12] In those same decades, Methodists carried their movement from the DelMarVa peninsula northward to Pennsylvania, Massachusetts, Vermont; south across Virginia, into South Carolina and Georgia; and west to Kentucky, Tennessee, and then the Old Southwest.[13] Although the growth certainly did not stop there, Methodism's early expansion provides an opportunity to see the creativity of believers in fashioning a new world.

Like John Wesley, American Methodists deemphasized theological speculation in favor of experience, discipline, and community. Although they self-consciously posed their open road to salvation against what they saw as the rigidity of Calvinists, they proposed the tenets of Arminianism as much in action as in exposition. Similarly, the Methodist notion of the good society was taught in part in lessons, but was conveyed more impor-

11. Henry Boehm, *Reminiscences, Historical and Biographical, of Sixty-four Years in the Ministry,* Rev. Joseph B. Wakeley, ed. (New York: Carlton and Porter, 1866), p. 32.

12. Wigger, *Taking Heaven by Storm,* p. 3. Edwin S. Gaustad gives the following figures on the growth of Methodism: 64,894 in 1800; 174,560 in 1810; 273,858 in 1820; 511,153 in 1830 (*Historical Atlas of Religion in America* [New York: Harper & Row, 1962], pp. 79-82).

13. In spite of expansion into all regions of the country, Russell Richey correctly notes that early Methodism acquired a "Southern accent" (*Early American Methodism,* pp. 47-64).

tantly through experiences: who worshiped with whom, who testified, what emotional bonds were forged, and where Methodists saw truth in action.

Accordingly, an orthodoxy on social issues did not automatically emerge any more than did orthodoxy in belief. Creating Methodism out of experience and behavior meant that the conclusions about a proper Methodist life were heavily reliant on the point of view of the person experiencing or observing. Methodism opened the way for varied interpretations of the right paths through life. One way that contests over those differences played out was through the claiming of spaces and the creation of places in which one could be properly Methodistical.

THIS ESSAY BUILDS UPON what scholars have labeled the "spatial turn" in the study of cultures. That turn followed several decades of work by geographers and others who elaborated the perception that giving meaning to physical space was a factor in the creation of identities, in the forging of relationships, and in the claiming of power. Yi-Fu Tuan initiated much of this study in the 1970s, when he proposed going beyond the view of space as an artifact and exploring the possibilities of seeing place as "as center of meaning constructed by experience."[14] The distinction between space and place is itself a helpful one that allows the use of the shorthand *space* for physical locations and *place* for meaning-filled locations. If early Methodism emerged in liminal metaphorical space, then it is possible to see productions and constructions of Methodism playing out in literal spaces that became Methodist places.

If we ask where Methodists experienced religious power in the eighteenth and early nineteenth centuries, we find ourselves looking in characteristically Methodist places to understand how worship created experience, social ideals, and community. The physical spaces in which Methodists experienced religion roll outward from the individual to the broader society: Methodists found religious experience in the body, in the class meeting, and in the love feast as well as in regular preaching services. Early in the nineteenth century, Methodists, along with Baptists and

---

14. Yi-Fu Tuan, "Space: An Experiential Perspective," *Geographical Review* 65, no. 2 (April 1975): 152. See also Jonathan Z. Smith, *Map Is Not Territory: Studies in the History of Religions* (Chicago: University of Chicago Press, 1993). For an example, see Belden C. Lane, *Landscapes of the Sacred: Geography and Narrative in American Spirituality* (New York: Paulist Press, 1988). The theme of the 2005 annual conference of the American Studies Association was "Groundwork: Space and Place in American Cultures."

Presbyterians, added the camp meeting to the spaces that opened religious experience and community.

Methodists reported religious experience in graphic phrases that communicated the power of the spirit to burn into all parts of the believer — into the body as well as the soul. William McKendree of Tennessee, later a bishop of the Methodist Episcopal Church, South, met a spirit who both "made cold chills run over me" and "waked all my interlectual [*sic*] powers to attention." After his encounter, he wrote, "my sp[iri]t fluttered, my heart beat — all my powers was a wake [*sic*] and Selistial [*sic*] fire ran through ever [*sic*] power of my body."[15] Virginia Methodist Sarah Jones similarly recorded a moment of spiritual ecstasy which engaged and fused all parts of her being: "my soul melted, my heart flaming, my tongue oiled, my spirit fluttering." She concluded, "Glory seemed woven in my clay."[16] Nor was such experience a once-in-a-lifetime possibility. Early Methodists sought to duplicate — and succeeded in duplicating — such powerful moments in their lives. Long after his initial conversion and call to preach, James Meacham attended a class meeting in North Carolina at which "my Soul felt the Holy Sanctifying Streams of love."[17] Jones's letters recount a series of ecstatic moments and a continual quest to rediscover the flame.[18] Richard Graves's specific experience of sanctification was but one way that Methodists found for framing experience beyond conversion.[19] For early Methodists, then, life ideally was punctuated by repeated experiences of spiritual wholeness. Bodily raptures signified spiritual ecstasy.[20]

15. William McKendree, Diary, June 7, 1790, William McKendree Papers, Vanderbilt University.

16. Sarah Jones to William Spencer, December 5, 1791, in *Devout Letters: or, Letters, Spiritual and Friendly, Written by Mrs. Sarah Jones,* Jeremiah Minter, ed. (Alexandria, Va.: Printed by Samuel Snowden, 1804), p. 100.

17. James Meacham, "The Journal of James Meacham," August 3, 1789, in *Historical Papers of the Trinity College Historical Society,* series 9 (Durham, N.C.: Duke University, 1912), p. 83.

18. For example, Jones to Jeremiah Minter, January 26, 1790, in Minter, *Devout Letters,* p. 8; Jones to Minter, n.d., in Minter, *Devout Letters,* p. 33.

19. Graves's July 2, 1799, experience is cited in Lyerly, *Methodism and the Southern Mind,* p. 32.

20. Ann Taves argues that European Americans did not "elaborate and institutionalize dissociative experience at the heart of their worship life" as African Americans did (Taves, "Knowing Through the Body: Dissociative Religious Experience in the African- and British-American Methodist Traditions," *Journal of Religion* 73, no. 2 (April 1993): 213), but she does note that early Methodists, both black and white, placed "dissociative experience" at the center (*Fits, Trances, and Visions,* pp. 76-117). A common scholarly error reduces religious experience among Methodists to the conversion experience; in fact, both the lives and hopes of

Such experience came to the individual, indeed, but Methodists recounted experience as testimony also to the permeable and not the isolated self.[21] First, they sought moments when they were no longer separated from God. James Meacham both yearned to be "swallowed up in God" and found his "Soul . . . bountifully filled with God."[22] The metaphors chosen by Methodists to describe spiritual experience often pointed explicitly to a sense of permeability, as the spiritual crossed or erased the boundaries of flesh and individuality. Itinerant John Wesley Childs celebrated his sense that "Surely God has come unusually near me, and in me."[23] Sarah Jones provides perhaps the best example of a Methodist who repeatedly lost her sense of self in the melting raptures of experience. "Ecstatic raptures would creep through my heart," wrote Jones, "and Heaven slide through my crimson life."[24] At such moments Jones described herself as "a-kin to nothing, a-kin to dust, and yet engulphed in love to Christ."[25] If Jones found "golden chains" had "bound my head, my heart, my hands," that limitation led to a bursting of boundaries when "I feel my widening soul a sacrifice to love."[26] The frequently used metaphor of flames implied, similarly, that the separate self was burned away in the conflagration of experience.[27]

---

early Methodists were experience-drenched well beyond conversion. Sylvia Frey, for example, refers to all ecstatic experiences as conversion experiences in "Shaking the Dry Bones: The Dialectic of Conversion," in *Black and White: Cultural Interaction in the Antebellum South,* Ted Ownby, ed. (Jackson: University Press of Mississippi, 1993), pp. 23-44. Ann Taves, on the other hand, emphasizes experience throughout Methodist spiritual and religious life and attributes this in large part to the Methodist belief in and quest for sanctification (*Fits, Trances, and Visions,* p. 85).

21. Mechal Sobel discusses the transition from "a permeable or collective sense of self to a far more individual and interior one" in *Teach Me Dreams: The Search for Self in the Revolutionary Era* (Princeton: Princeton University Press, 2002), p. 18.

22. Meacham, "Journal," August 20 and 22, 1789, pp. 89-90.

23. Childs quoted in John Ellis Edwards, *Life of John Wesley Childs: For Twenty-three Years an Itinerant Methodist Minister* (Richmond and Louisville: John Early, 1852), p. 101.

24. Jones to Minter, quoted in Lyerly, *Methodism and the Southern Mind,* p. 27. Lyerly sees these descriptions of experience as pointing toward individualism and the exaltation of the self; it is possible to see the experiences equally as hearkening back to the premodern "we-self" of which Sobel speaks (*Teach Me Dreams,* p. 18).

25. Jones to Minter, quoted in Lyerly, *Methodism and the Southern Mind,* p. 27.

26. Jones to Dromgoole, n.d., Dromgoole Papers, Southern Historical Collection, University of North Carolina (hereafter SHC, UNC), Chapel Hill, N.C.

27. For example, Rebecca Ridgeley quoted in Lester Ruth, *Early Methodist Life and Spirituality: A Reader* (Nashville, Tenn.: Kingswood Books of Abingdon Press, 2005), p. 74; Jones to Minter, n.d., *Devout Letters,* p. 34.

Although Methodists cherished individual experience located dramatically within the body as central to their lives, they valued community at least as much as individuality. In fact, Methodist leaders learned that an emphasis on finding experience within — or even engulfing — the body combined with an excess of solitude proved dangerous to the values of the greater Methodist community. Unfortunately, although solitary experience taught many Methodists about the love of God and the power of spiritual experience, solitary experience taught some Methodists lessons for life that the community sought to suppress. Methodist preachers, in particular, may have been tempted to take the elevation of the spirit and the concomitant mortification of the body to extremes. Early circuit riders often arose well before dawn for solitary prayer; they remained on their knees without food or drink or physical comforts sometimes for hours on end.[28] The celibacy of the circuit rider was practical — one could hardly ride all week and attend to a family as well — but also served as a spiritual discipline.[29]

Yet worship, perhaps especially solitary worship, could lead to unwelcome conclusions about the life to follow after one arose from his knees. John Wesley Childs, for example, began by limiting what he would eat. He then chose to walk beside his horse rather than to ride in order to demonstrate his willingness to suffer for his calling and to try to heighten his religious experience through subjecting himself to trials.[30] Childs came under censure for this choice — perhaps his superiors found such behavior self-promoting as much as self-abnegating, perhaps they worried about competitive mortification of the flesh. A more dramatic case of such mortification was that of Jeremiah Minter, Methodist preacher in eastern Virginia. Minter took Scripture to heart in a way that went beyond the readings of the wider group when he took literally the 12th verse of the 19th chapter of Matthew, which celebrates those who have "made themselves eunuchs for the kingdom of heaven's sake."[31] Minter suffered excommunication for his act.

28. Francis Asbury warned against indulgence in eating or drinking in a letter to Ezekiel Cooper, January 2, 1795, in *The Letters*, vol. 3 of *The Journal and Letters of Francis Asbury*, J. Manning Potts, et al., eds. (Nashville: Abingdon Press, 1958), pp. 132-33.

29. William Spencer to Asbury in *Letters*, p. 125 n. 18.

30. Edwards, *Life of Rev. John Wesley Childs*, pp. 102-3 and 71-72.

31. Minter, *Devout Letters*, p. 86 n; see also Minter, *A Brief Account of the Religious Experiences, Travels, Preaching Persecutions from Evil Men, and God's Special Helps in the Faith and Life, &c., of Jerem. Minter* (Washington: Printed for the Author, 1817; Early American Imprints, Second series, no. 41451).

Faced with such fruits of solitary worship, Methodists had yet one more reason to redirect individual experience into community. In any case, as Russell Richey has argued, early Methodists experienced their religious movement as "profoundly social, collective, corporate."[32] They developed and repeatedly found new life in a number of collective worship opportunities, including the class meeting, the love feast, regular circuit preaching, and the camp meeting.

John Wesley's class meeting traveled across the Atlantic intact in form although perhaps altered slightly in purpose. As in England, Methodists in America gathered in class meeting to examine one another's spiritual and moral direction. Some early class meetings brought together men and women, blacks and whites, but by the 1790s most class meetings were segregated by sex and by race. Convened by the class leader, a class meeting generally opened with singing and went on to prayer and examination of individual members. Each person spoke to his or her spiritual state as well as transgressions in behavior. The intense sense both of personal significance and identity and of scrutiny was heightened by the fact that one could only enter a class meeting with a ticket — a literal piece of paper or card stock that identified one as a member — and that a ticket could be denied if one's attendance or behavior consistently fell beneath Methodist standards. In the American context, what followed that "methodistical" disciplinary phase may have been more important. After members testified to their spiritual and moral triumphs and tragedies, the class might begin to praise God as if they were in regular worship services. Testimony to the workings of the spirit in one's life followed logically from examination and discipline.[33] Ideally, the result was that "our hearts melted and ran together" in a freshly created community of experience and discipline.[34]

Though it bore some resemblance to the class meeting, the love feast was a specifically Methodist innovation that broadened the creation of community and place through shared religious experience. The love feast usually occurred as a part of two-day quarterly meetings that brought together ministers and lay people. Believers gathered to share a simple meal of bread and water, but the sharing of food was by all accounts less impor-

32. Richey, *Early American Methodism,* p. 16.

33. Watson, *The Early Methodist Class Meeting;* Ruth, *Early Methodist Life and Spirituality: A Reader;* Wigger, *Taking Heaven by Storm,* pp. 98-103.

34. John Kobler quoted in Lyerly, *Methodism and the Southern Mind,* p. 35.

tant than the sharing of religious experience that followed. Methodists black and white, male and female, young and old, preacher and lay person — sometimes a "vast multitude"[35] — all came together into a single circle of believers at the love feast. People from any and all categories, groups, or walks of life came forward to recount their spiritual journeys and experiences.[36] These testimonies frequently set the stage for ecstatic expression of religious experience, often called the shout.

Of course Methodists often worshiped in regular — and irregular — preaching services. Since the early Methodist ministry was largely itinerant, adherents heard preaching when and where they could. A preacher might stop on a Sunday or any other day of the week. He might find a chapel in which to preach, or he might preach in a barn, a house, or a field. In any case, when Methodists heard that the preacher had an appointment in their vicinity, they gathered from some distance to hear the word. The preacher began with a Bible verse selected for the occasion; it was considered a special gift to be able to select biblical passages effectively.[37] The preacher then would expound upon the Bible verse either according to plan or extemporaneously. When ordained preachers could not get to a neighborhood, others filled in. Some who were not fully preachers themselves read the sermons of ministers to the flock.[38] More typically of Methodism, lay people with talent for speaking, often called exhorters, arose to call their brethren to repentance, to faith, and to sanctification. In the end a Methodist might have a wide experience of preaching loosely understood, including the reading, praying, and exhorting of blacks and women as well as white men.[39] As in the case of the class meeting, Methodists often embraced ecstatic experience as the ultimate measure of the quality of preaching.

Although later participants and observers have emphasized the camp meeting as the original ground of evangelical growth and enthusiasm, the camp meeting actually emerged a little later in Methodist development, in the 1790s. They soon became central to evangelizing and to revitalizing

35. Boehm, *Reminiscences,* p. 53.

36. Ruth, *A Little Heaven Below;* see also Richey, *Early American Methodism.* Asbury recorded that "simple and loving testimonies" were given at a love feast in the northern neck of Virginia in 1787 (*Journal* 1:531, January 6 and 7, 1787). Henry Boehm was brought to conversion at a love feast (Boehm, *Reminiscences,* pp. 52-53).

37. See, for example, Boehm's comment on Asbury (Boehm, *Reminiscences,* p. 440).

38. John Wesley Young, Autobiography, SHC, UNC.

39. Wigger, *Taking Heaven by Storm,* pp. 25-36.

spiritual communities.[40] At camp meetings, seekers and adherents — and often scoffers as well — retreated to a space carved out for preaching, prayer, singing, and fellowship that would last for days. Often preachers and people from several denominations cooperated in the creation of a camp meeting, so that the new institution endowed similarities in evangelical tone across denominations. Methodists and others found at the camp meeting opportunities to testify to their religious experiences, to seek renewed experience of the Spirit, and to bring others into the fold of the godly. Pitching tents and gathering to worship was in many ways a classic experience of carving sacred place out of woodsy space.[41] Like class meetings, on the other hand, camp meetings pointed toward a future of racial segregation which prefigured a sense of the creation of a different kind of community than that envisioned by the likes of James Meacham. In any case, camp meetings famously offered opportunities for participants to pray, sing, speak, testify, and, of course, to shout.

That string of verbs underscores the larger truth that Methodist community forged itself through sound, especially through voice.[42] Although emphasis on the Word was the norm within the Protestant tradition, Methodist preachers spoke not just of the Word but also of their "liberty" in preaching.[43] That is, they found their ability to preach rooted in their own and their listeners' religious experience. Ideally, God would be "in the word and in the sound."[44] Preacher John Wesley Young attributed his ability to "Speak with some degree of Power" not to his own capacities but to the "Spirit of God."[45] Whites often attributed the power of African-American voices to the spirit of God working in and through them; if the black prayer leader or preacher were illiterate, whites saw his ability to speak with power as a special spiritual force. Voice broke through the limi-

---

40. Dickson D. Bruce, *They All Sang Hallelujah: Plain-Folk Camp-Meeting Religion, 1800-1845* (Knoxville: University of Tennessee Press, 1974); Paul K. Conkin, *Cane Ridge: America's Pentecost* (Madison: University of Wisconsin Press, 1990).

41. Lane, *Landscapes of the Sacred.*

42. On Methodism as a movement of the voice, see Richey, *Early American Methodism,* pp. 82-83.

43. Diane H. Lobody, "'That Language Might Be Given Me': Women's Experience in Early Methodism," in Richey et al., eds., *Perspectives on American Methodism,* p. 134.

44. Childs to Claiborne, July 24, 1829, in Edwards, *Life of Rev. John Wesley Childs,* p. 59.

45. Young, Journal, April 24, 1836. See also Ruth Alden Doan, "John Wesley Young: Identity and Community Among 'The People Called Methodist,'" *The Human Tradition in Antebellum America,* Michael A. Morrison, ed. (Wilmington, Del.: Scholarly Resources, 2000), p. 30.

tations of the body and became the conduit of the spirit.[46] Such empowered preaching could reach directly into the souls of listeners and bring conversion, sanctification, or other religious experience.

Voice created the Methodist community not just through the preaching in liberty of the minister himself, but more important through the voices of the congregation. James Meacham recounted that singing and praying preceded the happy experience when "the Lord broke into our Souls,"[47] and Meacham knew that "the God of Heaven was there" when "crying and shouting was on every side."[48] The shout was perhaps the most characteristic Methodist expression and experience of spiritual power.[49] The urge to give vocal and physical expression to the presence of the spirit could come to an individual, as it did to James Jenkins in 1790.[50] But the shout more often carried whole congregations out of this world and into another.[51]

The shout was so familiar to early Methodists that they rarely described it. Rather, they summarized that expression of ecstasy in simple references: "we raised a shout,"[52] or "the shouts of happy believers."[53] Methodist minister John Jeremiah Jacob did tell of riding from meeting to meeting when his wife began a shout, after which Jacob cried, "The Lord is here!" and a companion followed with, "Yes! Glory to God! I know the Lord is here! Oh, that all the world knew how good the Lord is! O, God is a God of love. I love every body, etc. Oh this is the best day I ever saw, etc."[54] Even when he recorded the verbal substance of the shout, the specific words were not of overriding importance to Jacob — many could simply

---

46. Sobel, *Teach Me Dreams*, p. 89. One observer commented about William Adams, who testified at a love feast in Virginia in 1777, "His words seemed like fire that flowed from a heart glowing with the love of Jesus and ran through many a happy soul then present" (Ruth, *Early Methodist Life and Spirituality*, p. 121); see also Young, Journal, April 27, 1828.

47. Meacham, "Journal," July 5, 1790, p. 75.

48. Meacham, "Journal," July 13, 1790, p. 77.

49. Winthrop Hudson, "Shouting Methodists," *Encounter* 29 (Winter 1968), available at http://www.piney.com/Cane.Ridge.ShoutingMethod.html; Taves, *Fits, Trances, and Visions*, pp. 76-117.

50. Cited in Sobel, *Teach Me Dreams*, p. 89.

51. Meacham, "Journal," June 17, 1791, p. 70; July 3, 1791, p. 75; August 25, 1791, p. 91; Young, Journal, June 11, 1815; Ezekiel Cooper quoted in Ruth, *Early Methodist Life and Spirituality*, p. 87. See Ann Taves, "Knowing through the Body," *Journal of Religion* 73 (April 1993): 200-222.

52. Meacham, "Journal," August 16, 1789, p. 89.

53. Jesse Lee quoted in Wigger, *Taking Heaven by Storm*, p. 114.

54. In Ruth, *Early Methodist Life and Spirituality*, p. 167.

be left as "etc." Instead, the shout as an expression of spiritual joy took precedence over the simple meaning of the words. Henry Boehm remembered that the widow Eliza Airey felt the Holy Ghost descend "in copious effusions," and as a result she "shouted aloud for joy and was greatly strengthened and encouraged."[55]

Usually a shout incorporated physical as well as vocal activity, as when a woman "took a regular jumping shout."[56] Worshipers experienced the shout as a power running through the body which resulted in a verbal outburst — quaking, shaking, falling, and jumping, along with calling out praise, became part of a single experience of being filled with the Holy Spirit. As Meacham wrote, "the dear black people was filled with the power & spirit of God," and that collective experience of the spirit led to "a great Shout to give Glory to God."[57] One critic of Methodist enthusiasm may have been making distinctions that were more precise than those caught up in the experience would have recognized when he denounced "screaming" and "jumping up and down in the same place" and "shouting"[58] as separate expressions. On the other hand, as Ann Taves has noted, Methodists did not use the word "shout" to refer to just any vocalization, with or without bodily effects. Rather, the shout was the expression of the glorying upward movement of a believer who may have groaned and screamed his or her way through a sense of conviction.[59] After falling, often literally, worshipers would "spring up with heaven in their eyes and music on their tongues, overwhelmed with love divine."[60] No wonder a worshiper might sing her hope to "die a shouting Methodist."[61] In the rapturous sound of the shout, a body of Methodists created community and created a living sacred place.

Although the voice of the preacher helped to create a community of worship, then, neither preacher nor people saw his individual leadership as the key to that creation. The voice of the preacher drew empowerment from the congregation; indeed, without a sense of power arising from his hearers, the preacher failed to find the "liberty" to preach.[62] As Thomas

---

55. Boehm, *Reminiscences*, p. 61.
56. Quoted in Wigger, *Taking Heaven by Storm*, p. 86.
57. Meacham, "Journal," p. 94.
58. In Ruth, *Early Methodist Life and Spirituality*, p. 187.
59. Taves, "Knowing through the Body," pp. 208-11.
60. Ezekiel Cooper quoted in Boehm, *Reminiscences*, p. 72.
61. Full text of this hymn is in Ruth, *A Little Heaven Below*, p. 231.
62. On liberty in preaching, see Jeremiah Norman Diary, June 5, 1793, and September

Rankin found at least once, the spiritual power of the congregation could intensify to the point that the preacher became obsolete: Rankin and fellow preacher Brother Shadford "could only sit still and let the Lord do his work."[63] Divine power in the congregation could, in fact, subvert what might have been the expected relationship between preacher and people. James Meacham faced this in 1789 when he "strove to meet" a class meeting, but "could not, the Lord would not let me, he willed the people should praise him."[64] Jesse Lee may also have been perplexed as well as pleased when he arrived at a quarterly meeting only to find that "The divine power was felt among the people before the preachers came together."[65] The people of Methodism created places of spiritual power — places where experience brought that power and places where the power could be expected to bring forth experience. As Thomas Rankin testified in 1774, the sound-filled place created through the voices raised at a love feast was "none other than the house of God" and "the gate of heaven."[66]

THE CREATION OF PLACE through shared religious experience implied a fluidity in the experience of race. When early Methodists gathered in class meetings, love feasts, and preaching services, they worshiped in both biracial and segregated contexts. African Americans participated in Methodist worship in numbers disproportionate to their representation in the total population.[67] As a result, black Methodists experienced the carving out of sacred places both on their own and in collaboration with white Methodists. When worshiping separately, blacks more than whites, of course, faced a lack of officially designated houses of worship. They raised

---

22, 1793, Stephen B. Weeks Collection, SHC, UNC; Thomas Mann, Journals, April 22, 1805 [typescript] SHC, UNC; "The Journal of Benjamin Lakin," July 22 and August 16, 1795, in William Warren Sweet, ed., *Religion on the American Frontier*, vol. 4, *The Methodists* (Chicago: University of Chicago Press, 1946), pp. 208 and 209. Mathews points out that the authority of the preacher depended upon and drew from "the response from the congregation," in "Evangelical America," in Richey et al., *Perspectives on American Methodism*, p. 29.

63. Rankin quoted in Tucker, *American Methodist Worship*, p. 37.

64. Meacham, "Journal," May 6, 1789, p. 70.

65. Lee quoted in Richey, *Early American Methodism*, p. 2. Taves, in *Fits, Trances, and Visions*, points to the "interactive" nature of such gatherings (pp. 86-90).

66. Rankin in Asbury, *Journal*, 1:221, June 30, 177[7] (also quoted in Taves, *Fits, Trances, and Visions*, p. 87). Asbury himself found that "power" among the people led him to feel "as if I was let into heaven" (*Journal*, 1:552, October 29, 1787).

67. Richey cites 1,890 black Methodists in 1786 and 12,215 in 1797 (*Early American Methodism*, p. 60).

their voices in kitchens, in quarters, in woods, and there created places of meaning for themselves.[68] A number of scholars have argued that African traditions provided a — perhaps the — primary foundation for ecstatic experience and specifically for the shout among Methodists.[69] Here the significant point has less to do with origins than with effects of ecstatic experience. African Americans received the spirit within, found in the spirit a source of their own voices, and built community out of those voices. Philip Bruce described slaves in Virginia crying out so that they "drowned out preaching," and then forming circles, the "happy" around the "careless," to create the place where they could "shout and praise God."[70]

When they worshiped together, whites often saw blacks as models or sources of religious experience. Itinerant James Meacham frequently sought out the "dear black brethren" because "God blest my soul with them"; on a similar occasion he rejoiced, "O what a heaven I felt within."[71] Thomas Rankin told the whites at a quarterly meeting in Virginia to look to the blacks seated separately but in the same chapel. The result of whites looking to blacks as models was that "the very house shook with the mighty power and glory of Sinai's God."[72] The melting unity of Methodist worship could thus join blacks and whites together into a spiritual community.

For some, such a transcendence of social boundaries was central to the experience of Methodist worship. As Jeremiah Norman recorded: "we had then a sermon to wives & Husbands, Children & Parents Servants &c — it

---

68. Meacham, "Journal," August 15, 1789, p. 88; Boehm, *Reminiscences*, p. 63.

69. Discussions of the African origins of African-American religion can be found in Albert J. Raboteau, *Slave Religion: The "Invisible Institution" in the Antebellum South* (New York: Oxford University Press, 1980); Sylvia R. Frey and Betty Wood, *Come Shouting to Zion: African American Protestantism in the American South and British Caribbean to 1830* (Chapel Hill: University of North Carolina Press, 1998); Michael A. Gomez, *Exchanging Our Country Marks: The Transformation of African Identities in the Colonial and Antebellum South* (Chapel Hill: University of North Carolina Press, 1998); Milton C. Sernett, *African American Religious History: A Documentary Witness* (Durham, N.C.: Duke University Press, 2000); Albert J. Raboteau, *Canaan Land: A Religious History of African Americans* (New York: Oxford University Press, 2001).

70. Frey, "Shaking the Dry Bones," p. 38. See also Robert Simpson, "The Shout and Shouting in Slave Religion in the United States," *Southern Quarterly,* 23, no. 3 (1985): 34-48.

71. Meacham, "Journal," July 23, 1789, p. 79; August 22, 1789, p. 90; see also July 24, 1789, p. 80.

72. Frey, "Shaking the Dry Bones," p. 32.

was a melting time around the Lord's table."[73] When "the Lord pour'd down his Spirit on the poor people both white and black,"[74] Methodists experienced not only spiritual brother- and sisterhood but also a model of social relationships that they could choose to carry out from worship to everyday life. For Meacham, the experience of sharing sacred place with slaves led directly to feeling the "weight of oppression" that "proud whites" imposed upon blacks.[75] He believed that coming together in spiritual unity should lead directly to a commitment to end slaveholding, and he rejoiced when "our Dear honest Hearted bro. Seward" decided to act on that belief and "broke the yoke of oppression from off of his poor slaves."[76] Similarly, Sarah Jones's experience of worship at a quarterly meeting led directly to her conviction that slavery was wrong.[77] Yet Methodists again could disagree about the implications of religious experience. When Meacham tried to convince Brother O. Myrick of the logic that followed on the experience of spiritual unity, Myrick refused to go where Meacham would lead; he remained a "bloody oppressor" in the face of Methodist experience.[78] In the long run, as many historians have noted, the "bloody oppressors" dominated not only the South but the Methodist Church in the South as well. It was only for a moment that the liminal experience of Methodist worship opened the door for relative social equality.[79]

The creation of place through shared religious experience also implied that there was no preexisting sacred ground. Although early Methodists spent a great deal of time traveling through wilderness, passing through an unspoiled natural world, or retreating to the woods to pray, they did not

---

73. Jeremiah Norman Diary, October 20, 1793, Stephen B. Weeks Collection, SHC, UNC, Chapel Hill.

74. Meacham, "Journal," August 22, 1789, p. 90.

75. Meacham, "Journal," August 15, 1789, p. 88.

76. Meacham, "Journal," June 26, 1789, p. 73.

77. Jones in *Devout Letters*, December 1, 1788, pp. 1-2.

78. Meacham, "Journal," p. 68. Asbury discussed slavery and "the difficulties attending emancipation" with McKendree and others in Virginia, November 15, 1785, *Journal*, 1:498; Meacham engaged in conversation on the "Abominable Custom of Slavery," "Journal," July 25, 1789, p. 80.

79. Donald G. Mathews, *Slavery and Methodism: A Chapter in American Morality, 1780-1845* (Princeton: Princeton University Press, 1965); Mathews, *Religion in the Old South*; Ann C. Loveland, *Southern Evangelicals and the Social Order, 1800-1860* (Baton Rouge: Louisiana State University Press, 1980); John B. Boles, "Evangelicalism in the Old South: From Religious Dissent to Cultural Dominance," in *Religion in the South*, Charles R. Wilson, ed. (Jackson: University Press of Mississippi, 1985).

learn from the Methodist community to perceive the natural world as a source of spiritual experience in itself. Circuit riders rode past trees, stumbled on rocks, forded streams, and there they found . . . nothing but trees and rocks and streams. Asbury once commented, "O what a world of swamps, and rivers, and islands, we live in here!" but showed no inclination to unpack the metaphors that seem obvious in retrospect. Instead, later in the same entry, he simply wrote, "Three miles on the water, and riding three more on roads under the water (such is the inundated state of the country), made our jaunt unpleasant."[80] A later generation, embracing a romantic sensibility about nature, found this early generation's failure to perceive the spiritual in the natural as peculiar at best. A biographer of circuit preacher Peter Doub, for example, was struck by the fact that, "In the multitude of his days, surrounded by earth and sky of ever changing mood, in sunshine and storm," Doub never mentioned in his journal "the gorgeous pageantry of nature."[81] On the contrary, if early Methodists ever found anything of spiritual significance in nature, it was as likely to be an embodiment of the devil as an opportunity for spiritual uplift.[82] Methodists found nature rough, challenging, dangerous; it was backdrop rather than source. The experience of melting community posed religious experience against or away from any specific physical setting.

The dearth of physical spaces set aside for worship faced Methodists of the late eighteenth and early nineteenth centuries with both trials and opportunities. The later-romanticized circuit rider emerged in part out of the necessities thrown up by distance, dispersal of believers, and lack of houses of worship. Circuit riders thus often traveled miles every day in order to cover preaching appointments. Each place where the traveling preacher led worship offered lessons in spiritual community to those who came to participate. When Methodists did find buildings in which to worship, they were as often as not shared with other evangelical groups.[83] The building itself was not consecrated, therefore; the consecration of Methodist worship always arose out of the gathering and the sharing in the spirit of those who came to worship there.[84] As an early twentieth-century historian of

---

80. Asbury, *Journal,* 1:534, February 13, 1787.

81. Rev. M. T. Plyler, "Peter Doub, Itinerant of Heroic Days," in *Historical Papers,* p. 43; see also Edwards, *Life of the Rev. John Wesley Childs,* pp. 189, 213-14.

82. Freeborn Garretson met both the "blessed spirit" and the "evil spirit" in the woods (Ruth, *Early Methodist Life and Spirituality,* p. 79).

83. Wigger, *Taking Heaven by Storm,* p. 37.

84. Kyle B. Roberts points out that Methodists in New York City were willing to replace

Methodism noted, "The old pioneers preached in barns, outhouses, on the roadside, anywhere they could find hearers."[85]

Not surprisingly, Methodists could gather outdoors as well as indoors to create spiritual community. Even where a chapel existed, Henry Boehm once observed a large crowd "obliged to go in a grove" to have room to carry on with their quarterly meeting and love feast.[86] Students of Methodism — indeed, students of American history more generally — are familiar with the camp meeting ground or the sacred grove as the original or foundational space for the creation and re-creation of Methodism. As traveling preachers followed their circuits, they also led worship in smaller gatherings in the homes of society members. Sometimes worship in the home involved a preaching service; more often worship in the home consisted of individual or small-group prayer and conversation — and perhaps shouting. If we follow adherents rather than preachers through the spaces carved out for Methodist worship, we can observe some of the lessons they learned about the nature of Methodist society and community — and the implications that Methodism sometimes had for the broader society, as well.

One implication of creating sacred places through prayer, through voice, and in experience seems to have been, for women in particular, that redefining space through practices of worship opened a path for reconceiving social as well as religious space.[87] Certainly, the late eighteenth and early nineteenth centuries saw renegotiations of appropriate roles for women, which renegotiations involved reconceptualizing female space. For many early Methodists, that process took place in the context of the agrarian society of the Chesapeake, not in the march toward separate spheres of the northern urban middle class.[88] In the Chesapeake and far-

---

their meeting houses in part because they did not see the building itself as sacred or as the source of religious experience and truth ("Creating an Evangelical Space: The John Street Meetinghouses and the Development of Methodist Identity, 1768-1858," paper presented to the Society for Historians of the Early American Republic, Montreal, July 2006).

85. L. L. Smith, "Methodism in Albemarle," in *Historical Papers*, p. 58. See also Asbury, *Journal*, 1:531, January 11, 1787.

86. Boehm, *Reminiscences*, p. 53.

87. Thus this essay speaks — more literally than perhaps she intended — to Beth Barton Schweiger's call for study of how women and slaves carved out "dissident spaces" through evangelical religion ("Max Weber in Mount Airy, Or, Revivals and Social Theory in the Early South," in *Religion in the American South: Protestants and Others in History and Culture*, Schweiger and Donald G. Mathews, eds. [Chapel Hill: University of North Carolina Press, 2004], pp. 48-49).

88. The classic statement is Barbara Welter, "The Cult of True Womanhood," in *Dimity*

ther South, the household continued to be the locus of both production and reproduction well into the nineteenth century.[89] The shattering of eighteenth-century patriarchal modes did not reach fully into the Chesapeake household; rather, Methodists in Virginia, for example, entered into a society that still affirmed ideals and practices of the domination of fathers and husbands over wives, children, and slaves. That form of patriarchy was expressed in the space of the plantation and the farm.

Yet women south of the Mason-Dixon line, like those to the north, also lived amid wider discussions of the roles of women in the creation of the new republic and their responsibilities for the nurture of strong republican male citizens.[90] Thus for Methodist women the renegotiations of womanhood overlapped with the emergence of Methodism itself to create a place to rethink how women and households might fit into the new society and the new religious community.[91] Sarah Jones modeled the process. Having learned in love feast, preaching service, and shared prayer that sacred place could be created wherever experience might erupt, Jones had a prayer house built on the plantation where she might retreat to seek religious experience. In that house, she could close the door and find "my soul melted, my heart flaming, my tongue oiled, my spirit fluttering."[92]

Jones's own sense of the spirit working within and her own ability to voice it with her oiled tongue allowed her to make a prayer house that went

---

Convictions: The American Woman in the Nineteenth Century (Athens: Ohio University Press, 1977).

89. Elizabeth Fox-Genovese, *Within the Plantation Household: Black and White Women of the Old South* (Chapel Hill: University of North Carolina Press, 1998).

90. Linda Kerber, *Women of the Republic: Intellect and Ideology in Revolutionary America* (Chapel Hill: University of North Carolina Press, 1980); Jan Lewis, "The Republican Wife: Virtue and Seduction in the Early Republic," *William and Mary Quarterly* 44, no. 4 (1987): 689-721; Carol Lasser, "Gender, Ideology, and Class in the Early Republic," *Journal of the Early Republic* 10, no. 3 (Autumn 1990): 331-37; Anya Jabour, *Marriage in the Early Republic: Elizabeth and William Wirt and the Companionate Ideal* (Baltimore: Johns Hopkins University Press, 1998).

91. Jan Lewis, *The Pursuit of Happiness: Family and Values in Jefferson's Virginia* (Cambridge: Cambridge University Press, 1985); Rosemarie Zagarrie, "The Rights of Man and Woman in Post-Revolutionary America," *William and Mary Quarterly* 55 (1998): 203-30; on openness for women in religion specifically, see Catherine Brekus, *Strangers and Pilgrims: Female Preaching in America, 1740-1845* (Chapel Hill: University of North Carolina Press, 1998). A different point of view is represented by Susan Juster, *Disorderly Women: Sexual Politics and Evangelicalism in Revolutionary New England* (Ithaca, N.Y.: Cornell University Press, 1994).

92. Sarah Jones to William Spencer, December 5, 1791, in Minter, *Devout Letters,* p. 100.

beyond a little structure for quiet meditation to become a sacred place of worship. Although Jones's experience came to her in solitude, she often read her spiritual experience as emerging from relationship. In particular, she perceived her relationship with her mentor, Jeremiah Minter, as the context through which her experience might be inspired. A letter or a journal entry written by Minter, for example, served as the social link that carried experience almost as effectively as his physical presence.[93] Jones's remarkable religious experiences allowed her to redefine her relationship with her husband and thus her role in the household as well. When she became a Methodist, her husband, Tignal (or Tygnal) Jones, refused to follow. Over time, however, she succeeded in leading Tignal into Methodism. Just as William McKendree had gone to the woods not to stay there but to find a new spiritual identity to carry back to his community, Sarah Jones went out to her little house to build the spiritual power that allowed her to return to the big house to transform her family and household.[94]

Worship within the household had some of the most interesting and potentially transformative implications for Methodist society and the broader American world. When Sarah Jones returned home from her little prayer-house in the woods, she "found dear S E, sister K Jennet, and Mr. Jones all on fire" in worship together.[95] As Jones herself had come to Methodism first, with her husband ultimately following her into the new society, she became the spiritual leader and Tignal Jones the follower in their household.[96] This rearrangement of authority played out in other households as well. There is some evidence that women sought to build upon their roles in leading family members and sometimes whole congregations into the experience of Methodism to reconceptualize the role of the household in religious life.

Historians of Methodism adhere to a long tradition of celebrating the "Mothers in Israel," those women who helped to spread, nurture, and reinforce the Methodist movement, and especially to support their ministers, in the movement's early decades. Francis Asbury frequently noted the significance of women both in providing him physical care and in inspiring

---

93. Jones to Minter, January 25, 1790, and May 11, 1790, in Minter, *Devout Letters.*

94. Jones's influence over Tignal was limited, however: she did not succeed in persuading him to free his slaves.

95. Jones to Minter, January 25, 1790, *Devout Letters,* p. 6.

96. Lyerly discusses Sarah and Tignal Jones in *Methodism and the Southern Mind,* pp. 109-10; see also George Coles, *Heroines of Methodism; or, Pen and Ink Sketches of the Mothers and Daughters of the Church* (New York: Carlton and Porter, 1857), pp. 165-66.

him to higher spiritual development.[97] Many circuit riders did not just mention but glorified the women who offered them food and housing, cared for them in their days of illness, led them in prayer, and even gave them spiritual advice.[98] Without these women, it was clear, the system of itinerancy could not have survived through those early decades. Thus there was already a tradition of celebration before George Coles wrote *Heroines of Methodism* in 1857, a work that praised over a hundred women.[99]

More recently, professional historians have explored the significance of the Mothers in Israel.[100] Historian Cynthia Lynn Lyerly points to Methodist women who hosted prayer meetings, supported clergy, experienced visions, "reproved sin," testified, and exhorted.[101] Through such examinations, scholars have come closer to understanding the dynamics of leadership and the creation of Methodist community in the new republic.

One remarkable instance of a Mother in Israel transforming space into place comes in a selection from Benjamin Lakin highlighted by historian Diane H. Lobody. Lakin described a woman who first "got so happy that she hung upon her husband in raptures of joy," and then "ran through the [meeting] house." Most significantly, in Lobody's interpretation, "the house could not hold her" and "she rushed out the door to invite others to come to Jesus."[102] As Lobody argues, "the house could not hold" her is a statement about identity, liberty, and power. It also implies that claiming identity, liberty, and power has a spatial dimension.[103] Lakin's Methodist woman became a leader of others, a conduit to conversion, through her movement out of the meeting house and her choice to bring others in.

Thus, when we read stories of Mothers in Israel as narratives told from

97. Mathews, "Francis Asbury and Women of the Spirit."

98. Boehm, *Reminiscences,* pp. 60-61; Wigger, *Taking Heaven by Storm,* pp. 160-68; Lyerly, *Methodism and the Southern Mind,* pp. 98 and 101-2.

99. Coles, *Heroines of Methodism.*

100. For example, Mathews, "Francis Asbury and Women in the Spirit."

101. Lyerly, *Methodism and the Southern Mind,* pp. 94-118.

102. Lobody, "'That Language Might Be Given Me': Women's Experience in Early Methodism," in Richey et al., eds., *Perspectives on American Methodism: Interpretive Essays* (Nashville: Kingswood Books, 1993), p. 134.

103. Contrast the comment of Rachel Stearns, a northern Methodist of a later generation: "I long for any opportunity to shout God's praises. I never could shout in an improper place." (Quoted in Candy Gunther, "The Spiritual Pilgrimage of Rachel Stearns, 1834-1837: Reinterpreting Women's Religious and Social Experiences in the Methodist Revivals of Nineteenth-Century America," *Church History* 65, no. 4 [December 1996]: 586.)

the point of view of the women, that movement in space as a way of claiming social place becomes clearer. If the house of Mrs. Mary Addoms was "ever open to receive the ministers of Christ, with whom she delighted to converse on spiritual subjects," then Addoms may have seen her role as one of mentor and teacher, and the invitation into her house as a transformation of her house into a religious place.[104] The probably quite formidable Sarah Roszel of Loudon County, Virginia, etched out a place for herself as teacher and built meaningful place through communal experience when she brought her neighbors into the local schoolhouse for singing, prayer, exhortation, and class meeting.[105]

Mother Elizabeth Russell found in Methodist experience a source for new ways of living. Russell took on the role of Mother in Israel: she brought ministers home with her, advised, and prayed. Beyond this, she found in her experience at Methodist worship a new vision for the physical and functional nature of her household. Left to her own devices in widowhood, she literally rebuilt her home, reconfiguring its space into both domestic and spiritual place. She not only provided spaces where ministers and congregants could sleep but created a special room for religious worship. When ministers came to stay, she ordered a pulpit to be brought forward into the "big room" of her house so that the visitor could preach. When no preacher came, Mother Russell led those gathered in prayer.[106] Finally, like a number of other Methodists, she chose to free the slaves over whom she had legal control.[107]

Early American Methodist women did not seek the "Domestication of American Methodism" of which A. Gregory Schneider speaks.[108] Neither in the United States as a whole, nor in the Chesapeake region in particular, had the separate spheres of the mid-nineteenth century been carved out by 1800 or 1820. Without the sense of an isolated domestic, nurturing, pious female sphere, there was no context that required women to conceive of their religious roles and religious places as carried out within that particu-

---

104. Coles, *Heroines of Methodism,* pp. 156-57.

105. Coles, *Heroines of Methodism,* pp. 194-95.

106. Coles, *Heroines of Methodism,* p. 36; Julia A. Tevis, "Sixty Years in a School-room," in Coles, *Heroines of Methodism,* pp. 42-43. See also Wigger, *Taking Heaven by Storm,* pp. 164-66.

107. Thomas L. Preston, *A Sketch of Mrs. Elizabeth Russell, Wife of General William Campbell, and Sister of Patrick Henry* (Nashville: Publishing House of the M.E. Church, South, 1888), p. 26.

108. Schneider, *The Way of the Cross Leads Home.*

lar version of home. Instead, as in the larger social debate over domestic and public spaces, Methodist women took the opportunity to envision new spaces and places that would grow out of and validate new relationships. The new space implied by Russell's actions was neither solely domestic nor solely public. It was multifunctional, just like the household of the early South. If the household could be the locus of production and reproduction, and the head of household could be the head of economic pursuit and the head of family life, then it was also possible, in the universe opened up by early Methodism's world of worship, to envision physical space not limited by old categories of church and household nor yet driven into the narrow future categories of domestic and public.

EARLY METHODISTS SHARED the intense experience of the spirit of God within. They shared with equal intensity the sense of the community as the locus of spiritual experience and source of meaningful relationships. Out of those shared experiences, Methodists drew varied conclusions about the nature of the good life and the nature of the good society. The disputes into which they entered were not always carried on as debates. Methodists often asserted their visions of how and where to live through behavior rather than through wordy expositions. Their sense of the fluidity of the self, the fluidity of social relationships, and the fluidity of space and place grew out of their religious experience of producing the gate of heaven wherever they gathered. For a moment in the early republic Methodists found that they could shout out a new social world.

Horizons of Faith: San Antonio Tejanos in the Texas Republic

Timothy Matovina

The tolling bells of San Fernando parish in San Antonio solemnized the afternoon of February 25, 1837. A year earlier Mexican troops under General Antonio López de Santa Anna had defeated the garrison at the old Alamo mission, only to subsequently lose the decisive battle of San Jacinto which won independence for Texas. Now local residents could finally hold an interment ceremony for the fallen Alamo defenders. The organizer of the event was native San Antonian and Texas military officer Juan Seguín, a San Jacinto veteran who had escaped death in the Alamo battle only because he was sent through enemy lines to seek reinforcements. In his official report of the funerary rites, he stated that the remains of his fallen comrades had been left in three heaps after Santa Anna ordered San Antonio's mayor and residents to burn the corpses. Seguín had the ashes which still remained placed in a coffin marked with the names of famed Alamo defenders William Barret Travis, James Bowie, and Davy Crockett. He then had the coffin adorned with a Texas flag, a rifle, and a sword and laid out for public viewing at the parish church. On February 25 soldiers, civic authorities, clergy, musicians, relatives of the deceased, and the general populace processed with the coffin from the church back to the site of the ash heaps. Colonel Seguín gave a speech to the crowd in Spanish, while Major Thomas Western addressed them in English. Soldiers fired three volleys of musketry over the spots of the funeral pyres, interred the coffin, and then marched back into the town.[1]

---

1. Juan Seguín to General Albert Sidney Johnston, March 13, 1837, Johnston Papers, Howard Tilton Memorial Library, Tulane University, New Orleans; *Columbia* (later *Houston*) *Telegraph and Texas Register*, March 28, April 4, 1837. Seguín's speech and letter are also

At first glance this interment ceremony appears rather typical for a military funerary rite, enmeshing elements of patriotism and religious faith. Seguín finished his oration with the bold claim: "The venerable remains of our worthy companions as witnesses, I invite you to declare to the entire world, 'Texas shall be free and independent, or we shall perish in glorious combat.'" Western asserted that the Alamo defenders' "souls are with God in the regions of bliss, their memory is engraven [*sic*] on the heart of every votary of freedom throughout the universe, and their names are inscribed on the brightest shaft on the pinnacle of the temple of fame."[2]

Yet in at least one respect the public ritual to inter the Alamo slain was a remarkable event: the mutual participation of San Antonio natives who had just been through a civil war that divided friends and even families in their loyalties. Gregorio Esparza fought for Texas and died in the Alamo, where he had taken his wife Anna Salazar Esparza and their four small children, all of whom survived the battle. His brother Francisco fought on the Mexican side. José Antonio Navarro was a signer of the Texas Declaration of Independence whose brother Eugenio enlisted in the Mexican army. The local pastor, Father Refugio de la Garza, was a former representative to the Mexican National Congress and he too sympathized with the Mexican cause. But on this occasion those whom the crucible of war had turned into supposed enemies now joined in common worship, exhibiting a unity that is especially noteworthy when compared to the years of ongoing spite following similarly fratricidal conflicts like the U.S. Civil War.

Still, the capacity of worship to unify diverse parties was far from absolute, as Seguín's emphatic assertion about Texas independence to a crowd encompassing Mexican national sympathizers illuminates. Subsequently both Seguín and José Antonio Navarro repudiated Father de la Garza to Roman Catholic authorities, the Texas government arrested the priest for corresponding with Mexican military leaders, and he fled to Mexico. The year after the interment ceremony an Anglo-American named Tinsley denounced Eugenio Navarro as a traitor and instigated a fight in which the

---

in *A Revolution Remembered: The Memoirs and Selected Correspondence of Juan N. Seguín,* Jesús F. de la Teja, ed. (Austin: State House, 1991), pp. 156, 161-62. For San Antonio mayor Francisco Antonio Ruiz's account of the disposal of the corpses after the battle and other San Antonians' eyewitness accounts of the battle and its aftermath, see Timothy Matovina, *The Alamo Remembered: Tejano Accounts and Perspectives* (Austin: University of Texas Press, 1995).

2. *Columbia* (later *Houston*) *Telegraph and Texas Register,* April 4, 1837.

two combatants mortally wounded each other. When he came on the scene Eugenio's brother José Antonio urged the gathering crowd not to engage in retaliatory violence, but his conciliatory response did not purge his anguish and that of his family. The Navarros buried Eugenio in San Fernando church with a marker that to this day testifies he "fell an innocent victim, by a shot from the pistol of a vindictive adversary."[3]

During the period of the Texas Republic (1836-45), the Tejano[4] or Mexican-descent population of San Antonio adapted to significant political, economic, social, and ecclesiastical changes. Numerous elements of their social life intersected in public rituals like the Alamo interment ceremony: political views, communal relations, local religious traditions developed over the century since the settlement's founding, and the common struggle for survival in a time of social upheaval. Their worship for established annual feast days like that of Our Lady of Guadalupe reflected the reconfigured social relations as San Antonio entered the first stages of transition from an agricultural town into a more pluralistic urban locale. Funerals, processions, and other religious practices mirrored and responded to the tumult of violence, disease, and physical deprivation that were constant dangers in what in Spanish is called *lo cotidiano*, literally "the quotidian" but also connoting the trials and struggles of daily life. Such expressions of faith are enacted more independently of ecclesial and societal norms than the more liturgically regulated weekly Sunday Eucharist, providing a rich source for examining their practitioners' life and wor-

---

3. Juan Seguín, "Affidavit on Parish Priests of Béxar and La Bahía," January 5, 1839, in De la Teja, ed., *A Revolution Remembered,* p. 172; John Timon to Anthony Blanc, January 17?, 1839, University of Notre Dame Archives, South Bend, Indiana (UND); Timon, "Narrative of the Barrens," p. 39, Vincentian Archives, St. Mary's of the Barrens, Perryville, Missouri; "Señor Navarro Tells a Story," in *Rise of the Lone Star: A Story of Texas Told by Its Pioneers,* Howard R. Driggs and Sarah S. King, eds. (New York: Frederick A. Stokes, 1936), pp. 272-75; John J. Linn, *Reminiscences of Fifty Years in Texas* (1883; reprint, Austin: State House, 1986), pp. 345-46; "San Fernando Cathedral Deaths," Book 3, May 7, 1838, Catholic Archives at San Antonio, Chancery Office, Archdiocese of San Antonio (CASA).

4. The term "Tejano" was extant in primary documentation as early as 1824, although most nineteenth-century references to people of Mexican heritage in Texas name them Mexicans or *mexicanos*. Contemporary historians have employed the word Tejano to designate the regional identity of Texas residents that began to evolve during the eighteenth century. In this essay I follow their usage and employ the term and its feminine form Tejana in reference to native-born and long-term ethnic Mexican residents in San Antonio. Adán Benavides, "Tejano," in *The New Handbook of Texas* (Austin: Texas State Historical Association, 1996), 6:238-39.

ship. As Virgilio Elizondo has noted, "the ensemble of beliefs, rituals, ceremonies, devotions, and prayers which are commonly practiced by the people at large . . . express the deepest identity of the people."[5] In the wake of the Alamo battle and Texas independence, common worship was a core element in the vital interplay between Tejanos' everyday lives, theological worldviews, and faith expressions, all of which were in flux.

The Evolution of the Guadalupe Feast

San Antonio Tejanos had long celebrated annual feasts on the Roman Catholic liturgical calendar, especially feast days for patron saints deemed to have a particular relationship with their community. One such feast was San Antonio de Padua, the renowned Franciscan preacher whose June 13 feast fell on the day in 1691 when Spanish subjects first visited the future site of the Texas town that would bear his name. Another was San Fernando, the namesake of Ferdinand VI, a future heir to the Spanish throne whose father decreed and funded the formal establishment of a *villa* or town on the San Antonio River in 1731. Ferdinand bore the name of San Fernando, the thirteenth-century saint and king noted for his piety and recapture of territories from the Moors. Feast-day celebrations at San Antonio included religious ceremonies like Mass, dances, and other holiday festivities. The frequency, fervor, and festive ambiance of San Fernando parish's antebellum feast-day celebrations made them one of the most memorable features of life in San Antonio during this period. Well into the following century, area residents like Enrique Esparza recalled wistfully that "we had many saint days. Then we would visit with relatives and friends . . . [and] join in the fiesta around San Fernando." Sarah French, who settled at San Antonio with her family in the mid-1840s, remembered that during her early years in the town local customs included "the observing of certain Saints' days." Prominent among these days was the December 12 feast in which "the image of a woman, Saint Guadalupe, the patron saint of Mexico, was carried around the streets."[6]

5. Virgilio Elizondo, "Popular Religion as Support of Identity," in *Beyond Borders: Writings of Virgilio Elizondo and Friends,* Timothy Matovina, ed. (Maryknoll, N.Y.: Orbis, 2000), p. 126. See also Elizondo and Matovina, *Mestizo Worship: A Pastoral Approach to Liturgical Ministry* (Collegeville, Minn.: Liturgical Press, 1998); Orlando O. Espín, *The Faith of the People: Theological Reflections on Popular Catholicism* (Maryknoll, N.Y.: Orbis, 1997).

6. "Esparza, the Boy of the Alamo, Remembers," in *Rise of the Lone Star State,* Driggs

Devotion to Our Lady of Guadalupe dates from the sixteenth century and the original chapel built in her honor on the hill of Tepeyac in Mexico City, where she reportedly appeared to the indigenous neophyte Juan Diego in 1531. According to the Nahuatl-language Guadalupe apparitions narrative, the *Nican mopohua* (a title derived from the document's first words, "here is recounted"), Guadalupe sent Juan Diego to request that Juan de Zumárraga, the first bishop of Mexico, build a temple at Tepeyac in her honor. At first the bishop doubted the celestial origins of this request, but came to believe when Juan Diego presented him exquisite flowers that were out of season and the image of Guadalupe miraculously appeared on the humble *indio's tilma* (cloak).[7]

Guadalupan devotion was initially concentrated in Mexico City and its environs and then gradually expanded toward the north. By the time of Mexican independence in 1821 the devotion had spread throughout the viceroyalty of New Spain. Guadalupe's feast was the only Marian or saint day on a list of official national holidays which the Mexican Congress decreed in 1824. The observations of foreign visitors to the newborn Mexican Republic reveal that this legal prescription was accompanied by her widespread acclaim as a national patroness. One newcomer described Guadalupe as "the most venerated saint in Mexico, especially since independence" whose image was so popular that it was "found not only in churches but even in establishments alien to the faith."[8]

As the devotion spread northward the contingent of *mestizo* (mixed blood) parishioners at San Fernando made theirs the first congregation in what is now the United States to honor Guadalupe as a primary patroness.

---

and King, eds., p. 219; "Mrs. French's Reminiscences of Early Days in Béxar," in S. J. Wright, *San Antonio de Béxar: Historical, Traditional, Legendary* (Austin: Morgan, 1916), p. 98.

7. The Nahuatl original and an English translation of the *Nican mopohua* are in Lisa Sousa, Stafford Poole, and James Lockhart, eds. and trans., *The Story of Guadalupe: Luis Laso de la Vega's Huei tlamahuiçoltica of 1649* (Stanford: Stanford University Press, 1998), pp. 60-93.

8. National Congress decree on religious feasts and civic holidays, November 27, 1824, "Mission San Antonio de Valero Marriage Register, 1709-1788, 1797-1811, 1825," item #618 (second to last page), CASA; Jean Louis Berlandier, *Journey to Mexico during the Years 1826 to 1834*, trans. Sheila M. Ohlendorf, Josette M. Bigelow, and Mary M. Standifer (Austin: Texas State Historical Association, 1980), 1:127. For the gradual expansion of Guadalupan devotion and its nationalistic overtones, see Timothy Matovina, *Guadalupe and Her Faithful: Latino Catholics in San Antonio, from Colonial Origins to the Present* (Baltimore: Johns Hopkins University Press, 2005), pp. 4-12; Jacques Lafaye, *Quetzalcoatl and Guadalupe: The Formation of Mexican National Consciousness, 1531-1813* (Chicago: University of Chicago Press, 1976).

Observed since the first decades after the parish's foundation in 1731, by the nineteenth century the Guadalupe feast had grown to become the settlement's most prominent annual celebration. December was known as "la temporada de fiestas" (the season of feasts) as devotees extended the celebration of the Guadalupe feast into a prolonged period of rituals and revelry that lasted through the Christmas season. The boisterous crowds, aroma of *caldo* and *cabrito,* sound of hands patting out *masa* into *tortillas,* taste of *aguardiente de caña* (rum) and children's much-loved *piloncillo* (brown sugar cane), festive clothing, dramatic spectacle of bullfights, and dances, games, and general frivolity on the two plazas surrounding San Fernando church conjoined with solemn Masses, the singing of traditional hymns, and prayers of thanksgiving and supplication. As Jesús F. de la Teja has observed, the festivities were "timed to coincide with the break between the late maize harvest and the early-year cattle branding and planting preparations," thus enabling the local populace "to celebrate another year of survival as a community" and express its hope for future protection and sustenance.[9]

The 1830 census of San Antonio revealed that on the eve of Texas independence more than 60 percent of employed residents were farmers. In the following decades devotees continued to invoke Guadalupe's intercession for assistance with agricultural pursuits. One local Tejana spoke to Guadalupe when rain was needed and annually had a Mass offered and the church bells rung to honor her patroness. Although the woman was poor, she went from house to house with the Guadalupe image collecting donations to cover the expenses of her celebration. Another Tejana reportedly held a Guadalupan image over the San Antonio River and induced floodwaters to recede. A newcomer to San Antonio later recalled that

> . . . the gardens or farms were so close to the city that if we listened at the first streak of dawn we could hear the laborers going forth to work and humming a song of praise to María Santíssima [*sic*], protectress of the field:

> Thou art the Shepherdess,
> Lovely and fair,

9. "Minutes of the City Council of the City of San Antonio, 1830 to 1835, Spanish Minute Book Two" (typescript), December 1, 1831, Center for American History, University of Texas, Austin (CAH); Jesús F. de la Teja, *San Antonio de Béxar: A Community on New Spain's Northern Frontier* (Albuquerque: University of New Mexico Press, 1995), p. 149; Matovina, *Guadalupe and Her Faithful,* chap. 2, "Patroness of *la Frontera,* 1731-1836," pp. 46-64.

The sun that surpasseth
The moon and the stars.[10]

Nonetheless, during the period of the Texas Republic San Antonio entered a period of transition from a relatively homogeneous Mexican Catholic agricultural settlement to an increasingly diverse urban milieu, a process which would culminate in the arrival of the first railroad four decades later. The association between Guadalupe and the raising of crops was already beginning to diminish. Fewer residents engaged in farming, the town limits expanded, the sight of farmlands in the distance grew increasingly rare along the Guadalupe procession route, and evening dances replaced the former festivities of food booths and games on the plazas which had distinguished the Guadalupe feast as a harvest festival. As Tejanos organized their annual feast within an evolving social situation and welcomed newcomers into their worship traditions, the Guadalupe celebrations were transformed even as they helped reconstitute interrelations in the local populace. Like the Alamo interment ceremony, the participation of diverse groups and persons, even those who conflicted with one another in other social arenas, was a noteworthy characteristic of Tejano feasts and worship.

San Antonio's most important demographic characteristic during the Texas Republic was that it was a predominantly Tejano town in a primarily Anglo-American nation. The only official census of this period was conducted in 1840, but it lists land holders only and does not indicate the overall population. Travelogues and travelers' accounts vary in their estimates of San Antonio's population but consistently indicate that the town was a Tejano stronghold with a comparatively small but influential and growing group of Anglo-American newcomers. Population estimates ranged from a high of two thousand to under a thousand. These discrepancies are partly due to differences in perception, but they also reflect the actual population flux during times of peace and hostility. After the Texas Revolution, for example, a Houston newspaper reported that "many of the Mexicans who fled the country at the time of the invasion are returning. . . . [They] fled to the settlements on the Rio Grande, not so much on account of hostility to us, as to withdraw their wives and children from the scene of

---

10. Gifford White, *1830 Citizens of Texas* (Austin: Eakin, 1983), pp. 79-112; Catherine McDowell, ed., *Letters from the Ursuline, 1852-1853* (San Antonio: Trinity University Press, 1977), pp. 272-73; Sarah Brackett King, "Early Days in San Antonio Recalled by a Pioneer Resident of the City," *San Antonio Light*, February 4, 1917, p. 14 (quotation).

war." The 1850 census enumerated residents like one San Antonio Tejano family which had five minor children, three born in Texas and two in Mexico in 1837 and 1842, respectively, apparently on occasions when the family was waiting in Mexico for a time of peace so they could return to Texas.[11]

Ongoing contact with Mexico is reflected in eyewitness accounts of the Guadalupe feast during the years following Texas independence, which reveal that it featured colorful pageantry, vivid religious imagery, lively devotional expressions, enthusiastic participation, and an unmistakably Mexican ambiance. Announced a day in advance with extensive cannonading and bell ringing, Guadalupe feast-day processions flowed out of San Fernando parish into the town's plazas and streets. The principal ritual object was a "richly and gorgeously dressed" image of Our Lady of Guadalupe that Tejana devotees "loaded with all the necklaces and jewellery [*sic*] of the town" and "placed upon a bier elegantly adorned." Young girls dressed in white and bearing candles and flowers served as the immediate attendants of the Guadalupe image. Fiddlers and other devotees upholding a cross and Marian banner also participated, along with the parish clergy, large crowds of devotees, and men carrying rifles and pistols for devotional salutes. As they proceeded along their route, members of the entourage intermittently prayed the rosary, sang hymns in honor of their patroness, and acclaimed her with gun and canon tributes. The church bells pealed loudly as they arrived at the doors of San Fernando, where in preparation for this feast local women had generously provided "their most valuable ornaments for the decoration of their temple." Congregants then enshrined the Guadalupe image on its appointed altar and joined in Spanish- (and Latin-) language services: Mass, vespers, and further recitation of the rosary. Evening dances continued the festivities begun in these acts of worship.[12]

---

11. Gifford White, ed., *The 1840 Census of the Republic of Texas* (Austin: Pemberton, 1966), pp. 12-18; *Houston Telegraph and Texas Register,* May 19, 1838; V. K. Carpenter, comp., *The State of Texas Federal Population Schedules Seventh Census of the United States, 1850* (Huntsville, Ark.: Century Enterprises, 1969), 1:141, entry no. 509. For a fuller demographic profile of San Antonio during the period of the Texas Republic, see Timothy Matovina, *Tejano Religion and Ethnicity: San Antonio, 1821-1860* (Austin: University of Texas Press, 1995), pp. 25-26.

12. Rena Maverick Green, ed., *Memoirs of Mary A. Maverick* (San Antonio: Alamo, 1921), p. 53 (first quotation); Jean Marie Odin to Jean-Baptiste Étienne, February 7, 1842, in *The United States Catholic Magazine and Monthly Review* 3 (October 1844): 729 (last three quotations). A copy of this letter is in the Catholic Archives of Texas, Austin (CAT).

Guadalupe and Communal Relations

One small but significant group of newcomers to San Antonio who participated in the Guadalupe feast was European Catholic clergy. In 1840, Pope
Gregory XVI removed Texas from the Mexican diocese of Linares and declared it a prefecture apostolic under the diocese of New Orleans. French
priest Jean Marie Odin then assumed the leadership of the church in Texas.
Shortly after his 1840 arrival in Texas, Odin removed the two native-born
priests at San Fernando, Fathers Refugio de la Garza and José Antonio
Valdéz, claiming that their ministry was ineffective and that they had broken their priestly vows by having wives and children. He replaced the native clergy with Spanish priest Miguel Calvo, a fellow member of the
Vincentian religious order.[13]

Odin's first pastoral visit to San Antonio revealed the potential for ethnic and religious conflict as more newcomers arrived in the town. Born in
the wake of the French Revolution and formed for the priesthood during a
combative era for the French church, shortly before his 1822 departure for
the United States he wrote that his future mission field contained "millions
of idolators and Protestants, every day these wretched souls fall into hell,
and only fifty priests can lend them any assistance." His approach to
church discipline and Protestants led to controversy when, citing the dictates of Catholic canon law, he refused to allow the tolling of the San
Fernando church bells for the funeral of Colonel Henry W. Karnes, a hero
of the war for Texas independence from Mexico who was of Protestant
background. San Antonio mayor John Smith and other Anglo-American
residents held an indignation meeting and publicly denounced Odin and
his support of a church "principle which twangs more of the age of the in-
quisition than the liberality which characterizes the present era." According to Odin, the mayor and his supporters also sought to defy his authority
and reinstate Father de la Garza as San Fernando pastor. Perhaps due in
part to animosities between de la Garza and town leaders like Seguín and
Navarro, Tejanos neither participated in the effort to restore their former
pastor nor in the vilification of the French clergyman. After a century in
which nearly all disagreements among town residents were between

13. Odin to Timon, July 14, 1840, CAT; Odin to Blanc, August 24, 1840, CAT; Odin to Jo-
seph Rosati, August 27, 1840, CAT ; Odin to Étienne, August 28, 1840, CAT; Odin to James
Fransoni, December 15, 1840, CAT. For a fuller treatment of the native priests' removal, see
Matovina, *Tejano Religion and Ethnicity,* pp. 42-43.

Spanish-speaking co-religionists, the acrimonious denominational and ethnic conflict unfolding before their eyes was no doubt a bewildering spectacle.[14]

San Fernando was the only church edifice in San Antonio during the Texas Republic. Though Baptist, Presbyterian, and Methodist ministers visited the town, they did not establish congregations or conduct regular worship services before 1845. One Baptist visitor stated that the religious practices of San Antonio Catholics exemplified "the blindest superstition" and bemoaned the extent of Catholicism which "reigned without a rival" among the local populace. Odin lost no time in reaching out to the few Protestant residents in San Antonio, attracting "twelve children born of Protestant parents" who were "among my most faithful pupils" in catechism class. But Odin and Calvo concentrated the bulk of their efforts on Catholics, whom Odin opined "kept no more than a slight vestige of faith." Upon his arrival in San Antonio he initiated a vigorous campaign to vitalize Tejano Catholicism through catechetical instruction, regularizing common law marriages into sacramental unions, hearing confessions, promoting adoration of the Blessed Sacrament, and encouraging the reception of the Eucharist.[15]

Odin and other priests made energetic efforts to serve their Spanish-speaking co-religionists. Calvo's Vincentian confreres later claimed that, during his twelve years as pastor of San Fernando (1840-52), he "consoled and defended the native-born [Tejanos] against the cruelty of the yankees." Odin learned Spanish and was insistent that those coming to minister in Texas do the same. He was cautiously optimistic about Tejano response to his efforts to foster a lived Catholic faith through reception of the sacraments and catechesis. In 1842 he wrote that "there remains, no doubt,

14. Patrick Foley, "Jean-Marie Odin, C.M., Missionary Bishop Extraordinaire of Texas," *Journal of Texas Catholic History and Culture* 1 (1990): 42-60; Odin to Benoite (his sister), May 3, 1822, in Abbe Bony, *Vie de Mgr. Jean-Marie Odin: Missionaire lazarist, archeveque de la Nouvelle Orleans* (Paris: Imprimerie de D. Dumoulin, 1896), p. 39 (first quotation); *Austin Texas Sentinel*, August 29 (second quotation) and September 5; September 26, 1840; Odin to Blanc, August 24, 1840; Odin to Rosati, August 27, 1840; Odin to Étienne, August 28, 1840; Odin, "Daily Journal" (photocopy), pp. 6-8, CAT; P. F. Parisot and C. J. Smith, *History of the Catholic Church in the Diocese of San Antonio, Texas* (San Antonio: Carrico & Bowen, 1897), pp. 62-71.

15. Z. N. Morrell, *Flowers and Fruits from the Wilderness; or, Thirty-six Years in Texas and Two Winters in Honduras* (Boston: Gould and Lincoln, 1872), pp. 117, 118 (first two quotations); Odin to Étienne, February 7, 1842 (third and fourth quotations); Odin to Propagation of the Faith, March 28, 1852, CAT (last quotation).

much to be done at San Antonio: the reform which the country required is not yet as great and as general as we should desire; however, thanks be to heaven, our feeble efforts have not been fruitless, and already many abuses have been corrected." In contrast to other statements about Tejanos' lack of faith, Calvo and Odin were impressed with Tejano devotion, the latter writing after the 1841 Guadalupe feast that he had "seen few processions more edifying."[16]

While Catholic clergy attempted to inculcate their vision of authentic Catholicism among Tejanos, the participation of Odin and Calvo in the Guadalupe feast evidenced the Tejano desire both to continue their faith expressions and to initiate newcomers into their traditions. Indeed, with foreigners as pastors the persistence of local worship traditions like the Guadalupe feast was entirely contingent on sustained Tejano ingenuity. European clergy assigned to San Fernando may have been familiar with Our Lady of Guadalupe, since Pope Benedict XIV officially declared December 12 her feast day in 1754, but many local practices in celebrating her feast were new to them. As Odin himself wrote, in preparation for the feast "a good old man, together with some of his friends," took the initiative to approach him and offered to "bear the principal part of the expenses of the feast."[17] Moreover, the century-old practice of the town council overseeing feast-day celebrations abruptly ceased under the government of Texas, as Anglo-American newcomers were unaccustomed to elected officials organizing religious events. Since the settlement's relatively meager population and economic resources throughout its history had precluded the conventional Spanish Catholic practice of establishing a *cofradía* or pious society to organize the Guadalupe feast, the sudden collapse of the customary planning structures for this event placed its very existence in jeopardy. After the removal of San Fernando's Mexican priests, Tejano and Tejana devotees demonstrated their dedication to Guadalupe and their communal traditions as they took it upon themselves to raise funds, organize processions, adorn the church and the Guadalupe image, lead the rosary and other prayers, and invite the new European clergy to offer Mass and participate in their patroness's feast.

According to Odin Tejanos also attracted to the Guadalupe feast "a

16. Matovina, *Tejano Religion and Ethnicity,* pp. 39-41; Miguel Joaquín Calvo, Personal file, Archivo Matritense C.M., Madrid; Odin to Étienne, February 7, 1842 (last two quotations); Odin to Blanc, December 12, 1852, CAT; Odin to John Baptist Purcell, June 25, 1861, UND.

17. Odin to Étienne, February 7, 1842.

considerable number of Americans" from San Antonio, the surrounding area, and as far away as Austin some eighty miles to the north. Though Tejanos displayed their loyalty to Texas in public ceremonies like the funerary rites to honor the Alamo defenders, they clearly did not see the continuation of their Mexican Catholic traditions as inconsistent with Texas national allegiance. They refused to perceive themselves as foreigners after their political separation from Mexico, but rather as a "host society" whose longevity in their hometown dated back to their ancestors who had founded it. Thus they promoted the assimilation of European and Anglo-American immigrants — both Catholic and Protestant — into the practices established under their religious and cultural hegemony.[18]

As long as Tejanos remained numerically dominant in San Antonio, as they did throughout the period of the Texas Republic, their efforts to initiate newcomers remained viable. One new arrival, John Duff Brown, was about eight years old when his family moved to San Antonio in 1832. Shortly thereafter, he was baptized a Catholic. Although later in life he would observe religious practices learned from his Presbyterian grandmother, for the years his family lived in San Antonio he joined his classmates from the local school during religious celebrations and "marched with the pupils in double file to the cathedral [San Fernando parish] singing full-voiced some Catholic hymn." Other newcomers included the Samuel and Mary Maverick family, Episcopalians who moved to San Antonio in 1838. Mary Maverick wrote shortly after their arrival that "our only society are Mexicans." The Mavericks exchanged social calls with prominent Tejano families like the Navarros, Sotos, Garzas, Garcías, Zambranos, Seguíns, Veramendis, and Yturris. Mary Maverick's memoirs also contain a vivid description of the Guadalupe procession and feast, which she and her family attended. Afterward they went to a party and dance at the home of José Flores, where "the more prominent families[,] taking the Patroness along with them . . . danced most of the night."[19]

The incorporation of elite Anglo Americans into the Guadalupe cele-

18. Odin to Étienne, February 7, 1842. I have borrowed the phrase "host society" from the work of Milton M. Gordon. See, for example, his *Assimilation in American Life: The Role of Race, Religion, and National Origins* (New York: Oxford University Press, 1964).

19. John Duff Brown, "Reminiscences of Jno. Duff Brown," *Quarterly of the Texas State Historical Association* 12 (April 1909): 300; Mary Maverick to Agatha S. Adams, August 25, 1838, in *Samuel Maverick, Texan: 1803-1870. A Collection of Letters, Journals, and Memoirs,* Rena Maverick Green, ed. (San Antonio: Privately printed, 1952), p. 77; Green, ed., *Memoirs of Mary A. Maverick,* pp. 53-56.

brations, as well as into other ritual events like the Alamo interment ceremony in which Major Western was a featured speaker, advanced the political strategy of San Antonio Tejanos. While an overwhelmingly Tejano
electorate enabled them to retain control of the town council throughout
the period of the Texas Republic, those same voters selected only one
Tejano as mayor. They elected Samuel Maverick mayor the year after he
and his family settled in San Antonio. The other mayors were Anglo Americans who had married local Tejana women. Indeed, during this time of
transition "at least one daughter from almost every *rico* [rich] family in
San Antonio married an Anglo." These marriages offered Anglo Americans
the advantages of land and social status, while they offered Tejanos needed
allies within a new nation in which the language and legal system were un-
familiar and people of Mexican descent were vulnerable to accusations of
disloyalty.[20]

The marriage patterns and social interactions in San Antonio illustrate what David Montejano has called a "peace structure," that is, "a general postwar arrangement that allows the victors to maintain law and order
without the constant use of force." A primary element in this structure was
"an accommodation between the victorious Anglos and the defeated Mexican elite."[21] This accommodation did not substantially alter the traditional authority structures of Tejano society, but rather placed Anglo
Americans atop the existing hierarchy. The Mavericks' participation in the
Guadalupe procession and the festivities at the Flores residence symbolically expressed their incorporation into the Tejano inner circle and is consistent with Montejano's concept of peace structure.

Among Tejanos themselves, the Guadalupe feast-day celebrations reinforced internal divisions like class distinctions, as they had during previous eras. While the entire populace participated in the procession and
prayer services, the continuation of the celebration in evening festivities
divided the lesser and more prominent residents into two separate social
groupings. The upper class even reinforced their status by transporting to
their exclusive festivity the parish Guadalupe image, the principal ritual
object used in religious services. Men with the economic means to do so

20. Jane Dysart, "Mexican Women in San Antonio, 1830-1860: The Assimilation Process," *Western Historical Quarterly* 7 (October 1976): 370. Municipal election results for this
period are in "Minutes of the City Council of the City of San Antonio from 1837 to 1849,
Journal A" (typescript), CAH.

21. David Montejano, *Anglos and Mexicans in the Making of Texas, 1836-1986* (Austin:
University of Texas Press, 1987), p. 34.

also financially sponsored the Guadalupe feast, extending the longstanding practice of town-council members, other leading male citizens, and the parish clergy joining forces as the primary contributors and organizers for feast-day activities. The link between elite status and feast-day sponsorship is illustrated in the case of late eighteenth-century resident Antonio Rodríguez Baca, who advanced from his position as a soldier to become a successful merchant, the employer of various workers, and one of the area's major landowners. His selection as one of the sponsors for the Guadalupe feast came in the midst of his rise to prominence in the community. Sponsors usually occupied positions of distinction during feast-day celebrations. Though even the wealthiest residents had relatively modest economic means as compared to urban elites in Mexico City or Madrid, like other locales in the Hispanic Catholic world the privileged location of elite residents in worship tended to symbolically bolster a hierarchical social order.[22]

Women's leadership roles in Guadalupe celebrations contrasted with their subordinate social position, but also reinforced conventional views about womanhood. Though Spanish law allowed women more expansive property rights than codes of the Texas Republic based primarily on England's legal system, under Spanish and Mexican rule women endured inequalities in political affairs, the judicial system, and family life. The independence of Texas did not substantially alter the social and legal restrictions that kept Tejanas subservient. They were denied the vote and the right to hold public office and usually had their subordinate status in patriarchal households symbolically reinforced by wives eating separately from their husbands, but only after having served the men their meal. Female roles in planning Guadalupe celebrations, directing the rosary and other prayers, and accompanying their patroness as her immediate attendants provided them with a rare opportunity to exercise community leadership. Such prominence of leadership illustrates what Ana María Díaz-Stevens calls the "matriarchal core" of Latin American Catholicism, the exercise of autonomous authority in public prayer and devotion despite patriarchal structures that permeated social and family life. At the same time, however, women's leadership roles in the Guadalupe celebrations were limited, reflected an extension of domestic responsibilities into ritual, reinforced the notion that piety was primarily

---

22. Matovina, *Guadalupe and Her Faithful,* pp. 56-57, 61; De la Teja, *San Antonio de Béxar,* p. 132.

the responsibility of women, and in general did not substantially alter patriarchal social structures. They also symbolically linked the purity of young girls dressed in white with the Virgin Mary, a communal accentuation of feminine chastity that lacked a corresponding association between young boys and Jesus.[23]

Death and Divine Accompaniment

Whether female or male, young or old, or lower or higher status, in antebellum San Antonio daily sustenance and survival were cause for heartfelt gratitude. When residents woke up in the morning, they literally did not know if they would stay alive until the evening. Even in the most prosperous of times life expectancy was only about 40 years.[24] Medical conditions like appendicitis could cause death within hours. Epidemics like the devastating cholera scourges of 1833 and 1834 confirmed the sense that one's everyday life was in the hands of forces beyond human control.

The vigorous governmental and communal response to the 1830s cholera plight included public sanitation, medicine, quarantine from persons and products that might transmit the disease, and the mass distribution of mutton which was believed to prevent this malady. Residents also responded through their religious practices. Mayor Juan Seguín asked pastor de la Garza not to ring the church bells for the deceased lest the frequent tolling disturb the settlement's surviving population. Civic and religious leaders collaborated to organize a series of processions through the town streets as a "religious invocation to God for preservation from the cholera." A visitor to San Antonio noted that the Mexican Catholic participants in this ritual knelt in prayer at designated sites, possibly locales where friends and loved ones had contracted or succumbed to the disease. Their religious response to the epidemic reflected established worship traditions and attitudes about divine assistance and retribution, such as the

23. David J. Weber, *The Mexican Frontier, 1821-1846: The American Southwest under Mexico* (Albuquerque: University of New Mexico Press, 1982), pp. 215-16; Mark M. Carroll, *Homesteads Ungovernable: Families, Sex, Race, and the Law in Frontier Texas, 1823-1860* (Austin: University of Texas Press, 2001), pp. 99-101; Ana María Díaz-Stevens, "The Saving Grace: The Matriarchal Core of Latino Catholicism," *Latino Studies Journal* 4 (September 1993): 60-78.

24. Alicia V. Tjarks, "Comparative Demographic Analysis of Texas, 1777-1793," *Southwestern Historical Quarterly* 77 (January 1974): 309.

petitionary prayers and processions local residents had offered during a 1786 drought to "placate the Lord's ire."[25]

Funerary rites for deceased children revealed a more merciful image of a God who welcomes home the innocent, as well as a ritual means to engender hope amid loss. The night before the burial parents or other relatives laid out the deceased in the finest clothes available, decorated their remains with flowers, and received family and friends into their home, sometimes even with music and dancing. Children dressed in white, fiddlers, men firing gun salutes, and crowds of family and friends participated in the funeral procession the following morning. These festive elements were signs of the community's confidence that the deceased infant was experiencing the joy of heaven, since in Catholic belief a baptized child who dies is sinless and therefore goes directly to heaven. French émigré and artist Theodore Gentilz named his 1840s painting of such a San Antonio funeral procession "Entierro de un ángel" (funeral of an angel) to accentuate the belief that God mercifully gave eternal reward to departed children and thus averted their suffering the travails of adult life. Customarily the only mourner on such an occasion was the child's mother, who according to a visitor of another Tejano community "made loud and heart rending lamentations." Her bereavement evidenced the intimacy of the mother-child bond, but the overall joyful mood of these funerals constituted the community's faith response to high infant mortality rates.[26]

War and violence made life at San Antonio even more precarious. San Antonio's history includes more military battles fought in and around the city than any other place in the United States, about a dozen in all and most of them still in living memory during the period of the Texas Republic. José Antonio Navarro recalled revolutionaries publicly displaying the "blood stained jewels" from the brutal 1813 execution of the Spanish governor and his staff just outside the town, as well as the retaliation of Spanish

25. J. Villasana Haggard, "Epidemic Cholera in Texas, 1833-1834," *Southwestern Historical Quarterly* 40 (January 1937): 216-30; Juan Seguín to [José Antonio Salinas], October 29, 1834, Bexar Archives, CAH; Benjamin Lundy, *The Life, Travels, and Opinions of Benjamin Lundy* (1847; reprinted, New York: Negro Universities Press, 1969), pp. 54 (first quotation), 55; De la Teja, *San Antonio de Béxar,* pp. 93 (second quotation), 94.

26. Theodore Gentilz, "Entierro de un ángel" (funeral of an angel), painting, c. 1840s, The Daughters of the Republic of Texas Library, San Antonio; William F. Gray, *From Virginia to Texas, 1835; Diary of Col. Wm. F. Gray* (1909; reprinted, Houston: Fletcher Young, 1965), p. 97. A reprint of the Gentilz painting is in *Gentilz: Artist of the Old Southwest* (Austin: University of Texas Press, 1974), p. 83.

forces later that year in which numerous San Antonians suffocated in an inhuman confinement or were led before firing squads "for no more reason than having been accused of favoring [Mexican] independence." When Texas troops took the town from Mexican forces in a pitched house-to-house battle in December 1835, they broke through the walls of houses with battering rams rather than risk the open streets. One soldier recalled "how the women and children would yell when we knocked the holes in the walls and went in." Decades later eyewitnesses like Eulalie Yorba said of the March 1836 Alamo battle and its aftermath that "I used to try when I was younger to describe that awful sight, but I never could find sufficient language." Similarly, battle survivor Enrique Esparza, the son of Alamo defender Gregorio Esparza and his wife Anna, stated that "neither age nor infirmity could make me forget, for the scene was one of such horror that it could never be forgotten by any one who witnessed its incidents."[27]

If perchance some Tejanos' memories of past atrocities began to fade, in 1842 Mexican forces occupied San Antonio on two separate occasions. One Mexican general reportedly imprisoned the Tejano father of a sixteen-year-old daughter and "his liberation and life were pressed by the enamoured ruffian upon the anguished girl, as the reward of her acquiescence in his wishes." The predominantly Anglo-American Texan volunteer army forced the Mexican troops to retreat, but then proceeded "to commit the most shameful depredations" against Tejanos, leading the editor of one Houston newspaper to bemoan "that the government has not the means to station a company of soldiers near that city [San Antonio], to protect the citizens not only from the marauding Mexicans, but even from our own volunteers." Father Odin summed up the situation with the statement that "one is beginning to believe they [the Texas volunteers] will do more harm to Texas than a Mexican army."[28]

27. José Antonio Navarro, *Apuntes históricos interesantes de San Antonio de Béxar escritos por el C. Dn. José Antonio Navarro, en noviembre de 1853. Y publicados por varios de sus amigos* (San Antonio: Privately printed, 1869), pp. 16, 18; Sion R. Bostick, "Reminiscences of Sion R. Bostick," *Quarterly of the Texas State Historical Association* 5 (October 1901): 89-90; "Another Story of the Alamo," *San Antonio Express*, April 12, 1896, p. 13; "Alamo's Only Survivor," *San Antonio Express*, May 12, 1907, p. 14. A facsimile and English translation of Navarro's *Apuntes* is in José Antonio Navarro, *Defending Mexican Valor in Texas: José Antonio Navarro's Historical Writings, 1853-1857*, David R. McDonald and Timothy Matovina, eds. (Austin: State House, 1995); the Yorba and Esparza Alamo battle recollections are reprinted in Matovina, *The Alamo Remembered*, pp. 53-57, 77-89.

28. William Preston Stapp, *The Prisoners of Perote, Containing a Journal Kept by the Author* (1845; reprinted, Austin: University of Texas Press, 1977), p. 20; Odin to Étienne, June 17,

Writings of San Antonians and travelers are filled with descriptions of the frequent lethal conflicts with Native Americans. Odin wrote in an 1841 letter, "There is not a family [in San Antonio] who does not mourn the death of a father, of a son, of a brother, or of a spouse pitilessly slaughtered by the Comanches." One resident noted that the Comanches had killed nearly fifty people in or near the city during the first ten months of 1840. When representatives of the Comanches and the Texas government disagreed over an exchange of prisoners during March of that year, a battle called the Council House fight left thirty-five Comanches, six Anglo Americans, and one Tejano dead on the streets of San Antonio.[29]

Processions through the town streets and around the plazas on either side of San Fernando church inevitably encountered physical reminders of these sanguinary episodes, passing houses and other buildings which bore signs of violence such as the courthouse across the plaza from the church. One contemporary visitor noted that the plazas "have been [at various times] heaped with the slain. The houses that surround the square, and the church, which occupies the center are perforated by hundreds of musket and cannon shot . . . numerous heaps of ruins both in the town & neighborhood marke [*sic*] the places where houses once stood." Another visitor remarked that he met several Comanche children among San Antonio families and, "on asking one, a boy who was assisting a stone mason in the Plaza, how and when he came there, he replied, pointing to the Court House, 'My father was killed there.'" Participants in processions also encompassed relatives and former companions of those killed in battle. Like this child, they were silent reminders of past combat at San Antonio and the loved ones who no longer took their place among their fellow worshipers.[30]

Daily reminders of divine care and sustenance were juxtaposed with these potent remembrances of violent incidents, filling the imaginations of

1842, CAT; *Houston Morning Star,* June 9, 1842; Odin to Blanc, July 4, 1842, CAT. See also Joseph Milton Nance, *Attack and Counter-Attack: The Texas-Mexican Frontier, 1842* (Austin: University of Texas Press, 1964).

29. Odin to Étienne, April 11, 1841, CAT; Odin, "Daily Journal," p. 10; *Austin Texas Sentinel,* March 23, 25, April 15, 1840; *Houston Telegraph and Texas Register,* April 8, 1840; Green, ed., *Memoirs of Mary A. Maverick,* pp. 31-37; J[osé] M[aría] Rodríguez, *Rodríguez Memoirs of Early Texas* (1913; reprinted, San Antonio: Standard, 1961), pp. 24-26.

30. William A. McClintock, "Journal of a Trip through Texas and Northern Mexico in 1846-1847," *Southwestern Historical Quarterly* 34 (October 1930): 146; W. Eugene Hollon and Ruth Lapham Butler, eds., *William Bollaert's Texas* (Norman: University of Oklahoma Press, 1956), pp. 229-30.

worshipers with divergent and potentially competing symbolic representations. San Fernando church's location at the heart of the town was an architectural testimony to the centrality of faith in the lives of San Antonio's founders; its tower and clanging bells continued to shape the rhythms of daily life in the town. The parish's sacred images included the Mexican national patroness Our Lady of Guadalupe and a "wooden figure of a Mexican representing Christ on the cross," representations that symbolically connected congregants to their loving celestial mother and to Jesus whose solidarity in suffering could make their afflictions more bearable. One visitor noted that physical markers of faith were literally inscribed on Tejanos' bodies, observing that "every Mexican professes to be a Catholic and carries about his person the crucifix, the rosary, and other symbols of the mother church." Another visitor perceived the inscription of faith in bodily gesture, stating that as he followed along in a funeral procession for an adult "all the Mexicans we met fell on their knees and uncovered their heads." Processions on other solemn occasions also elicited Mexican devotional fervor; when the tolling San Fernando church bell signaled that the priest would take the consecrated communion host to the home of a sick person in danger of death, "the people hastened to the holy place in order to accompany Our Lord through the streets." These and other processions brought ritual objects like crucifixes, saints' images, candles, and the Eucharist itself right into the arenas where residents' homes and persons had been violated, asserting a truth about God's accompaniment larger than the sum of their collective anguish and symbolically consecrating anew the defiled places of daily life.[31]

Even Tejanos' religious legends reinforced their conviction about a God who accompanied them in daily life. One such legend "believed by all the old Mexicans about San Antonio" described the miraculous escape of a priest from the Comanches by the parting of river waters "as the Red sea [*sic*] did for the Israelites of old." Native San Antonian Antonio Menchaca recounted two legends about the legacy of the early Spanish Franciscans in Texas. In the first a band of Franciscans is beset with a large and hostile group of Native Americans, until the renowned missioner Antonio Margil de Jesús lifted up his eyes and "in the twinkling of a bed post the Savages

---

31. Otto B. Engelmann, trans. and ed., "The Second Illinois in the Mexican War: Mexican War Letters of Adolph Engelmann, 1846-1847," *Journal of the Illinois State Historical Society* 26 (January 1934): 383-84 (first and third quotations); Andrew Forest Muir, ed., *Texas in 1837: An Anonymous, Contemporary Narrative* (Austin: University of Texas Press, 1988), p. 103 (second quotation); Odin to Étienne, April 11, 1841 (fourth quotation).

were transmogrified into deer." The second recounts a traveling group of friars who were thirsty after passing several days without water, came upon a grape vine, prayed over it, pulled it out, and to their delight saw water come bursting forth. These legends of miraculous assistance for Spanish friars, which Menchaca states were also established tales among his Tejano contemporaries, accentuated the intervention of divine providence in human affairs. Not surprisingly, the legends address the misfortunes of Native American attack and drought, two of the San Antonio populace's most feared tribulations.[32]

At times confident assurance in the consistent involvement of heavenly beings in earthly dealings led to bewilderment and anger when prayers were not answered as expected. The aforementioned female supplicant who sought the favor of rains through the intercession of Our Lady of Guadalupe reportedly "beats the image of Our Lady" in the event "the rain do [*sic*] not come." In the most striking case in extant records, a few years after the U.S. annexation of the Texas Republic a Tejano reportedly went into a Catholic mission station which San Fernando parish clergy served and began to destroy the images of Jesus and the saints. After some Tejana women stopped his destructive spree, the man explained that "the Mexican Gods could neither eat, walk or talk, and were no Gods at all, consequently he wanted to put them out of the way." He added that "if the Mexicans had worshipped the true and only God, the 'gringos' could never have taken Texas." Although the precise motives of this man's agitation remain unclear, his observations reflect the conviction that Tejano Catholics suffered divine punishment or abandonment because their faith and traditions were a mere illusion in comparison to the potent, "true" God and religion of ascendant Anglo-American Protestants.[33]

A Theology of Divine Providence

Since San Antonio's founding settlers there had followed the Spanish Catholic practice of developing "a unique [ritual] calendar built up from the settlement's own sacred history," as William Christian has docu-

32. George William Bonnell, *Topographical Description of Texas. To Which Is Added, An Account of the Indian Tribes* (1840; reprinted, Waco: Texian Press, 1964), pp. 82-83; Antonio Menchaca, "Memoirs" (original manuscript), pp. 153-55, CAH.

33. McDowell, ed., *Letters from the Ursuline*, p. 273; *Alamo Star* (San Antonio), September 2, 1854.

mented.[34] From the vast array of feast days, saints, and Marian images in the Catholic tradition, devotees especially honored heavenly intercessors deemed to have a particular interest in their community. The San Antonio case illustrates typical ways that devotees and their patrons came to be linked, as local residents designated for their celestial benefactors San Antonio, the saint on whose day Spanish subjects first arrived in the area; San Fernando, the namesake of a royal benefactor's son; and Our Lady of Guadalupe, the cherished Marian image of early settlers in the area. Far from perceiving the emergence of their patrons as mere historical coincidence, the parishioners of San Fernando espoused the Spanish Catholic belief that God's providence provided these blessed protectors to accompany them and assist them in their struggles.

The theology of divine providence associated with venerating patron saints asserted that celestial beings and God's assistance were not distant but, as Ana María Díaz-Stevens demonstrated in her study of Puerto Rican Catholics, "constantly manifested in daily occurrences, in the forces of nature, in the seeming ease with which, season after season, the once dormant seeds woke up to warmth and sunlight."[35] This theology envisioned that all was in the hands of God — rain, drought, harvest, health, torment, good fortune, protection from enemies, communal well being. In fact, this sense was so prevalent that residents even presumed social divisions and one's state in life reflected a divine plan in which human relations mirrored the hierarchical ordering of the heavenly dominion. By God's design the earthly world imitated the celestial realm: the world was ordered in such a way that natural occurrences, social rank, and human events all conformed to a higher reason and purpose. In the most extreme cases these beliefs led devotees to "punish" their patron saints for unanswered prayers, presume God was angry at them when they faced undesired circumstances, or adopt a fatalistic view about their lot in life.

Yet theological convictions about divine providence did not lead all believers to blindly embrace a rigidly deterministic view of the world. Birth as a female or a male of lower class could lure Tejanos to accept their second- (or third-) class status with fatalistic resolve, but those of marginal social rank also strove to improve their position and even symboli-

34. William A. Christian, Jr., *Local Religion in Sixteenth-Century Spain* (Princeton: Princeton University Press, 1981), p. 3.

35. Ana María Díaz-Stevens, *Oxcart Catholicism on Fifth Avenue: The Impact of Puerto Rican Migration upon the Archdiocese of New York* (Notre Dame, Ind.: University of Notre Dame Press, 1993), p. 46.

cally authenticated their advance through assuming public roles in feast-day celebrations like those for Guadalupe. Deeply held convictions of a divine plan and ordering of the universe were tempered by human experiences that led believers to conclude that fortune, chance, perseverance, or sacrifice could alter one's situation in life. Fervent prayer and the performance of ritual duties could also influence life outcomes. But for most Tejanos faith was not a simplistic equation of a cause-and-effect relationship between intercession and heavenly assistance, since supplication for needs like safety from attack, good crops, and an end to epidemics was not always answered in the time and manner desired. The understanding of providence was a fluid theology adaptable to believers' longing for security, changing social conditions, and aspirations for social advancement. In the shifting terrain between belief in a divinely ordained plan for the world and the possibilities of human initiative and divine intervention, Tejano Catholics forged, fostered, and refashioned a theology of divine providence through their daily struggles and their collective and personal acts of worship.

Retrospectively, one can see in the theology of divine providence and the invocation of patron saints inherent in Tejano life and worship a tendency present within Christianity since it became the official religion of the Roman Empire in the fourth century. Rome was a socially stratified society in which more powerful patrons did favors for their weaker clients, who in turn repaid their benefactors by offering them their loyalty and homage. As Elizabeth Johnson has noted, "Given the church's inculturation into this social system, it is perhaps not surprising that patronage began to govern its transactions not only on earth but also with the realm of heaven."[36] Similarly, just as intermediaries like influential acquaintances or, after Texas independence, Anglo-American husbands and son-in-laws were often necessary for Tejanos to deal successfully with government officials or other elites, patron saints linked their devotees to the power of divine succor. Like numerous other believers before and since, Tejano Catholics projected their communal relations and social structures onto God and the heavenly household of faith.

Yet within the horizon of their collective imagination Tejanos continued to develop their view of God's presence and God's personal stake in their everyday affairs. During the period of the Texas Republic the Tejano

---

36. Elizabeth A. Johnson, *Truly Our Sister: A Theology of Mary in the Communion of Saints* (New York: Continuum, 2003), p. 316.

parishioners of San Ferando were a worship community in transition. The residual association of Guadalupe with agricultural concerns gave way to the role of her feast in the reconfiguration of communal relations. Moreover, they confronted in a particularly poignant way what anthropologist Clifford Geertz deemed "the Problem of Meaning," which "is a matter of affirming, or at least recognizing, the inescapability of ignorance, pain, and injustice on the human plane while simultaneously denying that these irrationalities are characteristic of the world as a whole. And it is in terms of religious symbolism . . . that both the affirmation and the denial are made."[37] Faced with shifting demographics, recurrent violence, and uncertainty about their wellbeing, the traditions of Mexican Catholic worship and belief enriched even as they limited and defined the religious imagination of San Antonio Tejanos and, more important, strengthened their assurance that the symbolic world of their faith illuminated a truth larger than the visible realities of their daily lives.

37. Clifford Geertz, "Religion as a Cultural System," in *The Interpretation of Cultures: Selected Essays by Clifford Geertz* (New York: Basic Books, 1973), p. 108.

"You Better Set Your House in Order": Worship Ritual and Black Church Life in Jim Crow Georgia

Paul Harvey

Evangelical Christianity in the South, according to the renowned scholar Samuel S. Hill, Jr., historically has been characterized by a reliance on the Bible as the "sole reference point of belief and practice," a stress on "direct and dynamic access to the Lord," an individualistic sense of morality, and informal "low-church" worship styles. Southern orthodoxy, according to Hill, aims at individual conversion, rather than social reform or other broader purpose, as the central role of religious institutions. Best enshrined in the Southern Presbyterian doctrine of the "spirituality of the church," this idea spread through the southern denominations during the era of sectional tensions prior to the Civil War. It became more firmly implanted in subsequent decades, as most southern denominations defended a conservative vision of the relationship of the church and the social order.[1] Meanwhile, black Christians in the South have maintained an intense relationship with an evangelicalism that has both oppressed and sustained them. For them, the "spirituality of the church" masked the clear implications for social power inherent in the church's involvement with society. Thus, while conservative in theology, Afro-Christianity has invited a more expansive reading of the social implications of the Gospel, and its cultural forms have left an indelible mark on twentieth-century American culture.

In the generations after the Civil War, religious practice in the American South was both priestly and prophetic. If its formal theology generally sanctified the regnant hierarchies, its spirit could subtly undermine the

1. Samuel S. Hill, Jr., *Southern Churches in Crisis* (New York: Holt, Rinehart & Winston, 1967); Samuel S. Hill, "Religion," in *The Encyclopedia of Southern Culture,* Charles Reagan Wilson and William Ferris, eds. (Chapel Hill: University of North Carolina Press, 1989), p. 1269.

dominant tradition. In one sense, the seeds of subversion against the segregationist order were embedded in the passionate individualism, exuberant expressive forms, and profound faith of the region's evangelical believers. These seeds were nurtured, across the color line, by black worship patterns that had been born out of the nexus between African styles of expression, an evangelical culture emphasizing spiritual liberation, and the temporally restrictive measures of slavery.

This essay explores the meaning and practice of that black southern faith in the years of Jim Crow's apogee, from the 1870s to the 1930s, an era that historian Rayford Logan has rightly declared to mark the "nadir of race relations" in the history of the nation. During this time, segregation statutes swept the laws and constitutions of the southern states, black voters were kept from the polls through means both dubiously legal and unabashedly illegal, and a reign of terrorism gripped the southern countryside and cities in the lynchings and race massacres that are commonly mislabeled "race riots." For African Americans, save for church and some fraternal communal organizations, there was no safe space, no means of recourse, and virtually no arena to exercise a voice or cast a meaningful vote.[2] As Jim Crow rose, so did the South's image as the "Bible Belt" — an ironic juxtaposition scathingly noted by numerous social critics. The long march of southern evangelicalism from marginality to dominance was well underway during the antebellum era, but only after the Civil War did it achieve true cultural dominance. Defeat in the war inspired a new generation of southern whites to sacralize the Confederacy under a new civil religion with its own theology, myths, rituals, and saints. In this context "Redemption" served as the perfect term to describe the end of Reconstruction, for it married the political events of the 1860s and 1870s to the religious imagery increasingly favored by white southern conservative elites. White southern Christians viewed their Redemptionist activity as essentially religious, an extension of the cosmic struggle between order and disorder, civilization and barbarism, white and black. Thus, southern conservatives celebrated the often violent restoration of Democratic governments as a "Christian triumph."[3]

2. For a gripping portrayal of black life under the regime of Jim Crow, see Leon Litwack, *Trouble in Mind: Black Southerners in the Age of Jim Crow* (New York: Alfred A. Knopf, 1998).

3. Christine Heyrman's Bancroft–prize winning book *Southern Cross: The Origins of the Bible Belt* (New York: Alfred A. Knopf, 1997), explores the early years of southern evangelicalism as the "origins of the Bible Belt." For the post–Civil War extension, see especially Charles Reagan Wilson, *Baptized in Blood: The Religion of the Lost Cause, 1865-1920* (Athens:

White southern theologians extended divine sanction to the hard fight that tried to secure the Jim Crow order. In the process, they entertained notions of scientific racism that their forebears had considered theologically heterodox. The fear of race mixing, particularly between white women and black men, was a brutally effective justification for segregation and a pervasive specter that haunted southern folklore. Nowhere was the violence enforcing white supremacy more gruesomely displayed than in the horrific acts by which white men claimed to preserve the honor of the race — that is, in lynching black men. Well over 4,000 lynchings (4,786 by one count) occurred in the United States from 1880 to 1950, and black men were the most common victims. The best known of these incidents were "spectacle lynchings" — solemn, quasi-religious rituals in which dozens, hundreds, or even thousands engaged in acts of purification. (Hence the frequency with which lynching victims were *burned,* and the invocations pronounced at such events by clergymen.)[4]

How did black communities survive so relentless an onslaught? The question may be answered in a number of ways, but surely the church would be at the center of any response. Or would it? If America once was called a nation with the soul of a church, the black church has been called the "church with the soul of a nation," and indeed, during the civil rights era black Christians moved the nation socially and politically. On the other hand, black churches have formed, in the words of the late seminary professor James Melvin Washington, a "frustrated fellowship." For much of the post–Civil War era, the potential collective power of black Christians seemed to be untapped, their worship spiritually exuberant but practically impotent. Accordingly, a long stream of proposals for reforming black worship arced across this era, aimed most often at specific behaviors of shouting and dancing that were deemed too emotionally enthusiastic. The frequent parodying of "jackleg" ministers in black music, literature, and film accented a steady rhythm of complaints against black churches being more devoted to building their own institutions than reforming the society around them. In short, from Reconstruction through Jim Crow, black Protestantism was as beleaguered as it was powerful; its

University of Georgia Press, 1980); and chap. 1 of Paul Harvey, *Freedom's Coming: Religious Culture and the Shaping of the South, From the Civil War through the Civil Rights Era* (Chapel Hill: University of North Carolina Press, 2005).

4. Grace Hale, *Making Whiteness: The Culture of Segregation in the South* (New York: Random House, 1997), discusses "spectacle lynchings" with penetrating insight.

fiercest critics, like its most eloquent and elegiac defenders, came from within the black community.[5]

In this light the recent push by scholars to extend the history of the civil rights movement back into the formerly untold story of black activism from World War I to 1950 invites a second look at the black churches of this era. To be sure, like the revisionist "long history of the civil rights movement," the revaluation of black church life can be romanticized. Critics of the institutionalized black church from W. E. B. DuBois in the early twentieth century to Gayraud Wilmore in the 1960s did have a point in urging churches in their own time to work at improving black life in this world and not just in the next. There is something to their argument that to the extent religious practice performed its historic role of providing communal solace in a harsh world, churches could serve as impediments rather than incentives toward social protest. Their thesis does not account, however, for the way in which urban black churches functioned as intermediaries between the black community and white governmental establishments. Nor did the critics fathom that the very worship rituals they condemned as "otherworldly," irrelevant, or embarrassingly ecstatic, were not only instrumental in sustaining black communities through soul-destroying times but eventually empowered a generation to overthrow one of the most pernicious systems of racial oppression in the western hemi-

---

5. James Melvin Washington, *Frustrated Fellowship: The Black Baptist Quest for Social Power* (Macon, Ga.: Mercer University Press, 1985). For a comprehensive exploration of black Christianity, see C. Eric Lincoln and Lawrence Mamiya, *The Black Church in the African-American Experience* (Durham, N.C.: Duke University Press, 1992). The critique by theologians and sociologists of African-American worship patterns as emotionally compensatory but pragmatically fruitless is evident in an older tradition of scholarship exemplified by Hortense Powdermaker's *After Freedom: A Cultural Study in the Deep South* (New York: Atheneum, 1968 [1939]), and Charles Johnson, *Shadow of the Plantation* (Chicago: University of Chicago Press, 1934), which portrayed African-American Protestantism in this era as essentially otherworldly and ineffectual. Out of the 1960s, critics such as Gayraud Wilmore updated this view (*Black Religion and Black Radicalism: An Interpretation of the Religious History of the Afro-American People* [Garden City, N.Y.: Doubleday, 1972]). Wilmore stressed the radicalism inherent in the black religious tradition and by contrast decried the deradicalization of the church in the early twentieth century and the consequent secularization of black radicalism. In Wilmore's view, it was precisely the emphasis on deliverance from sin into the glories of the next life that tended to inure black southerners to their oppressed condition rather than inspire them to feats of protest. After the initially exciting period of organization and political activism during Reconstruction, black church life turned inward. Ministers and parishioners accommodated themselves to the socio-political realities of American apartheid.

sphere. So we need to look at these rituals again to distinguish between a worship and church life that shrank from addressing fundamental moral evils such as segregation and practices that provided the spiritual sustenance necessary to people caught in exhausting turmoil.

To better understand the intersections of worship and worldview of black churches from Reconstruction to the Great Depression, this essay will focus on particular individuals and congregations in Georgia, especially those in the coastal entrepot of Savannah, the working-class inland town of Augusta, and the explosively growing railway and educational hub of Atlanta. The state of Georgia experienced much of the worst of Jim Crow, including the nationally infamous lynching of Sam Hose in 1893 and the Atlanta race riot in 1906. At the same time, Georgia boasted a highly cultivated and talented black intellectual class (including W. E. B. DuBois during his tenure at Atlanta University), a tradition of black political activism dating from Reconstruction, and a legacy of evangelical churches stretching back to the pioneer black Baptist churches in eighteenth-century America. The rural poverty and racism of Georgia defined the very meaning of the cotton South, hopelessly mired in the inefficiencies of tenant farming and sharecropping. At the same time, the low-country of Georgia around Savannah, including the Sea Islands off the coast, fostered a society of extremely wealthy white planters surrounded and hugely outnumbered by poor rural black people who were closely connected to African cultural roots. Black religious life there took on a particular flavor distinguishing it from that of the inland counties. Finally, the boosterism of Atlanta, and the number of black educational institutions in that rapidly expanding railroad center, gave Georgia an expansive urban hub unusual in the surrounding states.

In short, Georgia was a cross-section of southern geography, economy, and demography. Likewise, its black churches ranged from the "praise houses" in the circumference of Savannah, to the standard one-room Baptist and Methodist congregations in the cotton countryside, to the impressive urban elite congregations in Atlanta. Further, Georgia reveals the paradox at the heart of black religion. If the church was central to black life, that very fact made it difficult for black churches to undertake civil rights projects during the Jim Crow era. Churches so inwardly focused on building community feared the risks of challenging the apparently impregnable system of segregation. Only later, with the rise of black secular organizations, the destruction wrought by the Depression, and the emergence of a new reformist generation of ministers could black church life and rituals be harnessed to the civil rights movement. But then they did so, and shook the entire nation.

This conclusion would startle the pioneer sociologists of black religion as well as the church people they studied. The irony of black southern history is that the most "otherworldly" of institutions and the seemingly most spiritually ecstatic of ritual practices eventually empowered the most radical challenge to American racist ideology and practice of the post–Civil War era. In fact, to oversimplify only a little, the black church fostered the most important social movement of twentieth-century American history, and religious ritual provided the cadence, the sound, of the movement. As historian David Chappell puts it, the religious faith cultivated under slavery and developed during the reign of Jim Crow made the civil rights "movement" *move.*

AFTER THE CIVIL WAR, black churches imparted a powerful message: that freedpeople were equal citizens under the law. To white Redemptionists, this was subversive preaching, especially given the connection of black churchmen to the Republican Party. Nine ministers of the African Methodist Episcopal church attended the post-war constitutional convention in Georgia, and more than 230 black clergymen would hold local, state, or national office during Reconstruction. In Augusta, Georgia, black churches served as meeting places for laboring men who mixed religious sentiments and working-class politics. Some eighty black laborers in the growing town of Augusta sent this account of their proceedings to a northern missionary ally: "Was meet at the time apointed the meting Was open by Reading the 78 Chapter of Psalm, and singing o god our help in ages past our help for years to come by the Rev. Charles R. Edwards and pray by Rev. John Megee after witch Rev. Charles R. Edwards stated the call of the Meting one month ago fore to unit[e] the laboring men in the country into associations." As in countless other cases, Afro-Protestantism undergirded and supported the incipient organizing struggles of the freedpeople.[6]

In this context black and white missionaries in the post–Civil War South pursued the work of "political evangelization," to secure religious and political rights for the former bondspeople. Notable among them was

6. Meeting of the Colored Mens of the Mechanic and Laboring Men Association of Georgia, in John Emory Bryant Papers, box 2, folder for 1868-69, Special Collections Library, Duke University. An enumeration of the occupations of black men who held office during Reconstruction may be found in Eric Foner, *Freedom's Lawmakers: A Directory of Black Officeholders During Reconstruction* (New York: Oxford University Press, 1993).

the black Methodist stalwart Henry McNeal Turner. Remembered later for his caustic editorials that advocated black American emigration to Africa and that denounced the American flag as a "rag of contempt," the Constitution as a "cheat, a libel, . . . to be spit upon by every negro in the land," Turner, in fact, gave his life to establishing the African Methodist Episcopal Church in the South. Born free in 1834, in the 1850s Turner moved to Georgia where biracial crowds eagerly gathered to hear his powerful preaching (some incredulous whites pronounced him a *"white man galvanized"*). Following service as a Union army chaplain, Turner established himself as a prominent churchman, missionary, legislator, newspaper editor, and rhetorical firebrand. He was foremost among the emissaries that the AME and its sister competitor, the African Methodist Episcopal Zion Church (AMEZ), deployed to bring to the supposedly waiting masses of freed-people the leadership of venerable black ecclesiastical bodies. Turner and his fellows envisioned their religious work as essential to securing full citizenship rights for the freedpeople. That is, civil rights, church organization, and racial uplift would go hand in hand. Turner expressed this sentiment when defending the continued use of the word "African" in the AME denominational title. "The curse of the colored race in this country, where white is God and black is the devil," he insisted, was in "the disposition to run away" from blackness. "In trying to be something beside themselves," he said, black Americans would "never amount to anything." Turner advocated a different course: "honor black, dignify it with virtues, and pay as much respect to it as nature and nature's God does." Or more succinctly: "respect black." Not surprisingly, historians "rediscovered" Turner in the 1960s as a progenitor of the "black power" and "black theology" movements then beginning to garner national attention.[7]

Turner also served as a delegate to the postwar constitutional convention in Georgia and briefly in the state legislature before being illegally evicted from the state House by white opponents. With his political career forcibly terminated, Turner settled into three more decades of tireless work for the AME in the South and, later, South Africa. He traveled constantly, edited the official denominational hymnal, and eventually was elected bishop. The *Hymn Book of the African Methodist Episcopal Church* that he

---

7. Stephen Angell, *Bishop Henry McNeal Turner and African-American Religion in the South* (Knoxville: University of Tennessee Press, 1992), p. 24; *Star of Zion*, September 10, 1886. For a useful compilation of Turner's speeches and writings, see Edwin S. Redkey, ed., *Respect Black: The Writings and Speeches of Henry McNeal Turner* (New York: Arno Press, 1971).

compiled in 1876 was the first the church published after the Civil War. Famous later for his proclamation that "God is a Negro" and for his refusal to sing "Wash Me and I Shall Be Whiter than Snow," Turner included in his hymnal two selections celebrating emancipation, including "Freedom's Morn," with lyrics set to a meter for "My Country, Tis of Thee":

> All hail! Fair Freedom's morn,
> When Afric's sons were born,
> We bless this day.
> From Slavery we are freed,
> No more our hearts will bleed —
> Lord make us free indeed
> To Thee We pray.

Yet Turner also esteemed the revival songs of his era, for reasons that he gave in justifying their inclusion in the book:

> This may elicit the disapproval of some of our poetic neologists. But they must remember we have a wide spread custom of singing on revival occasions, especially, what is commonly called spiritual songs. . . . To remedy this evil, and to obviate the necessity of recurring to these wild melodies, even to accommodate the most illiterate, these time honored and precious old songs . . . have been as it were resurrected and regiven to the church. Besides, I am not ashamed to say that I love those good old soul-inspiring songs a thousand fold more than I do these later day operatic songs.[8]

Throughout the late nineteenth century, Turner fought internecine battles with northern bishops over the degree of education necessary for ministerial ordination and the place of women in the church; in both cases, he argued for democratizing church polity by extending opportunities to those historically excluded from leadership. When southern-style racism swept the country in the 1890s, Turner blasted American hypocrisy. Turner died in 1906, memorably eulogized by his fellow Georgian W. E. B. DuBois as "a man of tremendous force and indomitable courage. . . . In a

---

8. Jon Michael Spencer, *Black Hymnody: A Hymnological History of the African-American Church* (Knoxville: University of Tennessee Press, 1992), pp. 12-14. For more on Turner and the rise of the African Methodist Episcopal Church in South Africa, see James Campbell, *Songs of Zion: The African Methodist Episcopal Church in the United States and South Africa* (New York: Oxford University Press, 1995).

sense Turner was the last of his clan: mighty men, physically and mentally, men who started at the bottom and hammered their way to the top by sheer brute strength."[9]

Turner's career was indeed remarkable, yet hardly singular. Among the dozens of equally significant "political evangelists" across the South was William Jefferson White, a founder of black education in Augusta. The son of a white planter and a mother who was probably of mixed Native American and African-American ancestry, the ambitious young Georgian could pass as white but self-identified as black. In the 1850s he worked as a carpenter and cabinet maker, thus securing the artisanal economic base that sustained his independence into the era of black freedom. White served the African-American community as an educational leader, newspaper editor, and political spokesman, and the Augusta Baptist Institute that he founded trained talented students who would leave a significant mark on black Georgia, including Emmanuel K. Love, later pastor of Georgia's largest black Baptist church and a founder of the National Baptist Convention. But the school languished in Augusta, compelling its move in 1879 to the rapidly growing and more centrally located city of Atlanta. There it would take the permanent name of Morehouse College, honoring the white northern Baptist educator Henry Morehouse. It would serve as a base for the twentieth-century educator John Hope and trained Martin Luther King, Jr., Julian Bond, and other civil rights leaders.[10]

In 1880, White began publishing the *Georgia Baptist.* With its masthead reading "Great Elevator, Educator, and Defender of the People," the *Georgia Baptist* was one of the most widely distributed black newspapers in the late nineteenth-century South. White's use of "elevation" foreshadowed the concept of "uplift" that would become a predominant theme of black leadership, both secular and religious, in the early twentieth century. At the same time, "elevation" had a distinctive nineteenth-century sense of raising up one's self through one's own labor, á la Emersonian "self-reliance" and the Republican Party's "free labor" philosophy. The later usage of "uplift," by contrast, implied elites stretching their hands downward to lift up the struggling masses; hence the motto of the National Black Women's Club Movement: "Lifting as We Climb."

9. Quoted in Angell, *Bishop Henry McNeal Turner,* p. 249.

10. Bobby James Donaldson, "Standing on a Volcano: The Leadership of William Jefferson White," in *Paternalism in a Southern City: Race, Religion, and Gender in Augusta, Georgia,* Edward J. Cashin and Glenn T. Eskew, eds. (Athens: University of Georgia Press, 2001), pp. 139-40.

As a Republican Party activist and pastor of Harmony Baptist Church in Augusta, White aggressively defended black rights amid growing racial turmoil. He lent vocal support to streetcar boycotts that sprang up in a number of southern cities in the early twentieth century in response to the newly enacted segregation laws on public transportation systems. "The colored people of Augusta are keeping off the street cars because of the revival of Jim Crowism on them, and some of the white papers of the city are howling about it," he exclaimed. "They howl if colored people ride on the cars and howl if they stay off of them. What in the name of high heaven do the white people want the colored people to do?" In 1906, White joined W. E. B. DuBois, John Hope, and other race leaders to establish the Georgia Equal Rights League. The brutal Atlanta riot of that year again mocked their hopes for a racial truce. "Negroes like [W. J.] White ought to be made to leave the South," the local white newspaper opined. "The place for them is, either where there are no Jim Crow laws or where it is too hot for street cars. Augusta has no room for such incendiary negroes, and we should waste no time letting them know it." By the time of his death in 1913, White's Reconstruction-era hopes of equal rights for all were a distant memory.[11]

Reconstruction-era ministers and church organizers like Turner and White represented not only political activism but also a faith in respectability, "intelligent worship," and education as the conduits to black progress. They drew from the community of ex-slaves but attempted to lead them into a brighter future, including in their ways of worship. Their move from "elevation" to "uplift" was symptomatic of the class divide solidifying in postwar black communities. Increasingly, this defined black folk worship over against an urban, educated, elite style in black church life for much of the Jim Crow era. The pattern was particularly evident during the Progressive era, when what Evelyn Brooks Higginbotham has referred to as the "politics of respectability" was evident among educated black (and white) progressives.[12]

Recent scholarship has tended to valorize indigenous traditions of African-American worship, with their implicit rebuke of assimilation and "whiteness" and their maintenance of African-based rhythms, dances, and musical forms. At the same time, figures such as the great black intellectual

---

11. Donaldson, "Standing on a Volcano," pp. 135-77.

12. Evelyn Brooks Higginbotham, *Righteous Discontent: The Women's Movement in the Black Baptist Church, 1880-1920* (Cambridge: Harvard University Press, 1994).

W. E. B. DuBois, a resident of Atlanta in the early twentieth century, demonstrated what could be gained from balancing racial traditions with mainstream or "classical" culture. In his essay "The Conservation of the Races," an outline of the ideas presented more fully in his classic *The Souls of Black Folk* (1903), DuBois offered a spiritualized idea of race differences. The essay suggests that race is a "vast family" of human beings who share a "common history, traditions and impulses, who are both voluntarily and involuntarily striving together for the accomplishment of certain more or less vividly conceived ideals of life." DuBois argued that the various races had "messages" to give to the world, and insisted that Negro "destiny is *not* absorption by the white Americans," nor "a servile imitation of Anglo-Saxon culture." Rather, Black Americans were the "first fruits of this new nation, the harbinger of that black to-morrow which is yet destined to soften the whiteness of the Teutonic to-day"; or as he put it in *The Souls of Black Folk,* "we black men seem the sole oasis of simple faith and reverence in a dusty desert of dollars and smartness." DuBois was a defender of what we would now call "classical liberal culture" (which is why he writes, "I sit with Shakespeare, and he winces not"), but seems to have in mind a synthesis of world cultures as the end of the various races' "striving for manhood." DuBois appreciated, even exalted, folk traditions and the history and destiny of the Negro Church, while insisting that the doors of opportunity not be closed on the "talented tenth" who sought entrance into leadership positions in American society.[13]

During DuBois's time in Georgia, black churches still attracted African Americans of all classes. This enabled the black church to provide a public forum where members of the black community could plan their future and define their culture. Black elites, such as the ministers of Savannah's venerable Baptist churches, and Progressives, such as Henry Hugh Proctor of Atlanta's First Congregational Church, spearheaded campaigns for prohibition and public education, and against illiteracy, disease, and governmental corruption. Within their churches they promoted "intelligent worship," their term for the assimilation of Afro-southern religious practices into the American Protestant mainstream. The question that plagued them concerned the place of specifically Afro-Protestant practices, especially those involving physically demonstrative expressions of spiritual

---

13. W. E. B. Du Bois, "The Conservation of the Races," in *The Souls of Black Folk,* Norton Critical Edition, Henry Louis Gates and Terri Hume Oliver, eds. (New York: Norton, 1999), pp. 176-83.

enlightenment, in the respectable world of the New South. Black denominational reformers devoted much energy to repressing practices deemed embarrassing relics of a slave past. At the same time, the deeply congregational nature of most black church life — signified by the dominance of Baptist churches, which drew in about sixty percent of black churchgoers across the South — meant that the wishes and desires of congregants had to be respected. This tug of war between denominational reformers determined to enact their vision of a bright future on the one hand, and black congregants demanding spiritual voices for their deepest hopes and fears on the other, defined black religious life acrosss the Jim Crow era. The end result was a compromise at first precarious but eventually understood as representative of the varied traditions that went into the making of black religious institutions.

Henry Hugh Proctor offers a good example. Seeking to serve the body, mind, and spirit of his people at First Congregational Church in Atlanta, Proctor, a graduate of Fisk University in Nashville, took this pulpit in 1894. The church historically had been pastored by white clerics who oversaw biracial congregations. By Proctor's tenure, however, the congregation was exclusively black. Proctor immediately doubled its membership to four hundred, and launched a local chapter of the Christian Endeavor Society (a huge nationwide organization of Christian youth), a Working Men's Club, and other similar groups, in hopes of making religious institutions as enticing as the local dives. He sought to "hitch up the religion of the South," which was "sentimental rather than practical, individual rather than social," to solving the great problems of the age. "The spirit of cooperation, not only between the various wings of the race but also between white and black," he wrote in his autobiography, was the "chief contribution the First Church of Atlanta made to social betterment during the quarter of a century of my pastorate."[14]

Proctor led services typical for institutional churches; worship inculcated the same spirit of self-control, propriety, and uplift that characterized the ideology of the black "best men" and "best women" of the era. But Proctor also incorporated the tradition of the spirituals to provide a bridge between races and to raise money for his church. Since the days of the Fisk Jubilee Singers, the traveling choir from Fisk University that proved to be a fund-raising sensation for the fledgling Negro college, black choirs per-

14. Henry Hugh Proctor, *Between Black and White: Autobiographical Sketches* (Freeport, N.Y.: Books for Libraries Press, 1971 [1925]), p. 10.

forming carefully orchestrated versions of the spirituals had proven wildly popular with white audiences at home and abroad. The revamped spirituals combined formal singing styles (with carefully articulated consonants and classical harmonies) with vivid imagery in the lyrics. Capitalizing on this legacy, and honestly feeling they honored the sorrow and triumph of Negro history, Proctor sponsored spiritual concerts at the church as well as race festivals exhibiting varied black traditions in the arts. By 1913, however, Atlanta's black newspaper would no longer cooperate in promoting Proctor's festival, and by 1918, the church dropped the program. Proctor's efforts unintentionally reflected how music could contribute to and undergird a segregationist culture. Early folksong collectors cast their findings into preconceived racial molds — indeed, that is what inspired their research in the first place. Public performance of the spirituals exhibited the "genius" of the Negro, the biologically defined essence of a culture. Each "race" had its own music, and also its own place in social life.[15]

More important, race festivals and public performances of the spirituals could not douse smoldering racial tensions. The Atlanta Riot of September 1906, the single worst racist pogrom of the era, defeated Proctor's intention of mediating between racial communities. In three days of mayhem in the New South City, white mobs attacked blacks on the streets, in streetcars, and in their neighborhoods and homes, killing over twenty and injuring hundreds. Impromptu black militias fought back, driving white mobs from neighborhoods. Proctor remained faithful to his idea of biracial amity engineered by white elites and black spokesmen. "Some among my own people felt that I was giving away their case by seeking cooperation with the whites," he said of his role at that time, while "others thought that because I had openly denounced the conditions productive of riots that I had therefore produced the riot." After the brutal melee, Proctor served on a local "Committee on Church Cooperation," where he tried to dispel the "continuous rumors of approaching 'Race Riots' which creep like poisonous reptiles through the community." Normally circumspect, Proctor nevertheless condemned the white preacher as the "most cowardly character in the whole Southern situation. . . . If he would only speak out he could turn the tide." There was little to cheer in this regard. Proctor's white allies on prohibition or child labor turned their backs on the race issue. For Proctor, the reliance on uplift and cooperation with paternalistic

15. Gavin James Campbell, *Music and the Making of a New South* (Chapel Hill: University of North Carolina Press, 2003).

elites and Progressive reformers, supposedly the "best friends of the Ne-gro," proved to be a delusion.[16]

PROCTOR'S EFFORTS IN ATLANTA represented the apogee of the black progressive crusade, as well as the frustrations inherent in depending on bi-racial cooperation between elites within a system that at every turn re-inforced imbalances of power. As the twentieth century unfolded, black congregations in Georgia turned instead to strategies of race advance-ment, achievement, and uplift in a world increasingly separate from whites. They married black business and religion and concentrated on the internal separate development of the black community. The scholar Adele Oltman, who has compiled an impressive close study of black churches in Savannah during this period, calls the resulting ideology "Black Christian Nationalism." This kind of black nationalism, however, bore few resem-blances to its better known counterpart of the 1960s. The early twentieth-century version was elitist and full of "uplift," but it was also inter-class and corporate; it was black nationalist, but it also pressed hard toward an eventual full incorporation of African Americans into the larger "Ameri-can dream"; it encouraged black capitalism and business, but it did so while emphasizing the group over the individual; it disparaged black "folk" thought and religious practice, but not the black folk themselves; it represented a rejection of the racist southern social order, while it firmly bought into a theology that held much in common with white evangeli-cals in the South; it encouraged an inward-looking building of black in-stitutions encompassing all of black life, but in many ways it hindered de-velopment of a more politicized consciousness until a later generation moved away from some of its premises.[17]

The worship world of Savannah's black Baptist churches during the period cast the ambiguities in this model in clear relief. Savannah was the historic font of the black Baptist church in America, dating from the late eighteenth century, and black Baptist churches remained the port city's

16. Proctor, *Between Black and White*, pp. 102, 94, 106; Ralph Luker, *The Social Gospel in Black and White: American Racial Reform, 1885-1912* (Chapel Hill: University of North Carolina Press, 1991), p. 184; Henry Hugh Proctor Papers, box 4, Amistad Research Center, Tulane University, New Orleans, Louisiana; "Stop Burning Human Beings in America," Proctor Papers, box 3, folder 1; "A Colored Church and Its Colors," Proctor Papers, box 3, folder 1.

17. Adele Oltman, *Sacred Mission, Worldly Ambition: Black Christian Nationalism in the Age of Jim Crow* (Athens: University of Georgia Press, 2008).

largest and most influential black religious institutions. Savannah's First African Baptist Church, moreover, was the progenitor of numerous satellite and offshoot congregations in and outside the city, dating back to its role of organizing "praise houses" on surrounding plantations. First African later was instrumental in reviving the state NAACP, which had a brief flurry of activity just after World War I but then collapsed until the 1930s. Ralph Mark Gilbert, pastor of First African, convened Georgia's first statewide meeting of the four existing state NAACP branches in the late 1930s. He then traversed Georgia, creating or reviving more than fifty NAACP branches statewide and preparing the ground for significant black political activism. Gilbert used the pulpit to preach enthusiastic sermons which also contained political messages of uplift and activism. Like his more famous ministerial colleagues William Herbert Brewster in Memphis and C. L. Franklin (father of Aretha) in Detroit, Gilbert learned to employ the powerful euphonic and rhetorical devices of the African-American sermonic tradition — popularly known as the "whoop" — for a message of political empowerment. Later in the twentieth century Martin Luther King would emerge as the master of this synthesis.

Black Baptist churches dominated Savannah's religious landscape. In 1920, fifty-two Baptist churches were listed in the city directory, and this figure did not include any number of independent upstart Baptist congregations which frequently sprang up in black urban areas. The next closest local competitor, the African Methodist Episcopal churches, numbered but six. Savannah's most prominent black Baptist churches — First African Baptist, Bryan Baptist, and 2nd Baptist — attracted working-class worshipers, often recent migrants to the city, as well as black businessmen and an educated and cultivated elite. The churches were large and wealthy enough to hire ministers of education and standing.

For urban and urbane black churchgoers, the ironies were acute. On the one hand, over time black communities divided by class and wealth as did white neighborhoods and churches. Savannah's mainline black Baptist churches, for example, gradually fell under the control of educated men on the deacons' boards who marginalized the uneducated working-class men that formerly could assume positions of some leadership. The black elite, moreover, defined and enforced standards of respectable behavior. In the 1920s, Savannah's church leaders, for example, spied on and subsequently disciplined Baptist churchgoers who attended (for whatever reason) Charles Manuel "Daddy" Grace's revival services or expressed any interest in his House of Prayer for All People. Grace's ecstatic worship forms, outdoor baptismal processions, and raucous music all smacked of slavery times. On the other hand, the black community was not, and could not be, stratified, for black people were legally and socially defined as *negro*. As "the Negro" was a singular entity, Negro people were all in the same caste. This meant that a mixture of classes sat in the pews of even the most upstanding black Baptist churches in the city. Members of the black elite, moreover, understood theirs to be a corporate and interclass enterprise of uplifting the race as a whole. Thus, while the religious elite might condemn folk worship practices, they did not ostracize the folk themselves. Instead, by sponsoring nationally known lecturers, hosting classical music concerts, struggling to support black educational institutions (such as Central City College in Savannah), and disciplining wayward members, Savannah's black religious leaders fostered a culture of uplift and progress belying the dreadful oppression facing them. In their eyes, worship rituals would be central to the mission of creating a progressive black community that looked to the Kingdom of God in the future and not to the dismal tale of the enslaved past.

The question for black Christian leaders throughout this period thus was whether the folk tradition of enthusiastic worship could accompany or enhance uplift. Were the spirituals, for example, capable of delivering messages of respectability, or should they be dropped as relics of the slave past in favor of classical music and standard Protestant hymnology? The challenge for the progressive urban black congregation was to integrate folk materials into a progressive pageant of the present — not unlike what the Fisk Jubilee Singers had pioneered with their internationally renowned concerts of the spirituals. But the obstacles to "progressive" worship were formidable. Black and white believers shared spiritual beliefs that merged evangelical theology and biblical texts with personal visions and vivid supernatural encounters that could bring healing and harming. Black religious leaders in quest of respectability therefore had to confront practices such as vision quests, dreams, ecstatic conversion experiences and testimonies, spiritual dancing, ring shouts, and song-like sermonizing. A black clergyman in late nineteenth-century Savannah angered congregants because, "instead of teaching dreams and visions," he emphasized the necessity of an "intelligent Christian experience." Because of his refusal to countenance folk customs, he had been "cast out as an evil" by those who clung to a belief in "dreams, visions, and root-work superstition."

At the same time, the independent structure of Baptist church governance allowed for entrepreneurial spirits to create churches and build strong local followings. In response, Savannah's First African Baptist Church sent out apprenticed preachers to evangelize among the freed-eople in the Georgia low country. These emissaries supplied about a dozen "praise houses" (or "pray's houses") with ministerial leadership who reported back to the mother church. The basic conflict became especially acute in the countryside, for the public decorum and uplifting hymns prescribed by Savannah's religious elite there met deeply Africanized worship traditions which had long characterized cultural life on the islands, especially in rituals such as the ring shout.[18]

BLACK RELIGIOUS LEADERS KNEW that the materials of black history itself, such as the spirituals, provided rich resources and could not just be ignored or stamped out, for the repressed would return. Black music editors and publishers offered an important solution by publishing songbooks, song sheets, and hymnals that attempted to integrate and standardize music from the varied portions of the black past. The widely used collection *Gospel Pearls*, published in 1921 as the first official hymnbook for the nation's largest black denomination, the National Baptist Convention, showed the way by mixing spirituals from slave times, Moody-Sankey gospel songs, innovative choruses of Holiness-Pentecostal invention, and classics of Protestant hymnody. An introduction to one of its many editions warned against the "tendency to get away from that fervency of spirit and song that characterized the church and altar worship of other days, and which contributes so much to the stability of our religion." The hymnbook thus sought to preserve the "good old soul-stirring hymns of days gone by" while also providing space for newer compositions. The "Doxology" and "Holy, Holy, Holy" toward the front of the book mixed with late nineteenth-century revival songs such as "Rescue the Perishing" and "Softly and Tenderly Jesus is Calling" in the middle. Its back pages featured selections from A.M.E. minister and songwriter Charles Albert Tindley, the best known black gospel song writer of that generation, including his classic "We'll Understand it Better By and By." The third verse captures the sense of African-American struggle in the context of words that speak also to broader Christian themes:

Trials dark on every hand, And we cannot understand
All the ways that God would lead us to that Promised Land;

18. *Savannah Tribune*, May 14, 1898.

> But He guides us with His eye, and we'll follow 'till we die,
> For we'll understand it better by and by.

Some of *Gospel Pearls'* selections would become classics of white country gospel, such as "What Would You Give in Exchange for Your Soul?" later a hit for the Stanley Brothers bluegrass duo. Charles Jones, the black Holiness pioneer and a prolific songwriter, contributed "I'm Happy with Jesus Alone," later an anthem of sorts for the "Oneness" movement within Pentecostalism. Finally, *Gospel Pearls* featured, for the first time in black hymnology history, a fair selection of spirituals set to written music, including "Swing Low," "I Couldn't Hear Nobody Pray," "Steal Away to Jesus," "Wade in the Water," and "There is a Balm in Gilead."[19]

Gradually, the sacred forms of "white" hymns and folk religious harmonies from shape-note books, black spirituals, and gospel from both traditions mixed with the secular forms of the blues, reaching a synthesis in the gospel blues of the mid-twentieth century. Black religious music leaders created national organizations for choirs and choruses, aiming to train a generation in the norms of written music while giving specifically African-American tunes and lyrics a place in the Protestant musical canon. All of this effort symbolized a profound eschatological hope: that worship and ritual in church settings could symbolize and embody a collective effort to create a future recognizing but not acceding to the racist reality of Jim Crow America. The change happened across the interwar years, and the stylistic innovation was the combination of the blues with religious music — that is, importing blue notes, instrumental virtuosity, and the skills of charismatic soloists into what had been highly communal forms of sacred expression.

The classic example is Thomas Dorsey, who deserves the title often bestowed upon him, the father of black gospel music. Dorsey was born in Villa Rica, Georgia, to a father who held a prominent position as a minister on Sundays while toiling the rest of the week as a tenant farmer. Sponsored through Atlanta Baptist University by an education society to become a "race leader," Dorsey upon his graduation in 1894 became an itinerant preacher instead. "This abrupt change of course," Dorsey's biographer writes, "reflected a deep ambivalence toward assuming his duties in the acculturative church over which the Society had trained him to preside."

---

19. For more information on the information covered in this paragraph, see chap. 3 of Harvey, *Freedom's Coming*, and Spencer, *Black Hymnody*.

Dorsey's father was a powerful and emotional man in the pulpit; his quieter mother symbolized a simple day-to-day piety. In the family of the father of gospel music lay the same ambivalences that many black Baptist congregants felt between moving toward respectability and harboring the power of the expressive style.[20]

During his youth Dorsey paid the bills by spinning out hokum even while yearning to put his soul in the hands of the Lord. An ambitious musician, performer, and writer, he learned to emulate all sorts of styles around him, from the rollicking piano in clubs and brothels to the sophisticated jazz riffs of the 1920s. A series of personal tragedies, including the death of his beloved wife, convinced him that God would provide for a religious musician. In response he composed the classic anthem of God's reassurance of triumph over suffering, "Precious Lord, Take My Hand." The spectacular success of this moving song and his subsequent career justified his faith. Dorsey married blues feeling to gospel message. "Blues is as important to a person feeling bad as Nearer My God to Thee," he later said.

> I'm not talking about popularity. I'm talking about inside the individual. This moan gets into a person where there is some secret down there that they didn't bring out. . . . When you cry out, that is something down there that should have come out a long time ago. Whether it's blues or gospel, there is a vehicle that comes along maybe to take it away or push it away. [Aside from differences in the words,] you take that blue moan and what they call the lowdown feeling tunes and you shape them up and put them up here and make them serve the other purpose, the religious purpose.[21]

Beyond Dorsey alone, it was a coterie of people working together, writing hymns and performing them in the unique pastiche that was black gospel, who elevated the music to its place in the African-American sacred canon. Through the 1920s and 1930s, they defined the new style by employing many of the same tunes and words that had found their way into collections such as *Gospel Pearls*. "Gospel blues" followed the trains out of the South to northern cities such as Chicago. There, the waiting masses of black migrants took enthusiastically to a sound that drew on southern folk and blues roots, while adding sophisticated harmonies. They took advan-

---

20. Michael Harris, *The Rise of Gospel Blues: The Music of Thomas Andrew Dorsey in the Urban Church* (New York: Oxford University Press, 1992), p. 19.

21. Quoted in Harris, *The Rise of Gospel Blues*, pp. 99-100.

tage of church choirs trained in both "respectable" music and Afro-American rhythms and harmonies. The resulting combination revolutionized not only African-American religious music, but eventually American popular culture.

The train taking the migrants northward from Dorsey's Georgia was also the single most powerful metaphorical image in this music. In southern religious song imagery, trains were the vehicles delivering both physical and spiritual salvation. As the historian John Giggie explains, "when blacks sang of or imagined a conversion experience as going to heaven on a train, they understood the train as a vehicle of both spiritual and racial transformation, one bringing them to a time and place where the salvation included an end to racism." The train also symbolized transport in the other direction for sinners who were not right with God. In more than three hundred recordings made in the 1920s, the Reverend J. M. Gates, an Atlanta pastor who pioneered the art of the recorded chanted sermon, cut classics such as "Death's Black Train Is Coming." His rendition of the well-traveled song sold over 35,000 copies and helped to establish Gates as one of the best-selling artists for Columbia records. Just as Bessie Smith and other pioneers brought vocalizations of earlier eras to recorded blues, Gates imported African-American folk sermonic forms to his prolific output of three-minute record sides:

> O, The Little Black Train is coming.
> Get all you business right.
> You'd better set you house in order
> For that train may be here tonight.[22]

That trains found their way into countless southern gospel songs in both white and black traditions speaks to the deeply biracial traditions of southern religious culture. A famous example came from Georgia Holiness pioneer Charlie Tillman, a white gospel songwriter and author of classics such as "Give Me That Old Time Religion" (an adaptation of "Give

---

22. John Giggie, "God's Long Journey: African-Americans, Religion, and History in the Mississippi Delta, 1875-1915" (Ph.D. diss., Princeton University, 1997), pp. 120-40; Giggie, *After Redemption: Jim Crow and the Transformation of African-American Religion in the Delta, 1874-1914* (New York: Oxford University Press, 2007); *Complete Recorded Works of the Reverend J. M. Gates* (Document Records). Gates's version of "Death's Black Train Is Coming" may also be heard individually on *Roots 'n Blues: The Retrospective, 1925-1950* (Columbia Records), disc 1.

Me That Religion," a spiritual he overheard at a black revival service in Georgia). Tillman memorably used the railroad image in his 1891 classic "Life's Railway to Heaven," which found its way into both white and black communities. Racial interchange always had characterized southern religious culture. "Substantially the two races have the same religion," a white traveler wrote in the late nineteenth century, and her observation resonates through much of the literature of the Jim Crow era. White and black Christians organized into racially defined denominations, baptized their converted in separate pools, and buried their dead in segregated cemeteries. Yet within southern culture lay strata of white and black religious experience rarely seen in the institutional churches but evident in the interstices of community life. Racial interchange was especially strong in music and in the emergence of new religious traditions, especially Holiness-Pentecostalism. At these liminal points, the bars of race sometimes lowered, if only temporarily. When they did come down, they opened up possibilities for cultural interchange that fed a long-lived shared evangelical culture. White and black believers drew from common evangelical beliefs and attitudes, formed interracial congregations, and swapped oratorical and musical styles and forms. On occasion, they shared moments of religious transcendence, before moving back into the world where color delimited everything.

References both explicit and cryptic hint at the meaning of this biracial southern evangelical culture, and no better example may be found than in Georgia. In her life story scrawled out in the 1920s, Elizabeth Johnson Harris, a black resident of Augusta, recounted how aid from white and black residents after the Civil War had built her beloved home church, the Rock of Ages Colored Methodist Episcopal chapel: "I was young, but proud to be a member of the Church by true conversion and always proud to fill my seat in Church at every opportunity." Her faithfulness earned her the appellation "little pastor." When Dwight Moody came to town, white and black Augustans gathered together to hear the nationally renowned Christian crusader. He was, according to Johnson, "perfectly free and friendly as a man of God, with both white and colored. He extended a free invitation to one and all, to these services. The audience was sometimes mixed, the crowds were great, and the Holy Spirit seemed to be in such control over the house that the color of skin was almost forgotten for the time being." Harris devoted her life to cultivating God's Kingdom on her postage stamp of soil in Georgia. Accordingly, she seized on any indication of evangelical cooperation and said little about racial conflicts. Yet her account suggests that biracial religious gatherings could bring people other-wise separated into communal contact, even if carefully regulated and monitored.[23]

ULTIMATELY, OF COURSE, this counter-tradition of racial interchange could not break down the dominant world of racial segregation that in-cluded churches. Thus, in Georgia as in the rest of the South, racial inter-change at cultural events never translated into any self-consciously direct assault on the segregated order. In this sense, racial interchange pointed to but never spurred any fundamental revolution in the South. And yet, when the revolution came, it arrived in ways that whites instinctually under-stood, even when they resisted it. The evangelical language of the civil rights movement emerged from the same black churches that, for some scholars, stood convicted of otherworldliness and passivity in the face of oppression. The black churches of Georgia that we have explored were es-pecially notable as birthplaces of the movement — literally so, in the case of King's growing up years at Ebenezer Baptist Church in Atlanta. Ap-pealing to people nurtured even as they struggled amid violent locales in surrounding states, King and his many comrades and followers built a movement that indeed *moved*, drawing from, even as it transcended, the rich tradition of black worship.

23. Elizabeth Johnson Harris, "Life Story, 1867-1923," in Harris Papers, Special Collec-tions Library, Duke University, available online at http://scriptorium.lib.duke.edu/harris/.

Cultivating Soil and Soul: The Intersection of the National Catholic Rural Life Conference and the American Liturgical Movement, 1920-60

Michael Woods, S.J.

In a 1960 interview, Msgr. George "Alfalfa" Hildner, the beloved pastor of St. John Church in Gildehaus, Missouri, declared: "Plowing straight up and down the hills is like stabbing into the back of the soil. I told the farmers they would receive absolution for any sin they confessed, but God help them if they confessed plowing straight up and down the hills."[1] A "master conservationist," Hildner articulated an insight which the National Catholic Rural Life Conference (NCRLC) promoted from its earliest days: soil and souls — land and people — possess a unique affinity through which the Church's redemptive mission is expressed and lived out according to her liturgical and sacramental life. Supported by the Bible's agrarian imagery, the Conference taught, the liturgy makes use of the material creation in order to worship God. It is the fruits of the earth — water, wheat, grapes, and oil — that human hands fashion and God blesses for the building up of the Body of Christ and the manifestation of the Kingdom. The NCRLC sought to make farmers aware that, due to their unique vocation of working on the land, they were "partners with God" in bringing to fulfillment this lofty endeavor. That it drew life and liturgy so close together was a natural consequence of the mission that the Conference set for itself at its founding: "The salvation and sanctification of rural people in and through the circumstances of their own lives is the central aim and objective of the National Catholic Rural Life Conference."

It was also natural that the NCRLC discovered early on the American liturgical movement, with its agenda to reform and renew the Christian life

---

1. Quoted in *Jubilee*, August 1960, p. 14. Copy in Marquette University Archives, Monsignor Luigi G. Ligutti Collection, box F-2, folder "Correspondence H."

by way of the liturgy. A trans-Atlantic phenomenon that came to the United States in the 1920s, the movement sought to recover a more authentic spirit of Christian worship, one that fostered intelligent and active participation in the liturgy. The distinctive American contribution to this impulse was the insistence that liturgy help transform the daily life of Christians and contribute to a just social order. For its part, the NCRLC made public worship and devotions the animating force of its social agenda for rural Catholics. In nearly all Conference programs — farmer retreats, summer schools, priest institutes, etc. — the liturgy served as the principal spiritual component, imparting an authentic rural piety, while rural parishes additionally made wise use of the *Roman Ritual* with its numerous agricultural blessings to further integrate their religious and agrarian lives. The intersection of the NCRLC and the American liturgical movement thus constituted a unique attempt to meld liturgy, culture, and the quest for social justice among rural Catholics in the mid-twentieth century.

Finding Land, Tilling Soil, and Sowing Seeds: 1923-40

The liturgical and Catholic rural life movements not only arose about the same time but under the leadership of two men who had been born in the same state, Minnesota, just ten years apart. Fr. Edwin O'Hara, founder of the NCRLC in 1923, and Dom Virgil Michel, credited with launching the American liturgical movement in 1926, both had sweeping visions for revitalizing the Church and believed that the liturgical and sacramental life should occupy a distinguished place in that mission. Each one, being a faithful disciple of Pius X, firmly believed in the pope's motto *instaurare omnia in Christo* — to restore all things in Christ.[2] Very quickly the two became aware of each other's organization.

O'Hara (1881-1956) was reared on a Minnesota farm and schooled at St. Thomas Seminary in St. Paul, Minnesota, where he was greatly influenced by Archbishop John Ireland and Fr. John A. Ryan, two great promoters of Catholic social teaching. O'Hara went on to combine his farm experience and seminary formation to put forth a bold vision of ministry to the

---

2. Pius X, *E Supremi* (Vatican: Acta Sancta Sedis, 1903). Pius X stated: ". . . We proclaim that We have no other program in the Supreme Pontificate but that 'of restoring all things in Christ' (Ephes. i., 10), so that 'Christ may be all in all' (Coloss. iii., 2)." In *The Papal Encyclicals: 1903-1939*, Claudia Carlen, I.H.M., ed. (Wilmington, N.C.: McGrath Publishing, 1981), #4.

faithful in the countryside, who already in the 1920s were suffering economic depression and were a marginalized population in the Church besides.[3] Catholicism in the United States was largely an urban phenomenon but many immigrants from the European countryside continued to move westward to settle on the land. The territory was still something of a frontier and Catholics were often without parish or priest. It was to such isolated communities that O'Hara directed the efforts of the NCRLC.

Virgil Michel, O.S.B. (1890-1938), had been born and reared in a middle-class home in St. Paul and spent most of his life as a monk of St. John's Abbey in Collegeville, Minnesota. He founded the Liturgical Press which published the journal *Orate Fratres,* the liturgical movement's leading organ. Michel combined two insights from contemporary papal teaching into the movement's core agenda: "Pius X tells us that the liturgy is the indispensable source of the true Christian spirit; Pius XI says that the true Christian spirit is indispensable for social regeneration. Hence the conclusion: The liturgy is the indispensable basis of social regeneration."[4] The Mystical Body of Christ, shaped and sustained by the Church's worship, was to be the animating force behind a more just social order. The movement's mission was all the more urgent, Michel thought, because American Catholics too often kept the Church's worshiping life separate from its social teaching, misunderstanding their intrinsic interrelationship.[5]

The leaders of the American liturgical movement were not attempting to initiate anything radically new. Rather, through their study of liturgical history they wanted the Catholic Church "to return to its roots in the early Church where the lives of Christians, both individually and corporately, were formed and shaped by the worship in which they participated, living

---

3. On O'Hara, see Timothy Dolan, *Some Seed Fell on Good Ground: The Life of Edwin V. O'Hara* (Washington, D.C.: The Catholic University of America Press, 1992); Dolan, "The Rural Ideology of Edwin O'Hara," *U.S. Catholic Historian* 8 (Fall 1989): 117-29. On the NCRLC, see Raymond P. Witte, *Twenty-Five Years of Crusading: A History of the National Catholic Rural Life Conference* (Des Moines: National Catholic Rural Life Conference, 1948); and David Bovée, "The Church and the Land: The National Catholic Rural Life Conference and American Society, 1923-1985" (Ph.D. diss., University of Chicago, 1986).

4. Virgil Michel, "The Basis of Social Regeneration," *Orate Fratres* (hereafter *OF*) 9 (1935): 545; Pius X, *Motu proprio Tra le sollecitudini,* November 22, 1903 (Vatican City: *Acta Sancta Sedis*). Mark Searle wrote an excellent commentary on Michel's syllogism: "The Liturgy and Catholic Social Doctrine," in *The Future of the Catholic Church in America: Major Papers of the Virgil Michel Symposium,* John Roach et al., eds. (Collegeville, Minn.: Liturgical Press, 1991).

5. Michel, "Scope of the Liturgical Movement," *OF* 10 (1936): 485.

their baptismal dignity as partners in Christ's Mystical Body."[6] For centuries Catholic liturgy had been centered on the priest, leaving the laity without an active role to play. Thus, the faithful usually uttered private prayers and devotions *during* the Sunday (and daily) Mass; piety was rather individualistic. By contrast, Michel and his colleagues wanted the faithful to actively and intelligently participate in the Church's liturgy as social worship. Their work bore its most noted fruit at the Second Vatican Council (1962-65) and the promulgation of the decree on liturgy, *Sacrosanctum Concilium.* But a more active liturgical participation already before the Council impacted a wide array of other renewal movements in the Church — liturgical arts, music, education, and social justice. The distinctive American link of liturgy to social justice, in turn, came through a retrieval of the seminal insight attributed to Prosper of Aquitaine: *ut legem credendi lex statuat supplicandi,* often abbreviated *lex orandi lex credendi* — the law of prayer grounds the law of belief. Recent liturgical scholarship verifies that during the Middle Ages this fundamental relationship between liturgy and theology had been broken, with important consequences for Christian praxis. The liturgical movement thus saw *lex orandi lex credendi* needing to be supplemented with the *lex vivendi* (or *lex agendi*), as the latter helps to illuminate what the former entails for the believer's daily spiritual and moral existence.[7]

---

6. Keith Pecklers, *The Unread Vision: The Liturgical Movement in the United States of America, 1926-1955* (Collegeville, Minn.: Liturgical Press, 1998), pp. 44-45. Pecklers's work has become a standard reference for scholarship on the American liturgical movement. He uncovered the extensive network of relationships between the liturgical movement and many mid-twentieth-century Catholic social movements. One of the latter was the NCRLC. For a concise overview of the liturgical movement, see his entry in the *New Catholic Encyclopedia,* 2nd ed., "The Liturgical Movement I. Catholic," pp. 670-77; and Kathleen Hughes, ed., *How Firm a Foundation: Voices of the Early Liturgical Movement* (Chicago: Liturgy Training Publications, 1990). While the following list of people are readily identified with the liturgical movement, they also made contributions to the Catholic rural life movement: Virgil Michel, William Busch, Martin Hellriegel, Alcuin Deutsch, O.S.B., Godfrey Diekmann, O.S.B., Msgr. Joseph Morrison, Benedict Ehman, O.S.B. (Rochester, N.Y. Abbey), Michael Ducey, O.S.B. (Secretary of the Liturgical Conference), Reynold Hillenbrand, Hans Ansgar Reinhold, Lydwine van Kersbergen (American Grail), Fr. Philip Weller (translator of the *Roman Ritual*) , Bede Scholtz, O.S.B. (founder of the journal *Altar and Home*), Clifford Bennett (Gregorian Chant Society), Gerald Ellard, S.J., Maurice Lavanoux (Liturgical Arts Society), and Dorothy Day (Catholic Worker co-founder).

7. Pecklers, *Unread Vision,* pp. 81-150. Kevin Irwin, *Context and Text: Method in Liturgical Theology* (Collegeville, Minn.: The Liturgical Press, 1994), pp. 4, 44-46; Kevin Irwin, *Models of the Eucharist* (Mahwah, N.J.: Paulist Press, 2005), pp. 29-30.

This adaptation and its linkage to the NCRLC's work was spelled out in a pivotal article published by William Busch, an important collaborator of Michel, in early 1930, in the first months of the Great Depression. Writing about it to Michel in October 1929, the month of the Wall Street crash, Busch said: "Father O'Hara of Oregon has suggested to me an article on a topic which may sound surprising to those who have not thought deeply about the liturgical movement. It is: The liturgy and farm relief."[8] O'Hara solicited the piece to secure support from the U.S. bishops, as a body, for a new venture the Conference was promoting, a nationwide observance of Catholic Rural Life Sunday on the fifth Sunday of Easter. The bishops needed to be "strengthened in their attitude," Busch agreed, since some in the hierarchy were resisting the liturgical and rural life movements alike.[9]

Busch's article, "The Liturgy and Farm Relief," provided the Catholic agrarianism of the NCRLC with its liturgical and theological foundations and its social justice orientation. At the same time it evoked the liturgical movement's critique of the patterns of individualistic piety that had caught up American Catholics and explicitly invoked Prosper of Aquitaine's axiom as a corrective:

> Prayer not only implores and honors God, it also educates mankind. This is especially true of liturgical prayer. The liturgy well understood will show us the meaning of the Christian religion in all its scope. The *lex orandi* will help us to know the *lex credendi* and the *lex agendi* [*vivendi*]. We shall be conscious once more of our social solidarity in Christ. We shall see a transformation of social life, agricultural, industrial and political. If this is too much to hope for Christian nations, then the outlook of the modern world is dark indeed.[10]

By itself, Busch allowed, the liturgy was insufficient to correct unjust social structures; it provided no ready-made solutions to the world's problems. Rather, the liturgy was to heighten the Christian's awareness of social

---

8. William Busch to Virgil Michel, October 17, 1929, St. John's Abbey Archives, Virgil Michel Papers, Box Z 23 (hereafter SJAA). This collection is distinct from the St. John's University Archives (SJUA). Upon his ordination to the priesthood, O'Hara was sent to the Diocese of Oregon City, Oreg., due to the great pastoral needs there. He would, however, spend the first fifteen years working in an urban parish. In 1920 he was assigned to St. Mary's in Eugene, Oreg., where he labored among rural Catholics and conducted the affairs of the NCRLC for the first seven years.

9. Busch to Michel, March 19, 1930, SJAA, Virgil Michel Papers, Box Z 23.

10. Busch, "Liturgy and Farm Relief," *CRL* 8 (April 1930): 2.

ills so that, through worship and study, the faithful received the spiritual means to discern which course of action would be most beneficial to the common good. Specifically, the liturgy inspired a deep "social solidarity in Christ" which enabled the Christian to discern the best course of action to pursue — organically, from within one's culture, and in conjunction with a study of Catholic social teaching and other spiritual practices.[11]

Busch's article highlighted a favorite theme of the liturgical movement that had special resonance with Catholic rural life: the "sacramental principle."[12] The relationship between the material and spiritual dimensions of life (the natural and supernatural orders) was a theological pillar of both movements. Simply stated, farmers worked closely with the "materials" used in liturgical-sacramental celebrations, their "spiritual" sustenance. Besides liturgical materials, many aspects of their daily round deepened the spiritual life of farmers. Busch offered an eloquent insight which could have served as the theological *magna carta* for the convergence of the liturgical and rural life movements against the backdrop of the Great Depression:

> The liturgy long antedates modern industrialism and speaks in a language of an age more closely in touch with nature and filled with references to rural life. Like the parables . . . and the pastoral and nature imagery of all the Bible, the liturgy, true always to the sacramental principle, brings us through the things of nature to the things of grace. To the dwellers in the country the liturgy speaks in a familiar way, and to all of us in a way that tends to correct our modern life in which man is

---

11. For Michel, Catholic social teaching was expressed primarily in the papal encyclicals *Rerum Novarum* by Leo XIII and *Quadragesimo Anno* by Pius XI.

12. One contemporary definition of this principle states: "All reality, both animate and inanimate, is potentially the bearer of God's presence and the instrument of God's saving activity on humanity's behalf. This principle is rooted in the nature of a sacrament as such, i.e., a visible sign of the invisible presence and activity of God. Together with the principles of mediation (God works through secondary agents to achieve divine ends) and communion (the end of all God's activity is the union of humanity), the principle of sacramentality constitutes one of the central theological characteristics of Catholicism." See *The HarperCollins Encyclopedia of Catholicism* (San Francisco: HarperCollins, 1995), p. 1148; and Richard McBrien, *Catholicism* (New York: HarperCollins, 1994), pp. 9-11. Sacramentals encompass those "things" which are used in a liturgical-sacramental celebration proper (water, bread, wine, oil, etc.), and they included such things as ashes used during Lent, as well as ritual actions such as genuflecting or striking the breast. Blessings of anything (homes, soil, seed, harvest, tractors, etc.) are considered sacramentals.

divorced from nature while nature is mechanized and divorced from God. The appeal to nature is, however, only the method by which the liturgy instructs us regarding human relationships and regarding the relation of man to God. Nor is it instruction only, for the liturgy imparts the power to do what it teaches. It brings social enlightenment, it instills a sense of social responsibility, it prompts to social action. The liturgy is indeed a cosmos in which the individual, the parish community, the diocese and the universal Church find their life ordered and ennobled in Christ.[13]

O'Hara agreed that the faithful of the countryside had high esteem for the liturgy, also because its communal dimension helped overcome the isolation they often experienced. He saw how often active participation carried over from the liturgy to the Christian life in general. Thus, besides soliciting help from Busch, O'Hara wrote Michel for pamphlets from the Liturgical Press for a course in "Parish Sociology" that O'Hara was to teach at The Catholic University of America, a course that would focus on the rural parish. He hoped to discover "in what way we can go further in interesting the farmer in the liturgy or interpret the liturgy to the farmer through his occupation."[14] Such training was important for O'Hara had led the NCRLC, at its 1929 convention, to set forth an ambitious and comprehensive program: "Our general objective is Rural Life. By 'life' we mean a rounded Catholic life, with proper unity and proportion for its different factors . . . supernatural *charity* should inspire and ennoble all its manifestations and activities."[15] The "different factors" included health care, economics (cooperatives and credit unions), family life, religious life (for the lay and religious state), education, community life (parish centered), civic life (including relations with non-Catholics), relations with wider life, and liturgy.[16]

As regards the last two resolutions, among the "relations with wider life" the resolution specified work among and with "negroes," no doubt the influence of John LaFarge, S.J., who had been working among African Americans in rural southern Maryland. LaFarge was also closely aligned

---

13. Busch, "Liturgy and Farm Relief," pp. 2-3.

14. Michel to O'Hara, February 21, 1930; O'Hara to Michel, February 25, 1930, in The Catholic University of America Archives/Social Action Department (hereafter CUAA/SAD), box 53, folder 25, "Liturgical Movement and Rural Life Movement."

15. Witte, *Twenty-Five Years of Crusading*, p. 83.

16. Witte, *Twenty-Five Years of Crusading*, pp. 82-88.

with the liturgical movement. Thus he wrote O'Hara in April 1929 to ask special emphasis for the liturgy in the Conference's plan of action.[17] The "liturgy" resolution in turn urged "that the Fifth Sunday after Easter be nationally observed as Rural Life Sunday, and that the liturgical prayers and ceremonies of the ensuing Rogation Days be carried out . . . by the Catholics of this country."[18] Rogation Days (from *rogare,* to petition) originated in the fifth century and preceded the feast day of the Ascension. They were observed as days of prayer to avert plague and drought and to implore the blessing of God for good harvests. While they originally had a penitential dimension, more importantly their observance was public as the faith community went in procession through the fields chanting the litanies and other prayers, blessing the crops. Their present observance had become somewhat perfunctory and their wider social significance lost. Thus, aligned with the liturgical movement's principle of restoring the social character of Christian worship, its advocates, including William Busch in his seminal article on "Liturgy and Farm Relief," emphasized that Rogation Days produced their full effect when observed in connection with the Church's overall liturgical life, especially in close conjunction with the liturgical and natural cycles of time. Moreover, Busch argued, in view of the economic catastrophe of the day, the observance of Rogation Days could no longer be considered the interest of the agricultural sector alone but was relevant to the entire nation.[19]

The NCRLC's vision continued to mature throughout the 1930s. A resolution passed at the 1935 convention in Rochester, New York, stressed the role "economic cooperation" could play in advancing the common good. In the midst of the Depression, such an ethos of cooperation was crucial; thus, the NCRLC promoted credit unions and cooperatives, naming the Antigonish Movement of St. Francis Xavier University in Nova

17. Dolan, *Some Seed Fell on Good Ground,* p. 99, n. 58.

18. Witte, *Twenty-Five Years of Crusading,* p. 87. This resolution also noted that the Conference would participate "in a movement already widespread amongst our fellow citizens in the United States." A 1929 letter from Harrison W. Foreman of the National Council of the Protestant Episcopal Church encouraged O'Hara and the NCRLC to join President Hoover, the Agriculture Secretary, and many other religious and civic groups in observing Rogation Days as well as the Fifth Sunday after Easter as "Rural Life Sunday." The accompanying letter made suggestions for hymns, Scripture, prayers, plays, pageants, and a bibliography. H. W. Foreman to O'Hara, July 2, 1929, CUAA/SAD, box 53, folder 25, "Rural Life Movement and Liturgical Movement."

19. Busch, "Liturgy and Farm Relief," p. 2, and Adolf Adam, *The Liturgical Year: Its History and Meaning after the Reform of the Liturgy* (New York: Pueblo, 1981), pp. 190-91.

Scotia as an outstanding example.[20] Spiritually, the Conference adopted the image of the Mystical Body of Christ, formed by the communal celebration of the liturgy, as the best way of expressing such cooperation — religious and economic: "We urge likewise the study of the liturgy of the Church and the participation of our rural people in the liturgy according to the mind of the Church as the spiritual basis of the communal spirit and the source of Christ-like living and apostolic social action." This resolution prompted the Conference to invite Virgil Michel to the following year's convention at Fargo, where he delivered his talk on the liturgical and cooperative movements.[21]

For their part, in the mid- to late 1930s Michel and St. John's University undertook direct efforts to integrate the rural and liturgical apostolates. In the Benedictine tradition this was not too great a stretch, since the *labora* of the order's well-known maxim presumed wise and effective care of the land to support the monastery and its works. St. John's became a center for rural life activities, often in collaboration with the NCRLC, and *Orate Fratres* published many articles on liturgy and rural life. At almost every step of the way the liturgical life was understood to be constitutive. For example, Michel and Alphonsus Matt (publisher of *Der Wanderer*) established the Institute for Social Study at St. John's in 1934. Its weekend institutes, designed mostly for the laity, covered an array of social topics and were anchored by the Saturday evening "spiritual" conference on the Mystical Body of Christ and the liturgy. So, during one weekend the topic was "Consumer Cooperatives," in which participants studied various international cooperatives (mostly agricultural). The Saturday evening lecture was entitled, "The Social Nature of Communion [Eucharist]," which advanced the value of communal participative worship and its potential to overcome the individ-

20. The Antigonish Movement was the strongest Catholic Cooperative in North America. NCRLC president Fr. W. Howard Bishop was responsible for bringing its founder Fr. Coady and some co-op members to the 1934 St. Paul convention. After this meeting, the NCRLC formed the "cooperative committee." See Witte, *Twenty-Five Years of Crusading*, p. 107, and Christopher J. Kauffman, *Mission to Rural America: The Story of W. Howard Bishop, Founder of Glenmary* (New York: Paulist Press, 1991), pp. 92, 123.

21. "Resolutions Thirteenth Annual Convention, Rochester, N.Y.," MUA/NCRLC, Series 8/1, box 2, folder "Meetings and Conventions October 27, 1935-September 25, 1938," p. 159. Michel's Fargo address was later published in *Catholic Rural Life Objectives* (1936) and as "The Cooperative Movement and the Liturgical Movement," *OF* 14 (1939-40): 152-60. Immediately following the NCRLC's 1936 Fargo convention, Michel returned to St. John's where the first weekend of the Institute for Social Study was to be held October 17-18, 1936, one of the venues in which Michel specifically explored the agrarian question.

ualism that tended to drive capitalism. Thus, cooperatives, individualism, and Holy Communion were discussed in the context of a weekend featuring common prayer and meals throughout and concluding with the Sunday liturgy in which all were encouraged to participate. The weekend made for a *potentially* significant formative experience.[22]

By the end of the 1930s both the NCRLC and the liturgical movement had made good strides to integrate the liturgy and rural life, but still showed some limitations. Michel, who died in 1938 at age forty-eight, left on his desk an unfinished rural life curriculum that he wanted to establish at St. John's. In 1939 the NCRLC issued the *Manifesto on Rural Life,* its most authoritative statement to date and one of the more comprehensive social documents ever produced by a recognized Catholic organization. The *Manifesto* situated the rural question in the context of the papal social encyclicals of the day along with current socio-economic research. Yet it made no reference to liturgy or much else of a spiritual nature. This was especially surprising since two years earlier Michel had spoken at the Conference's Fargo convention to just this point. Furthermore, in 1937 the various committees responsible for producing the *Manifesto* had drafted their preliminary reports. One of those was titled "Christian Cooperatives" and was prepared by John LaFarge and Michel. Their draft proposal made a direct connection between ethical relationships in the agrarian-economic sphere and the Mystical Body of Christ. They suggested that the Church's liturgy could serve as a sound "model" for cooperation. For some reason these insights did not make it through the final redaction.[23]

---

22. Michel, "Cooperative Nature of Communion," Institute for Social Study Papers, SJUA 1771, University Topics Rf-T. Michel also conducted a series of seminars between 1937 and 1938 entitled "Course in Catholic Background and Current Social Theory." One of the seminars treated the "The Liturgical Movement, the Corporative Order, and the Distributist-Agrarian Movement." This was a particular attempt to integrate his liturgical and agrarian thought. Central to Michel's agrarian vision and its relationship to the liturgy was his sacramental worldview. See Michel, *Course in Catholic Background and Current Theory,* SJAA, Virgil Michel Papers, box "Works Published," 1937-1938. In 1935-36, Michel also wrote several articles on the "natural and supernatural" order, which, while not treating agrarianism proper, supported his agrarian views more generally and placed them on a more firm liturgical-theological basis. Key to that foundation was the sacramental principle. See Michel, "Natural and Supernatural Society: I. The Sacramental Principle as Guide," *OF* 10 (1936): 243-47; Michel, *Our Life in Christ* (Collegeville, Minn.: Liturgical Press, 1939), pp. 76-85, 180-89, esp. pp. 77 and 181.

23. "Catholic Planning for Rural Social Welfare," NCRLC, Richmond, Va., November 7-10, 1937. See MUA/NCRLC, Series 12/1, box 1, "1937." The liturgical and spiritual lacunae of

Harvesting the First Fruits, 1940-55

Such deficits would diminish significantly in the next decade. Beginning in 1940 the NCRLC witnessed a veritable explosion of programs and publications on liturgical and devotional life. Similar stirrings marked the Liturgical Conference, above all with its annual Liturgical Weeks. Movement pioneer Martin Hellriegel declared that the two movements "are like the two halves of a circle and the leaders of one should bring information and inspiration to the other. . . . The liturgical group is the 'husband' and the rural life group is the 'wife' and, what God has joined together, let no man put asunder. But right now they are divorced."[24] The *Missa recitata* (dialogue Mass) became a regular feature during the Liturgical Weeks and the NCRLC's annual conventions. Among many activities a few stand out as illustrating the variety and creativity of the movements.

The Grail was an international women's movement begun in the Netherlands in 1927, aimed at forming Christian women as apostles of the Mystical Body of Christ so as to transform the world. Lydwine van Kersbergen became its first president in Holland and brought the movement to the United States where it took on a decidedly rural character.[25]

---

the *Manifesto* did not escape the attention of Martin Schirber, O.S.B., a fellow monk from Michel's community and closely aligned to the rural and liturgical movements. In spite of the *Manifesto's* reliance on Catholic social principles, Schirber wondered if it had done so too narrowly: "It [the *Manifesto*] scarcely mentions grace, the supernatural life, the mystical body, life in Christ, the liturgy, sacraments, the Mass as community worship and sacrifice, and the Eucharist as the bond of social unity. Even the discussion of social charity leaves the impression that the writers have in mind merely a rural community chest campaign, whose purpose is to bolster up a faltering justice — with little to distinguish it from mere humanitarianism." See Martin Schirber, O.S.B., "Manifesto on Rural Life," *OF* 14 (1939-40): 93-94.

24. Martin B. Hellriegel, "A Pastor's Description of Liturgical Participation in His Parish," *National Liturgical Week, 1941* (Newark, N.J.: The Benedictine Liturgical Conference, 1942), pp. 82-83. The annual Liturgical Week in St. Paul, Minn., was being held at the same time as the NCRLC's Jefferson City, Mo., convention. This great liturgical leader's endorsement of the NCRLC would not be his last. Throughout the decade Hellriegel had his hand in several liturgical initiatives of the Conference, spoke at its annual meetings, and served on its board of directors from 1947 to 1950.

25. In 1940 van Kersbergen attended the NCRLC meeting in St. Cloud, Minn., where she listened to a speech by renowned Catholic rural life leader Msgr. Luigi Ligutti. Though generally impressed with Ligutti, she stood up and asked him why no one had said anything about the role of women on the land, pointing out to him that no renewal of life on the land would be possible without the support of women. Ligutti promptly made her a vice-president of the NCRLC. Ligutti was instrumental in obtaining land for the Grail in

One of the first initiates to the American Grail was Janet Kalven, a convert to Catholicism, who attended the first National Liturgical Week in Chicago and was especially moved by the celebration of the *Missa recitata*. The American chapter of the Grail, located in Loveland, Ohio, had a regimen of common work, meals, and prayer; the ultimate bonding factor, however, was the liturgy. The Grail saw the great harmony between the rhythms of nature and the liturgical cycle. The liturgical year provided the structure for their annual activities, while grace at meals, presided over by one of the members, brought one of the themes from the day's liturgy to the table. The meals were second only to the Mass as a source of unity and a means to nourish mind, body, and spirit. The Divine Office structured the day which allowed the women to stop working and pray in common. The week's work ceased at noon on Saturday in order to prepare for the worthy celebration of Sunday, the "day of the Lord . . . the eighth day . . . which set the rhythm for the whole week." Sunday meant a larger meal and some frivolity that included folk singing, dancing, plays, and poetry readings. "For us, life on the land gave new meaning to scripture and liturgy." The Grail women even experimented with liturgical dancing. The NCRLC published works written by Grail members and advertised for the "schools" they conducted. Grail women also gave talks at annual NCRLC meetings.[26]

At the NCRLC's 1949 Columbus, Ohio, gathering, Florence Berger conducted a workshop called "Liturgy and the Home." She arranged the exhibit in such a way that people would move from one table to the next, each representing a liturgical season or feast day. The order was Advent, Christmas, Epiphany, Mardi Gras, Lent, Holy Thursday, Easter, Pentecost, St. John's Day, Assumption, Halloween, and All Saints. The people then sampled her recipes designated for that time of the liturgical year. Berger became well known for her book *Cooking for Christ: The Liturgical Year in*

Loveland, Ohio. On the American Grail, see Alden Brown, *The Grail Movement and American Catholicism, 1940-1975* (Notre Dame, Ind.: University of Notre Dame Press, 1989); Janet Kalven, *Women Breaking Boundaries: A Grail Journey, 1940-1995* (Albany: State University of New York Press, 1999); Mary Jo Weaver, "Still Feisty at Fifty: The Grailville Lay Apostolate for Women," *U.S. Catholic Historian* 11 (Fall 1993): 3-12.

26. Kalven, *Women Breaking Boundaries*, pp. 14, 83, 87, 88. Kalven's most focused treatment of liturgy can be found on pp. 87-89. Some of the Grail publications include Josephine Drabek, *Love Made Visible* (Des Moines, Iowa: NCRLC, 1946); Drabek, *Rogation Days at Maranatha* (Des Moines, Iowa: NCRLC, 1951); Kalven, *The Task of Woman in the World* (Des Moines, Iowa: NCRLC, 1946).

the Kitchen.[27] The recipes were accompanied by liturgical commentary related to the season or feast day. Luigi Ligutti wrote in the preface: "This book is an extension of the Missal, Breviary and Ritual because the Christian home is an extension of the Mass, Choir and sacramentals."[28] Berger boldly declared in her introduction: "Cook you may call her. I prefer Christian in Action. To some it may seem sacrilegious to connect cookery and Christ but that is exactly what this book means to do."[29] Berger established a clear connection between liturgy and rural daily life, where the foodstuffs would have come directly from the land on which they were grown.

The liturgical year was another facet of the Church's life to which the liturgical movement brought deeper reflection and renewal. Rural Catholics had a special interest in and a natural affinity for the pulse of the Church's year since many of its celebrations coincided with nature's cycles of planting and harvesting.[30] Integral to the liturgical year were blessings that had the purpose of drawing the ordinary things and events of life into closer relationship to God's salvific plan.[31] They occupied a significant place among rural Catholic communities. In 1946 thirty-two blessings, particular to agricultural life and found in the *Roman Ritual,* were translated into English by Bishop Joseph Schlarman of Peoria, Illinois, and published by the NCRLC as *With the Blessing of the Church.* The book formed part of a larger effort that pressed for greater use of the vernacular in the liturgy.[32]

---

27. Florence E. Berger, *Cooking for Christ: The Liturgical Year in the Kitchen* (Des Moines, Iowa: NCRLC, 1949). In MUA/NCRLC, Series 5/1, box 2, folder "General Publications 1948-50." The book is still available from the NCRLC. In 1949 both the *New York Times* and *Time* gave it favorable reviews. See actual blueprint of her set-up in MUA/NCRLC, Series 8/1, box 7, folder "National Convention Columbus, Ohio, November 4-9, 1949."

28. Ligutti, in Berger, *Cooking for Christ,* preface.

29. Berger, *Cooking for Christ,* introduction.

30. The material that could be examined here is rather extensive. Therefore, several rural liturgical practices around St. Isidore's feast day (March 22) and within the Lenten season will be highlighted. Brief mention will be made of other feasts and blessings at other times of the year.

31. Paul Jounel, "Blessings," in *The Church at Prayer: The Sacraments,* ed. A. G. Martimort, one-vol. ed., trans. Matthew J. O'Connell (Collegeville, Minn.: Liturgical Press, 1988), pp. 263ff.

32. NCRLC, *With the Blessing of the Church* (Des Moines, Iowa: NCRLC, 1946). The blessings are as follows: Blessing of a Farm, Blessing of the Cornerstone of a New Building, Blessing of a New House, Blessing of a Water Supply, Blessing of the Hearth, Blessing of a

The season of Lent set in motion a particularly intense period of rural-liturgical celebrations. In the United States, the feast day for St. Isidore the Farmer, patron saint of the NCRLC, was celebrated on March 22 and always fell within Lent. Thus, around his feast day, rural Catholics could observe a number of liturgical, paraliturgical, and devotional activities that served to heighten awareness of the farmer's vocation and his place in God's redemptive plan.[33] The *Novena in Honor of St. Isidore Patron of Farmers* was prayed for nine days preceding the feast day.[34] Its primary purpose was to "inspire rural people anew with the dignity of their vocation," understanding that dignity as a veritable partnership with God in his creative work.[35] The novena had a strong catechetical thrust which empha-

---

Stable, Blessing of Horses and Other Draft Animals, Blessing of All Domestic Animals, Blessing of Diseased Cattle, Blessing of Diseased Animals, Blessing of Salt and Feed for Animals, Blessing of Bees, Blessing of a Mill, Blessing of a Spring or Well, Blessing for the Sprouting Seed, Blessing of Pasture, Meadows, and Fields, Blessing of Orchards and Vineyard, Prayer Against Harmful Animals, Blessing of the Barn and the Stored Harvest, Blessing of Herbs on the Feast of the Assumption; IN THE MACHINE AGE — Blessing of a Wagon or other Vehicle, Blessing of a Dynamo; BLESSING OF FOOD — Blessing of Eggs, Blessing of Bread and Cake, Blessing of Cheese and Butter, Blessing of Bacon or Lard, Another Blessing of Bread, Blessing of Poultry, Blessing of Grapes, Blessing of Fresh Fruit, Blessing of Wine, Another St. John Blessing of Wine, Blessing of Food in General.

33. St. Isidore the Husbandman (or Farm Laborer) was born in Madrid, Spain, around the year 1070 and was christened Isidore after the famous bishop of Seville. Poor and unable to afford any kind of schooling, Isidore began working as a farm-laborer on the estate of John de Vergas. Isidore differed from many farmers in that he made daily pilgrimages to several churches while en route to the fields. He regularly arrived later than the other workers, who, consequently, became annoyed and reported him to de Vergas. One morning the landowner hid himself near to where Isidore worked in hope of catching this "slacker" in his employ. True to his daily order, Isidore came late to the fields. De Vergas waited a few moments to watch Isidore begin his work. Just when he was about to confront him de Vergas noticed something strange. He saw a second team of oxen driven by two unknown figures (angels) plowing next to the one Isidore was working and accomplishing the work he was given. "St. Isidore the Husbandman," in *Butler's Lives of the Saints* (Collegeville, Minn.: Liturgical Press, 1995), p. 323.

34. It was also prayed during the days leading up to the August 15 celebration of the Assumption of the Blessed Mother and the days before the civil celebration of Thanksgiving Day (a harvest celebration).

35. NCRLC, *Novena in Honor of St. Isidore Patron of Farmers* (Des Moines, Iowa: NCRLC, 1954). The last page of this booklet suggests that the novena "is much more than a series of prayers. It is a manual of spiritual direction for rural people. It offers select passages from scripture which will renew the spirit and bring peace and joy to the rural family, home and farm."

sized the farmer's vocation and his responsibility to contribute to a just social order. The novena's acknowledgments of the expertise of "Fr. Abbot
and the monks of St. John's Abbey," who were responsible for its redaction
and composition, revealed the continued cooperation between the rural
life and liturgical movements. Clifford Bennett, director of the Gregorian
Institute, composed the "Hymn to St. Isidore" for the novena.[36] Each day
of the novena had certain set prayers, but otherwise the prayers were tai-
lored to a specific rural Christian theme and revealed the Conference's
comprehensive approach to Catholic rural life.[37]

The novena concluded on March 22 when the feast day of St. Isidore
was celebrated. The Blessing of Seed and Soil for the Feast of St. Isidore is
instructive on many fronts and underscores several of the liturgical movement's guiding principles. This rather "simple and noble" blessing ceremony also illustrates how the Church's *lex orandi* can potentially and more
directly inculcate right belief and action. The ceremony was fully
participative. It was led by the priest but provided significant roles for the
assembly — clearly dialogic and communal in nature. It may be argued
that the liturgy's procession actually began at home as soon as the people
gathered themselves and their gifts and directed their attention toward

36. NCRLC, *Novena in Honor of St. Isidore Patron of the Farmer*, p. 43. "Hymn to St.
Isidore": "O Lord, as you have made the earth/to man and beast have given birth/have given
sun and rain that thence/the soil might give them sustenance. We beg you make us willing
to/perform the law we get from you/that work of ours and grace of yours/may bring the increase that endures." Refrain: "Through Jesus Christ let this be done/who lives and reigns
our Lord your Son/whom with the Spirit we adore/one God with you for evermore."

37. Novena themes: Day 1: Partnership with God; Day 2: Family Life in Christ; Day 3:
Love of Neighbor; Day 4: Dignity of Work; Day 5: Walking in the Presence of God; Day 6:
Stewardship of Soil; Day 7: Rural Works of Mercy; Day 8: Trust in Prayer; Day 9: Sacrifice of
Praise. In the view of the NCRLC, essential to the vitality of the Mystical Body of Christ was
concern for the land; its stewardship was fundamental to a well-lived rural Catholic life. The
reflection for Day Six, "Stewardship of Soil," relied upon the thought of Liberty Hyde Bailey,
one of America's most famous agrarians and the founder of Cornell University's agricultural
college. This was a rather bold move for a Catholic devotional pamphlet in that Bailey was
not Catholic but had a Masonic background. Bailey even tended to blend into his science his
philosophy and theology, which could have been construed as Deist or pantheist. He saw no
conflict between evolution and religion. Nonetheless, he had a keen sense that proper care of
the earth was intimately bound up with human welfare: "He [the farmer] must handle all
his materials, remembering man and remembering God," NCRLC, *Novena in Honor of St.
Isidore*, p. 24. The quote from Bailey comes from his book *Holy Earth*. See also Alan Carlson,
*The New Agrarian Mind: The Movement Toward Decentralist Thought in Twentieth-Century
America* (New Brunswick, N.J.: Transaction Publishers, 2000), pp. 7-30.

God and the church. They brought something "material" from their homes and farms, which was, in the first place, a gift from God (soil and seed). Yet, it was properly theirs and central to their way of life. The blessing itself — words about God, creation, and the people who are creation's stewards — served as a solemn reminder of their dignity as baptized Christians and their unique vocation as farmers. The ceremony involved the key facets of liturgical prayer: blessing, petition, and thanksgiving. The assembly sang two songs, one about the work of the Spirit, the other beseeching God through Christ, in the Spirit, to make "that work of ours and grace of yours . . . bring the increase that endures."[38] While the blessing could be done in the home, its celebration with the gathered community was preferred.

The blessing oriented those who would use the soil and seed toward God and God's plan of salvation. The farmer and the community, as Christians, having already been made part of the redemptive narrative through baptism, the blessing enabled the farmer's unique life context to be more deeply joined to the larger salvific account, thus fortifying Christian identity. The farmer did not merely partake in a Blessing of Soil and Seed but, true to liturgical prayer, participated here and now in the realization of Christ's redeeming mission. The blessing liturgy helped to locate the particularities of one's life and culture within the universal action of the Eucharistic celebration. As steward of God's manifold gifts and partner with God, the farmer begs: "Take infertility from the earth, and fill the hungry with Thy gifts, which the fruitful earth will yield in fullness, that the poor and needy may praise the name of Thy glory forever and ever. Amen." Concern for the earth and the poor called rural Catholics to live out what they just celebrated.

In short, the Blessing of Soil and Seed provides one example of how communal prayer could straightforwardly express orthodox belief and encourage the practice of social charity *(lex orandi, lex credendi, lex vivendi)*. Furthermore, the prayers were uttered in a language reflective of a unique

---

38. Among the other blessings recited by the people were the Blessing of Seed — "To Thee, O Lord, we cry and pray; bless this sprouting seed, strengthen it in the gentle movement of soft winds, refresh it with the dew of heaven, and let it grow to full maturity for the good of body and soul" — and the Blessing of Soil: "We humbly beseech Thy clemency, O Lord, that Thou wouldst render this soil fertile with rains in due season, and Thou would fill it with Thy blessing, and do grant Thy people may be ever thankful for Thy gifts. Take infertility from the earth, and fill the hungry with Thy gifts, which the fruitful earth will yield in fullness, that the poor and needy may praise the name of Thy glory forever and ever. Amen."

rural culture. They were noble, simple, and intelligible. The work of God mediated through liturgical prayer was drawn into closer union with the daily work of human hands. Liturgy was expressive of God and life. In some respects, the liturgy began at home with things and people; both passed through the prism of the Church's prayer which is Trinitarian, paschal, and communal. The liturgy — prayer, things, and people — concluded at the farm-home where the blessed soil and seed were returned to God's good earth which brought them forth. A crop's growth as well as the Christian's was of the *one* salvific narrative.

On February 22, 1947, St. Isidore was declared the official patron of the NCRLC, even though he had long been claimed as patron saint of farmers. To honor the occasion, Fr. Joseph Urbain published *St. Isidore Patron of the Farmer*. The pamphlet contained the Mass Proper, the Prayer of the Christian Farmer, a Rural Family Prayer, a Christian Farmer's Creed, Suggested Family Practices, along with other suggestions for Participation in Rural Parish Life.[39] Urbain also composed the Litany of St. Isidore, which employed images from the life of St. Isidore and virtues extolled by rural Catholics. The Mass Proper had ample Scripture with agrarian imagery, making for an easy connection to the life of the farmer and affording pastors the opportunity to tailor the sermon for the rural faithful.[40] This liturgy espoused the virtues of patient faith and humility,

39. Joseph Urbain, *St. Isidore: Patron of the Farmer* (Des Moines, Iowa: NCRLC, 1947) in MUA/NCRLC, Series 5/1, box 2, "General Publications, 1947," 2. Two examples show how the NCRLC tried to meld rural life and piety. Prayer of the Christian Farmer: "O God, Source and Giver of all things, who manifests your infinite majesty, power and goodness in the earth about us, we give you honor and glory. For the sun and the rain, for the manifold fruits of our fields, for the increase of our herds and flocks, we thank you. For the enrichment of our souls with divine grace, we are grateful. Supreme Lord of the harvest, graciously accept us and the fruits of our toil, in union with Christ, your Son, as atonement for our sins, for the growth of your Church, for peace and charity in our homes, for salvation to all. Amen." A Christian Farmer's Creed: "We believe that: Farming is a noble Christian occupation. The farm home is the most suitable place for the rearing of a Christian family. The good earth is the greatest material gift of God to mankind. A farmer must be a conserver of soil, a steward of God's gifts, a producer of the essential elements of life for his family and society, a good neighbor, faithful parishioner, a good citizen. By good example, participation and sharing within the family we shall encourage the children to follow the vocation of farming. By assistance and organization within the parish and diocese we can increase the number of Catholic families living on the land. By neighborliness and Christian living we shall draw more to the faith."

40. The Mass Introit was taken from Psalm 92: "The just shall flourish like the palm tree. . . ." The feast's Scripture readings came from the letter of James 5:1-8, 11, 16-18: "Be pa-

which, while important for any Christian, possessed greater immediacy for the farmer. Even if the farmer did practice his art wisely, there were still many factors simply out of his control that required his deep trust and patience. Also of note were the references to justice, which came to the one who walked with humility (from Latin *humus,* earth, soil). No farmer's harvest was genuine which "overlooked the responsibility to be generous toward the poor."[41]

The celebration of *A Day of Christian Rural Living* was a fully participative liturgy that included prayers recited in unison, processions, and blessings.[42] It combined official blessings from the *Ritual* as well as specially crafted prayers (paraliturgical) which were recited by the assembly. These prayers were verbose yet instructive in their attempt to make direct reference to the work of farmers. The ceremony took place sometime during Lent, but it was unclear on which day, and none was suggested. One notable event, yet to be mentioned, was the proximity of the vernal equinox (March 21) to the feast of St. Isidore. There was a possibility that this ceremony could have been held in conjunction with the equinox as part of an entire week of rural devotions and activities.

The ceremony began: "IN THE NAME OF OUR LORD JESUS CHRIST — We welcome all of you to this Spring ceremony of the Rebirth of Man and Nature." This was followed by a brief introduction that wove a

---

tient, therefore brethren . . . the farmer waits for the precious fruit of the earth, being patient until it receives the early and late rain." The Gospel was John 15:1-7, "I am the true vine, and my Father is the vine-dresser. . . ." As John Hennig noted, "the vine-dresser represented the farmer; thus, in his very trade, the farmer imitates God." See John Hennig, O.F.M., "Prayers for Farmers," *OF* 18 (1943-44): 497. *Orate Fratres* was known for the artwork which adorned its pages. At the end of Hennig's article, one finds a papal tiara looking very much like a beehive (cross on top and small entrance below) with several bees busily at work.

41. Hennig, "Prayer for Farmers," p. 498.

42. *A Day of Christian Rural Living* (Franklin, Ill.: Catholic Rural Life Conference of Springfield, Ill., ca. 1951) in MUA/NCRLC, Series 5/1, box 2, "General Publications 1947." Hereafter, CRLC (IL), *Day of Christian Rural Living.* The basic structure went as follows: I. Why We Are Here; II. The Wonder of the New Life of Nature ("Men" enter center aisle bearing soil and seeds of wheat, corn, beans, hay, fruit and vegetables and place them on a table in the sanctuary); III. The Need for Re-birth within Ourselves; IV. The Joy and Love of Family and Home (Boy and girl enter bearing wedding rings, accompanied by servers with marriage ritual, and holy water); V. Gifts of Redemption (Men enter bearing image of Divine Infant, Crucifix, and Bible); VI. Sermon (optional); VII. Benediction of the Most Blessed Sacrament and Prayer to St. Isidore; VIII. Blessing of Soil and Seed (Blessing/Sprinkling of envelopes of soil and seed brought by the families); IX. Procession out of the church to bless/sprinkle tractors (vehicles), farm implements, and farm animals.

sound paschal theology with agrarian themes.[43] The ceremony's reference to the Mystical Body of Christ made for good ecclesiology as well: "The persons who bear the Symbolic Gifts up the aisle are the representatives of ALL OF US, of OUR ENTIRE DIOCESE." The presentation of the gifts, an ancient and important liturgical action, had long fallen out of use in the Roman Rite. The NCRLC played a central role in resurrecting this practice, related as it was to the community's offering of gifts for the Eucharistic celebration and to benefit the poor. Overall, the prayers put forward an easily understood theology of rural life, expressed in a manner that was at once cosmic and quotidian, universal and folksy.

The ceremony also addressed the need for personal and communal rebirth. Spring marshaled in new life; the good earth is born again but the people begged: "Lord, we too, need to be renewed." This prayer for rebirth equated the language of one who worked the fields with the discipline of Lent, so as to usher in a just and fruitful harvest.[44] At work here was an asceticism that has long been associated with agrarianism. The seasons were a given, but they regulated the farmer's life much more directly than an urban dweller's. As each season approached, farm life demanded specific tasks which governed the farmer's daily activities. To neglect or grow slack in such duties could adversely affect the farmer's livelihood. Most important, such asceticism was ultimately joined to the fruit of the physical and spiritual harvest. The asceticism set forth by the NCRLC was balanced, benefiting the farmer's overall life and health, and was rarely expressed in penitential terms alone. Days of fasting and discipline made those of feasting all the more joy-

---

43. CRLC (IL), *Day of Christian Rural Living* (emphasis original). The prayer stated: "The Season of Spring is the season of renewal. The plants and trees are reborn after the death-like sleep of winter. The farmer prepares for this rebirth by plowing and harrowing the fields, by pruning the trees. Similarly in the liturgical year of Christ's Mystical Body on Earth, Spring is a season of rebirth, climaxed by the Resurrection of Christ from the dead on Easter Sunday. And this too must be preceded by a season of preparation, plowing and harrowing through forty days of Lent, the time of penance and self-sacrifice, the season of inward renewal of the life that really counts. The full meaning of the ceremony is made clear in the words of the ceremony itself."

44. CRLC (IL), *Day of Christian Rural Living*, "The Need for a Rebirth within Ourselves." The prayer stated: "Just as the fields must be plowed and harrowed in order that the seed can bring new life and a good crop . . . so must we plow and harrow our own selves. By prayerful thought we must turn over the great truths of life in our minds. With the pulverizing harrow of fasting we must crush the hardness of our hearts. . . . We must pull out the weeds of passion and we must root up our habits of sin . . . to bring forth the harvest of peace here on Earth and the joy of life everlasting with you in our heavenly home."

ful. *A Day of Christian Rural Living* communicated, by way of a participative liturgical rite, themes such as the vocation of the farmer, soil as sacrament, stewardship, family life, and justice — liturgy gave expression to life.

Other liturgical seasons and feasts provided opportunities for rural liturgy as well. During the Advent-Christmas cycle came the Blessing of Wine on the feast of St. John, Apostle and Evangelist (December 27). It was a special privilege for the farmer who cultivated vineyards to provide wine for the Eucharistic celebration and common use. The blessing spoke of the Incarnation and temporal birth of the Christ so that he could "seek the lost and wayward sheep . . . and cure the man fallen among robbers of his wounds by pouring wine and oil . . . bless + sanctify this wine." Those who drank the wine were to receive strength of body and soul for their earthly pilgrimage. The Blessing of Stables (on or near the Nativity) had an obvious link to rural life.[45] Ember Days, observed four times a year, were clearly related to nature's cycles and were made a part of the Church's tradition. For reasons unknown, however, Ember Days never achieved the popularity that the Rogation Days did among rural Catholics.

The Easter season was a special time to bless food, especially food grown (or raised) by farmers. More generally, food is connected to the overall health and well-being *(salus)* of the people who consumed it. The new life associated with the Blessing of Eggs reminded one of Christ's resurrection. The Blessing of Bread and Cake brought to mind the Eucharist and the way in which "the early Christians brought bread to the altar at the offertory procession to receive a blessing after the consecration."[46] These bless-

45. "O Lord, Almighty God, who didst decree that Thy only-begotten Son, our Redeemer, should be born in a stable and laid in a manger between an ox and an ass, bless, we beseech Thee, this stable and preserve it from every deceit and snare of the devil that horses and cattle within it may be healthy and secure from all harm." NCRLC, *With the Blessing of the Church,* p. 9.

46. NCRLC, *With the Blessing of the Church,* pp. 22-27. Two other blessings not necessarily associated with Easter are especially striking. Blessing of Bees: "Thou who hast directed that the ministers of Thy holy Church should light candles made of beeswax when the holy sacrifice is offered . . . send down Thy blessing on these bees, that they may multiply and be fruitful and be preserved from all harm . . . so that the product of their labor may be used to Thy honor." Blessing of the Silkworm: "O God, Maker and Director of the universe, Who in creating living things didst endow each with the power of propagating its own species, bless + we pray, these silkworms, foster them, and let them multiply. May thy holy altars be adorned with the fruit of their industry. And let thy faithful servants resplendent in robes of silk acknowledge thee with heartfelt praise as the Donor of every Good. Who with thy Sole-Begotten Son and the Holy Spirit livest and reignest for all eternity. Amen."

ings helped to connect the liturgy at the altar to the liturgy in the home. As for the Rogation Days, despite being one of the most commonly observed rural liturgies, it would not be until 1953 that the Diocesan Rural Life Conference of Springfield, Illinois, prepared *A Manual of Ceremonies for the Parish Observance of the Rogation Days.*[47] The ceremony consisted simply of a procession through fields, during which the Litany of the Saints was recited or sung, followed by the celebration of Mass. The *Missal,* while noting when the days were to be observed, did not provide a rubric to bless anything, let alone fields and animals; rather, the blessing was presumed to be carried out based upon the ancient tradition and practice.[48] Of particular note in the introduction to the *Manual* was the emphasis on the ceremony's public character. Finally, in the Easter season, the feast of "The Finding of the Holy Cross" (May 3 or the Sunday following) afforded the opportunity to bless crosses that would be placed in fields, vineyards, or gardens. The blessing's theme united the suffering endured by Christ on the wood of the cross with the hope of a fruitful harvest.[49]

Throughout the growing season (Ordinary Time), blessings could be

47. *A Manual of Ceremonies for the Parish Observance of the Rogation Days* (Des Moines, Iowa: NCRLC, 1953), MUA/NCLRC, Series 5/1, box 2, "General Publications, 1951-54" (hereafter NCRLC, *Manual*). The *Manual* was yet another fruit of the Priest's Rural Life Study Club under the direction of Fr. Irvin Will in the Diocese of Springfield, Ill. Among the many articles in *Orate Fratres,* the following were especially relevant: A Sister of the Most Precious Blood, "The Apostolate: Ascension Week in the Classroom," *OF* 19 (1944-45): 279; Sister Mary Charity, OP, "Thanking for the Harvests," *OF* 23 (1948-49): 540; Martin Hellriegel, "Brief Meditations on the Church Year: Fifth Sunday After Easter," *OF* 18 (1943-44): 291-308; Hellriegel, "The Apostolate: Seasonal Suggestions," *OF* 30 (1955-56): 374-77.

48. The introduction to this *Manual* (catechetical in nature) implored God to protect body and soul, and declared that through the "Sacrifice of the Mass and the Procession on the Rogation Days" "we try: To move ourselves to penance, arouse confidence and trust in God, acknowledge publicly our dependence on God, ask for plentiful harvest, thank God publicly for the harvest, show publicly our faith, hope and love, and to realize that only through living according to God's will and commandments may they possess a happy, contented, peaceful existence" (NCRLC, *Manual*, Introduction).

49. "Almighty, everlasting God, Father of goodness and consolation . . . in virtue of the bitter suffering of thy Son . . . endured for us sinners on the wood of the Cross, bless + these crosses which thy faithful will erect in their vineyards, fields, and gardens. Protect the land where they are placed from hail, tornado . . . and every assault of the enemy, so that their fruits ripened to the harvest may be gathered to thy honor by those who place their hope in the holy Cross. . . ." The Blessing of Crosses on this feast held much potential because of its proximity to Good Friday — *Ecce lignum crucis!* See Philip Weller, ed. and trans., *The Roman Ritual: The Blessings in Latin and English with Rubrics and Planechant Notation,* vol. 3, no. 24 (Milwaukee: Bruce, 1946).

employed to beg God's ongoing protection of the crops. The celebration of the Assumption on August 15 was preceded by the Novena of St. Isidore (August 7-15). In 1955 the Conference published its *Blessings and Prayers for the Feast of the Assumption in Honor of Our Lady of the Fields.* The pamphlet's cover page showed the Blessed Mother standing in a wheat field holding a sheaf of the newly harvested crop. The fully participative blessing liturgy (in English) blessed the first fruits, focusing on the herbs and flowers and alluding to their healing or medicinal purpose. Praise and gratitude for the bounteous harvest that God gave to the farmer were coupled to the stark reminder that thousands of people in other countries "go without daily sustenance, have the poorest clothing, and hardly any shelter." The first of three prayers acknowledged God's goodness as the Creator, who brought forth all kinds of fruitfulness, both as food for creatures and as medicine for the sick: ". . . bless + these various herbs and fruits, and add to their natural powers the grace of thy new blessing. May they ward off disease and adversity from men and beasts who use them in thy name."[50]

Finally, Thanksgiving Day served as a natural and civic end to the growing season for most farmers in the United States. Already in 1925, H. F. Roney had suggested celebrating a Mass on Thanksgiving Day (or on the nearest Sunday) in gratitude for the harvest. He noted how it was fitting to close the year (which began with a blessing of soil and seed back in March) with a Mass of thanksgiving for the harvested fruits of the land. The Catholic Rural Life Conference of Springfield, Illinois, took the lead (again) and published the *Ceremony for the Parish Observance Thanksgiving Day* in 1953.[51]

---

50. The second prayer invoked the name of Moses, who ordered Israel to carry their sheaves of new grain and present them to the priests and thereby to God: "Hear thou our supplications and bestow blessings + in abundance upon us and upon these bundles of new grain, herbs. . . . Grant that men, cattle, sheep . . . find in them a remedy against sickness, pestilence, sores, injuries, spells. . . . May these blessed objects act as a protection against diabolical mockeries, cunnings and deceptions wherever they are kept. . . . May we laden with sheaves of good works, deserve to be lifted up to heaven." The final blessing prayer begged Mary to intercede on our behalf before the "fruit of her womb," Christ our Savior: "We pray that we may use these fruits of the soil for our temporal and eternal welfare — the power of thy Son and the patronage of His glorious mother assisting us." NCRLC, *Blessing and Prayers for the Feast of the Assumption.*

51. H. F. Roney, "A Thanksgiving Mass," *Catholic Rural Life* 3 (November 1925): 6. Roney's recommendation in 1925 anticipated the *Roman Missal* of Paul VI, which provided a Mass proper for this civil holiday. See also *Ceremony for the Parish Observance of Thanksgiving Day* (Sigel, Ill.: Catholic Rural Life Conference, 1953) in MUA/NCRLC, Series 5/1, box

Fr. Paul Brinker — A Saint of the Soil

The rural life movement numbered outstanding leaders who captured the vision and spirit of the NCRLC, promoted it, and implemented it. The defining traits of these leaders were many and varied, but all of them aimed for a vibrant liturgical life coupled to a penchant to reconstruct the rural social order. An exemplary leader who blended vision with personal charisma was Fr. Paul Brinker of the Diocese of Covington, Kentucky. Like George Hildner, Brinker was another of many city-born priests who became an outstanding rural leader.[52] From 1951 to 1957 he was pastor of St. Rose of Lima parish in rural Mays Lick, Kentucky. This small community was comprised mostly of tobacco farmers. Brinker knew little about farming but readily noticed that his flock's well-being was closely tied to growing tobacco. Thus he began his "worship-work program," and it was at St. Rose that he became known for celebrating the annual "tobacco Mass."

Brinker immersed himself in the life of his parishioners, visiting their homes and farms. He often asserted that there must be a direct connection between a "man's life and his liturgy, his cult and his culture." When he saw the spring burning of the tobacco beds (a procedure that prepares the ground for planting), he set in motion for the following Sunday a Blessing of Soil and Tobacco Seed which occurred during Mass. In the middle of the growing season he celebrated a Blessing of the Crops for their protection, susceptible as they were to severe droughts. The faithful processed to an altar set up in or near someone's tobacco patch where a blessing was given and the Litany of the Saints was recited or sung. Brinker's very brief report at the NCRLC's 1952 meeting in Saginaw declared: "Living the Liturgy on the Land seems to have been the theme of the Rural Life program for the past year in Covington. Blessing of seed, the tobacco fields, and the

---

5, "1951-55." Fr. Irvin Will, diocesan director of rural life in Springfield, Ill., reported that by 1957 over twenty thousand Rogation Day manuals had been distributed, and by 1960 over sixty thousand Thanksgiving Day pamphlets found their way into the hands of the faithful. See "Catholic Rural Life Bulletin, 1951-66," Diocese of Springfield, Illinois, Archives, 65, 96, 135, 171.

52. Born in 1910 in Covington, Kentucky, Brinker entered the seminary in 1928 and was ordained on June 7, 1936. Bishop William Mulloy called him one of the more gifted men of the diocese, intellectually and pastorally. After a number of assistant pastor assignments and chaplaincies, he became the diocesan director of rural life in 1945, a position he held until 1957. At this writing, Brinker is still living at age 96, although frail, and was not able to be interviewed. See the comments below of one of his parishioners, Dolores Donovan.

Thanksgiving ceremonies along with the dialogue Mass in the vernacular, were carried out with dignity and benefit to all participating."[53]

The annual Mass held to give thanks to God for the tobacco harvest demonstrated most strikingly how Brinker joined liturgy and life. On a Sunday in December after the crop had been harvested, farmers brought to church a "stick" of the finest "hands" of tobacco from their harvest. Depending on the size of the hands, one could place about eight to twelve hands on a single stick.[54] The farmer removed one or several hands for family members to carry forward during the Mass as part of the "offertory," laying them on a table in front of the altar. The choir sang the following Brinker-composed hymn while the congregation processed forward with tobacco in hand:

> Lady of tobacco fields,
> Golden leaves we offer thee;
> God has blessed our field of labor,
> In tobacco crops of gold.

Brinker composed other songs which he put to the tunes of familiar church hymns. They were appropriate to certain feasts and facilitated congregational singing. After Mass, all of the tobacco was taken to the market and sold. Sales of the crop went toward the purchase of insurance or coal to heat the church as well as "reserves" for the poor. Even the church was decorated with bouquets of beautiful golden tobacco leaves which flared from tall vases.[55]

This Mass as well as other feast days involved further liturgical innovation. During Advent and Lent, the seven o'clock morning daily Mass was in dialogue form and featured congregational singing accompanied by organ. Brinker's homilies throughout the year made an explicit connection between religion and rural life. He faced the people to say Mass while a lector narrated the Mass in English. Brinker believed that people could never be entirely happy in their religion until they achieved a sense of participation

53. Paul Brinker in "Summary of Diocesan Director's Reports, Saginaw Convention," MUA/NCRLC, Series 8/1, box 10, folder "National Convention Saginaw, Oct 17-22, 1952."

54. The entire plant is cut, or likely uprooted by "hand," hence the term. The stalk is split or speared and left to wilt on "sticks" in the field for a day or two before it is hung in a curing barn. Wilting the leaves helps to dry them out and to prepare them for curing. A "stick" is approximately 53-55 inches long.

55. Ruth Craig Moore, "Holy Mass of the Harvest," *The Louisville Courier-Journal*, December 27, 1953, p. 9.

and possession in their worship. In his petition to his bishop to face the people celebrating Mass, he argued: "I hope in this way to increase their active and intelligent participation in the holy liturgy. May I also occasionally use the offertory procession?" In September or October St. Rose also celebrated the Wheat Mass. The wheat was grown by the parishioners, who also cleaned and ground it before taking it to the local convent where the sisters baked the altar breads. A small portion of wheat was brought forward during the offertory procession and the surplus wheat was used for the poor.[56]

Beyond the sanctuary, this devoted pastor engaged in a wide array of activities on behalf of rural people, collaborating with a broad spectrum of society and eager to promote rural welfare. A glance at his diocesan director report for 1953-54 gives some indication of his zeal and the fervor he tried to inspire in other rural pastors.

> Worked to establish a new Catholic hospital [nearer to rural areas]; one credit union; Southern States Cooperative in two counties; Rural CYO [Catholic Youth Organization] organized; three new rural grade schools; Rogation Days observed (litany in English, paraliturgical); Feast of St. Isidore observed; St. Isidore Shrines in every home of St. Rose; Tobacco Masses — blessing of seed, blessing of crops with procession, harvest Mass facing people; four study groups for clergy; gave first broadcast in Soil Conservation Week, July 25-31, statewide 30-station hook-up; Aug 23-28, gave 30 minute broadcasts over station WFTM, World's Finest Tobacco Market, disseminating the Catholic rural philosophy; distributed 5000 pieces of literature at R.E.A. [Rural Electrification Association] Fair, July 28-29; Weekly article in diocesan newspaper; Dialogue Mass established in several places; collaborating with rural Life Committee of Diocesan Council of Catholic Women in promoting family shrines; Wheat Mass, every year at harvest time. Wheat used for altar breads; surplus for the poor.[57]

56. Brinker also made incremental requests for the use of musical instruments during the liturgy, beginning with the midnight Mass of Christmas. He started with the violin, and then added the flute and eventually a flute-violin ensemble for the feast of the Assumption later that year (1954); he did the same for the midnight Christmas Mass. In 1954 Brinker broadcasted the midnight Mass on a local radio station with his brother Maurice, also a priest of the diocese, serving as narrator. For the correspondence between Brinker and Bishop William Mulloy, see Diocese of Covington, Kentucky, Archives (hereafter DCA), folder "St. Rose of Lima, Mays Lick."

57. See Brinker, "Diocesan Rural Life Activities, 1953-54," MUA/NCRLC, Series 8/1, box 13, folder "Diocesan Director Reports, Davenport, Iowa, Oct. 8, 1954."

Brinker worked with Professor Howard Beers of the University of Kentucky Sociology Department on how to more effectively organize rural communities, helping to conduct the "Rural Leadership Institute" in 1948 at the university. Health issues being a perennial challenge to rural communities, he requested permission from Bishop Mulloy to work with legislators on a rural health bill, wanting to identify with them and add strength to the cause. More interesting, he pointedly asked Mulloy: "How far shall I go in recommending that this bill be extended to rural coloreds?"[58]

To modern sensibilities the concept of a Tobacco Mass could not be more politically incorrect. Yet Dolores Donovan, a parishioner at St. Rose during Brinker's pastorate, said of the beloved priest: "He could bring a dead ant back to life. He was simply the most personable man and knew everyone; he made you feel essential to the parish — all in order to keep the engine oiled." She added, "he'd also stare you down in church and 'call you out' if he saw you weren't singing."[59] Fifty years later one could hear in Mrs. Donovan's voice the joy that Fr. Paul Brinker imparted to his flock. More significantly, after all this time, one sensed the great impact left on her by the intelligent and active participation in the liturgy which he fostered. Of all the activities in this small but bustling faith community, liturgy made the greatest impact and it was explicitly joined to the daily lives of these tobacco farmers of St. Rose of Lima parish.

Conclusion

This chapter set out to identify the collaboration that existed between two vital twentieth-century Catholic movements, noting a few of their historical, liturgical, and practical associations. The NCRLC not only embraced the liturgical renewal initiated by Virgil Michel but went further in trying to adapt the liturgy and devotions to rural life and vice versa. Such adaptation was a form of liturgical inculturation that sought a deeper integration of religion and life. But the NCRLC was not founded for liturgical purposes; rather, the liturgy was one means among many that strengthened

---

58. Brinker to Mulloy, February 24, 1947, DCA, folder "NCRLC 1945-47." He also worked with sewage authorities to use a by-product of human waste for fertilizer; this was to help farmers improve their farms the "organic way." The project was considered quite progressive for its time in terms of conservation and sustainability.

59. Personal telephone conversation with Dolores Donovan, October 2006.

the vocation of the farmer, preserving the rural way of life and enabling Catholics to remain on the land. The Conference took a thoroughly "catholic" approach to ministering to rural Catholics, attending to their religious, educational, cultural, and socioeconomic well-being. The land took on a sacramental quality since it was the source of both the Church's sacramental life and the very livelihood of agrarians. Soil conservation was deemed the "11th Commandment." Msgr. George Hildner called the soil "sacred" and its conservation "a holy cause," adding: "By not conserving it, he [the farmer] has sinned against it. By conservation man is expiating his sin and making restitution. This makes soil conservation a pious act."[60] Indeed, as Anthony Adams, the Jesuit priest and rural life leader, said: "Soil and soul, both need saving!"

60. "Alfalfa George: A Rural Pastor Talks about God, the Land, and His People," *Jubilee* (August 1960): 19.

Rites of the Tribes: Two Protestant Congregations in a Twentieth-Century City

James D. Bratt

When a new ethnic consciousness arose in the United States around 1970, people discovered that Protestants could be tribal too. Typically, during the great century of European immigration (1830-1930) observers of American religion and politics had affixed the "tribal" label to communities begun by Roman Catholic and Jewish immigrants. Protestants, by contrast, were deemed "pioneers" or "settlers" who commanded not just a parochial turf but general public space, setting the norms to which later arrivals were bound to assimilate. In the late twentieth century, however, it became clear that sometimes these putative standard-bearers were just leading their own parish parade, that they had own distinctive customs, imputed ancestries, and tight institutional networks fully as much as did any group of southern or eastern European origin. Simultaneously, renewed scholarly interest in the history of immigration rediscovered Protestant groups in that flow as well, whether in the post-1880 "new immigration" or the truly new immigration post-1965.[1]

The amplest harvesting of these two discoveries came in the field of

---

1. Landmark volumes on the two sides of the new ethnic consciousness are Peter Schrag, *The Decline of the WASP* (New York: Simon & Schuster, 1971), and Michael Novak, *The Rise of the Unmeltable Ethnics* (New York: Macmillan, 1972). Important surveys of Euro-American immigration include Roger Daniels, *Coming to America: A History of Immigration and Ethnicity in American Life* (New York: Harper, 1991); Walter Nugent, *Crossings: The Great Transatlantic Migrations, 1870-1914* (Bloomington: Indiana University Press, 1992); John E. Bodnar, *The Transplanted: A History of Immigrants in Urban America* (Bloomington: Indiana University Press, 1985); Thomas J. Archdeacon, *Becoming American: An Ethnic History* (New York: Free Press, 1983); and John Higham, *Send These to Me: Jews and Other Immigrants in Urban America* (New York: Atheneum, 1975).

political history, where the ethno-cultural model recast American elections as battles between tribal coalitions. In these contests Protestants of Yankee derivation formed the hard core of Whig-Republican voters, as Irish Catholics did among Democrats. Immigrant Protestants fell somewhere in between, shifting across party lines from election to election depending upon which of the two core groups most threatened their customs and values. The ethno-cultural school succeeded at establishing clear affinities between a group's ethic and its political disposition, although some political historians found it less persuasive in linking voter coalitions with the parties' policy formulations. For their part scholars of religion could have pressed the model harder to demonstrate more fully how politics was grounded in communal lived practices. One set of terms commonly used to label the two sides — "pietist" and "liturgical," denoting Whig-Republican and Democratic affinities, respectively — invites the exploration of worship practices themselves for the roots, or at least the reinforcements, of political sensibilities.[2]

This essay will undertake that venture by investigating the histories of two congregations that have produced a significant share of the Republican — that is, "pietist" — party leadership in Grand Rapids, Michigan. The choice of site has three virtues. First, by treating what might seem to be the ritually less promising side of the religious divide, it will show that "pietists" too — perhaps especially — have liturgical habits. Second, midsized cities in the upper Midwest, like Grand Rapids, lie off the beaten trail of urban political historiography but offer considerable promise for testing theories. Finally, by following its patterns across the twentieth century, this essay shows that the ethno-cultural approach works beyond the

2. Richard J. Jensen, *The Winning of the Midwest: Social and Political Conflict, 1888-1896* (Chicago: University of Chicago Press, 1971), pioneered the "pietist" and "liturgical" (alternately, "ritualist") usage. Paul Kleppner, *The Cross of Culture: A Social Analysis of Midwestern Politics, 1850-1900* (New York: Free Press, 1970), and *The Third Electoral System, 1853-1892: Parties, Voters, and Political Cultures* (Chapel Hill: University of North Carolina Press, 1979), supplied the most elaborate studies. Daniel Walker Howe, *The Political Culture of the American Whigs* (Chicago: University of Chicago Press, 1979), and Robert Kelley, *The Cultural Pattern in American Politics: The First Century* (New York: Knopf, 1979), supplied the richest interpretations. Signal critiques of the approach include J. Morgan Kousser, "The New Political History: A Methodological Critique," *Reviews in American History* 4, no. 1 (1976): 1-14; James E. Wright, "The Ethnocultural Model of Voting: A Behavioral and Historical Critique," *American Behavioral Scientist* 16, no. 5 (1973): 653-74; and Richard L. McCormick, "Ethno-cultural Interpretations of Nineteenth-Century American Voting Behavior," *Political Science Quarterly* 89, no. 2 (1974): 351-78.

Progressive Era, when the professionalization of politics supposedly eroded the model's salience.

The two congregations selected for scrutiny represent the two sorts of Protestant tribes to be found in the urban North. Eastern Avenue Christian Reformed Church was founded in 1879 during the peak Dutch migration to the United States, and for several generations maintained the insular communalism associated with immigrant churches.[3] First, or Park, Congregational Church was founded forty years earlier, with the village of Grand Rapids itself, by Yankees who moved there directly from New England or via intermediate settlement among the Yankee diaspora in upstate New York and Ohio's Western Reserve.[4] Both rooted in Calvinist religious traditions, affiliated with the same Republican political party, and assuming local leadership in sequential, not overlapping, periods, the two churches nonetheless gave each other a wide berth on the local scene. Eastern Avenue's parishioners were newcomers to a bustling industrial city, finding work as laborers in its booming furniture factories or operating small businesses or truck farms on the edge of town. The people at Park Church, on the other hand, ran the city — its banks, schools, and factories — in conjunction with members of four other prominent downtown churches. The Christian Reformed tended to translate their social status into theological terms, faulting the compromises and creeping liberalism they saw corrupting orthodoxy at the tall-steeple churches. Park's people in turn would sigh over the "backwardness" of Christian Reformed theology, and the very insistence that theology was of the essence of religion. That the two bodies nonetheless could each take significant leadership in local politics speaks most obviously of changing circumstances in the local environment. But it speaks as well of the altered rituals by which each

3. The principal sources on this congregation's history include *75 Years on Eastern Avenue: Diamond Jubilee of the Eastern Avenue Christian Reformed Church* (Grand Rapids: Eerdmans, 1954); *100 Years in the Covenant: Eastern Avenue Christian Reformed Church, 1879-1979* (n.p.: n.p., n.d. [Grand Rapids: Eastern Avenue Christian Reformed Church, 1979]); *125th Anniversary: Our Memories, 1879-2004* (Grand Rapids: Eastern Avenue Christian Reformed Church, 2004); and the Eastern Avenue Christian Reformed Church files at Heritage Hall, The Archives of the Christian Reformed Church, Calvin College, Grand Rapids, Mich. (hereafter EACRC Files, CRC Archives).

4. The principal sources on this congregation's history include [Mrs. W. H. McKinney and Mrs. F. A. Baldwin, eds.], *Park Congregational Church: The Story of One Hundred Years, 1836-1936* ([Grand Rapids]: Park Congregational Church, 1936); James Van Vulpen, *A Faith Journey* ([Grand Rapids]: First (Park) Congregational Church, 1985); and the congregation's rich archive on site (hereafter PCC Archives).

church translated its tribal customs so as to better address a larger public. Put briefly, both churches found political salience after loosening some of their theological strictures and adopting more ecumenical liturgies.

*   *   *

The ritual that attended the birth of First Congregational Church in 1838 was a covenanting ceremony familiar to the two dozen people in attendance. Whether direct arrivals from Vermont, like Myron and Emily Hinsdill, who owned the pioneer hotel in whose parlor the gathering took place, or upstate New York transplants like William and Sally Haldane, who would be instrumental in starting Grand Rapids's furniture industry, First Church's founders were Yankees whose forebears had been forming fellowships this way for two hundred years in America and two generations before that in England. They pledged themselves to common doctrine and mutual discipline and sealed the covenant with a communion service carried out with ordinary tableware. They selected one of their own, James Ballard, as their first minister and won financial assistance from a New England home-missionary society to pay his salary. Ballard himself had benefited from an education at Williams College which had been founded by a similar society precisely to supply clergy and teachers for the frontier. For the next 133 years — until 1971 — every one of the thirteen ministers that followed Ballard to this pulpit could claim a New England birth or education; all but three had both.

The fledgling congregation scored a coup when it purchased the largest church building in town from the village's original settler, the French Canadian — and Roman Catholic — fur trader, Louis Campau. To finance the deal Ballard and his father-in-law, Stephen Hinsdill, conducted successful fundraising tours back in New England, appealing to their tribe's ancient anti-Catholicism. The targeted building "is the only Catholic establishment in Western Michigan," Boston's *New England Puritan* informed its readers in 1841. "By making this purchase, their further progress is stopped . . . and a young Protestant Church will be provided with a substantial and commodious place of worship." The building secured, Ballard improved the opportunity. He conducted a forty-day revival in the hard winter of 1842-43 to catalyze nominal members and win new ones. He thundered against alcohol consumption, card-playing, and the theater, and for dietary reform and the abolition of slavery. When he left the pulpit it was to head up that other arm of Yankee culture, public education; as principal of local schools he could count numerous First Church women among his teachers. All of these callings came together in Ballard's final phase as missionary teacher to freedpeople in the South after the Civil War. While one of his successors at First Church continued the revival campaigns, another, Stephen S. N. Greeley, a New Hampshire native by way of Dartmouth College and Andover Seminary, preached up the Civil War as a moral crusade, helped drill the congregation's young men on the town green, and eventually followed them to the front as chaplain of the Sixth Michigan Cavalry. In its first generation, in sum, First Church incarnated the Yankee heritage of evangelical religion, moral strictures, and righteous politics. Adding their plain-speech worship style to the picture, the flock qualified as "pietists" indeed.[5]

The next generation brought in fundamental changes, but quite in keeping with New England developments. Their avatar was J. Morgan Smith, pastor of First Church from 1863 to 1883, a cousin of financier J. P. Morgan, Yale class poet of 1854, and bearer of the anti-revivalist theology of nurture that Horace Bushnell had formulated in an epochal pastorate at Hartford, Connecticut. If his "new school doctrine" fazed some at First Church, they were mollified by Smith's "old school character." Orthodoxy needed to adapt doctrine to the progress of the times, he was fond of repeating, yet true religion had to resist the materialistic spirit of the [Gilded] age. Smith sought to strike that balance by combining energetic calls to moral earnestness with a construction project that succeeded in raising Grand Rapids's grandest church edifice directly across from its central green, thus replicating the New England town pattern. That the $75,000 "Gothic structure, dignified, correct, and beautiful," was paid off within ten years testifies at once to the refined taste and to the deep pockets that by now characterized "Park" Church's membership.[6]

The sanctuary's 1,025 seating capacity would be filled by the 750 new members who joined the church under Smith's pastorate. These included a heavy representation of the industrializing city's elite. The building project's single largest donor was Martin L. Sweet, a native of upstate New York, Grand Rapids's richest citizen and one-time mayor. The chair of the building committee and a perennial Park trustee, Vermont-born Solo-

5. McKinney and Baldwin, *PCC: One Hundred Years,* pp. 3-11; Van Vulpen, *Faith Journey,* pp. 1-12; quotation, p. 5.

6. McKinney and Baldwin, *PCC: One Hundred Years,* pp. 13-19; quotations, pp. 14, 19; Van Vulpen, *Faith Journey,* pp. 13-16; quotation, p. 13. For Smith's central theme of progress and stability, see his sermon "Farewell to the Old Church," November 18, 1869, PCC Archives.

mon L. Withey, occupied a pew with his wife, Marian Hinsdill, in whose childhood parlor the church had been founded twenty-five years before. After a term in the Michigan state senate, Withey was appointed by Abraham Lincoln to what became a twenty-four-year career as West Michigan's first federal judge. In another pew sat another New York native and previous mayor, state senator, and future Congressman, Wilder D. Foster. The most significant figure in the ranks, however, might have been Harvey Hollister, lineal descendant of a Puritan line that had been planted in Connecticut in 1642. Twenty years the church's treasurer as well as its longtime Sunday School superintendent, Hollister was also the most significant banker in town. First National, which he had co-founded with Martin Sweet, helped finance everything from the city's first railroad line to the logging boom in northern Michigan timber. Most of all, it served as the finance arm of the furniture cartel that put Grand Rapids on the map. With Hollister's eminence at both institutions, Sweet as the bank's co-founder, and two Park Church trustees, including Solomon Withey, on its board of directors, Park was well dubbed "First National Church." For Hollister, the interlocking directorate was nothing to be ashamed of; in his latter-day version of the Puritan ethic, all honorable earthly enterprise began from and circled back to Christian verities by way of an ethic of stewardship whose hallmarks were reliability, trust, and duty.[7]

The women of Park Church were equally prominent in local culture and philanthropy. Propriety labeled Marian Hinsdill "Judge Withey's wife," but she might have been the city's most able entrepreneur-organizer regardless of sex. She started Grand Rapids's premier (and one of the nation's earliest) women's guild, the Ladies Literary Club; managed the merger of smaller collections into a central public library; and helped found the United Benevolent Association Hospital, whose descendant is still part of the city's chief medical complex. Hinsdill-Withey came to these ventures from having managed the churchwomen's campaign to provide — either by their own hand or by producing items for sale — all the furnishings for Park Church's new edifice. The women were practiced in this line from having raised medical-care supplies for the Civil War wounded by the same means. Their ready transfer between ecclesiastical and public roles was well demonstrated by "the ladies" who taught in

7. See biographical entries in Albert Baxter, *History of the City of Grand Rapids, Michigan* (New York and Grand Rapids: Munsell & Co., 1891). Quotation, Van Vulpen, *Faith Journey*, p. 19.

Park's Sunday School on the weekends and the city's public schools during the week. They moved into politics proper when they joined women from the downtown Methodist and Baptist churches to lead the anti-alcohol crusade that dominated local public affairs in the mid-1870s.[8]

Such crusading set limits on Park Church's success in local politics, however. Among other things, alcohol consumption symbolically divided Protestant from Catholic, and Grand Rapids remained, as it had been from Louis Campau's start, a half-Catholic town. Thus, in the third of a century from 1873 to 1906, control of the mayor's office fell over half the time to nine different members of St. Mark's Episcopal Church, an obviously "liturgical" congregation that could mediate the Protestant-Catholic divide. Besides, St. Mark's candidates came from both political parties.[9] Park Church's strictly Republican, "dry" profile alienated too great a share of the city's voters, so that only three mayors came from its ranks, two of them prior to 1865 and two for only one term. It found better success in the wider orbit of county and statewide elections, where partisanship and attractiveness to rural Protestantism helped. From 1910 to 1946 Park Church put two successors to Solomon Withey on the federal bench, and for all but three terms between 1895 and 1939 two of its members successively occupied Michigan's Fifth Congressional seat. One of them, William Alden Smith, left that post to serve two terms (1907-19) in the U.S. Senate, where he had been preceded by Russell Alger, husband of a Park Church daughter. In 1928 Park's native son Arthur H. Vandenberg took over the seat. By the end of his four terms his impact literally reached the ends of the earth, for he led the Republican minority away from its isolationist posture during World War II and chaired the Senate Foreign Relations Committee during the birth phase of the Cold War, 1947 to 1951. All told, over the first half of the twentieth century, Park

8. On Hinsdill-Withey, see Baxter, *History of Grand Rapids,* pp. 247, 252, 353-54; Marian L. Withey, "Park Has Touched Me — I Have Grown" (loose-leaf collection of reminiscences from PCC's 150th anniversary, PCC Archives), #44 and #91. On early fundraising, see McKinney and Baldwin, *PCC: One Hundred Years,* p. 106; on the anti-alcohol crusade, see Baxter, *History of Grand Rapids,* pp. 199-202, 357-59.

9. James D. Bratt and Christopher Meehan, *Gathered at the River: Grand Rapids, Michigan, and Its People of Faith* (Grand Rapids: Grand Rapids Area Council for the Humanities/Eerdmans, 1993), pp. 81-87; Philip R. Vander Meer, "Religious Divisions and Political Roles: Midwestern Episcopalians, 1860-1910," in *Beliefs and Behavior: Essays in the New Religious History,* Vander Meer and Robert Swierenga, eds. (New Brunswick, N.J.: Rutgers University Press, 1991), pp. 222-26.

Church might have been the single most politically important congregation in the state of Michigan.[10]

What transpired in the church's life to help explain this status? Beyond party loyalties, Park's members by 1900 had accumulated powerful professional credentials — University of Michigan law degrees and corporate practices for the judges, successive editorships of Grand Rapids's morning daily, the *Herald,* for Smith and Vandenberg. As a mature church with native-born leadership, Park also won city-wide respect by assuming responsibility for the public weal. Two of its members, including banker Harvey Hollister, pioneered "organized charity" in town during the economic depression of the mid-1890s, the first severe test of Grand Rapids's industrial regime.[11] The actual provision of social services typically came from the hands of female volunteers coordinated by a few paid staff; the small circles ("Tens") into which many of Park Church's women members were organized fit the purpose exactly. The social-welfare function, furthermore, built upon a network of influence that an older generation of Park women had extended by planting Sunday schools in each of the city's four quadrants; in due time these grew into daughter churches.

The exterior reach of these endeavors should not blind us to their crucial functions *within* congregational life. The eight Tens of 1895, numbering 227 women, would proliferate into forty-six over the next century, chapters closing and opening with the life-cycles of their members, thus forming intense bonds within successive generations. The memoirs of these bands recount a ritual year of quilting bees, rummage sales, Christmas bazaars, strawberry festivals, bake sales, picnics, bandage-making, mission trips, and sorties into poor relief. If one of the chroniclers apologized that all this amounted to "nothing spectacular," only "years of steady service to our beloved church and happy companionship and love for one another," she in fact described the life-blood and sinews of the church body — put otherwise, the way enduring loyalty was created across generations of middle- and upper-middle class women who had the disposable

10. For the U.S. judges, see entries on Arthur Carter Denison and Fred Morton Raymond, in *History of the Sixth Circuit,* http://www.ca6.uscourts.gov/lib_hist/sitemap.html. For U.S. Members of Congress and Senators, see entries on Russell Alexander Alger, Wilder D. Foster, Carl E. Mapes, William Alden Smith, and Arthur H. Vandenberg in *Biographical Directory of the United States Congress, 1774-Present,* http://bioguide.congress.gov/biosearch/biosearch.asp.

11. Van Vulpen, *Faith Journey,* p. 23; McKinney and Baldwin, *PCC: One Hundred Years,* p. 36 (quotation); Baxter, *History of Grand Rapids,* pp. 675-78.

time to commit to these efforts and who bound their husbands and sons to the church in the process.[12] The men would be the foot-soldiers for Park candidates in formal politics, but their public work rested upon the foundations of female activism in the informal sphere. The bonds of affection that were (sometimes literally) knit there had the further function of providing moral regulation within the congregation and moral prescription for the larger community. Thus Park Church accumulated resources for service, prestige, and power.

The associational matrix extended but also altered Park's older tribalism. The alterations were most evident on the plane of theology, where J. Morgan Smith's Bushnellian innovations — themselves premised upon family nurture and, in Bushnell's own case, extrapolated into Yankee tribal imperialism — were followed by further creedal relaxation in subsequent pastorates. In 1917 Park voted for the overtly liberal creed recently passed by the National Association of Congregational Churches, in keeping with Smith's mantra to keep doctrine in tune with human progress. That human "progress" might have seemed dubious in 1917 was a matter of retrospect; Park's pulpit and pew alike greeted American entry into World War I with crusading enthusiasm.[13] A deeper source of theological accommodation had been manifest already a generation earlier, when the church admitted to membership the Universalist Charles Garfield. It wasn't only that Garfield was one of Grand Rapids's foremost citizens; more to the point, he was married to one of Park's favorite daughters. Tribe overtly trumped theology in the unanimous sentiment of the church council: "If Charlie Garfield is good enough for Jessie Smith, he's good enough for Park Church."[14]

Mores changed even more than theology. If Park's council had declared in 1857 that "the influence of the theater . . . especially upon the youth . . . is inherently, unmistakably, and irrevocably pernicious," J. Morgan Smith had not heard the news, for he taught Shakespeare to the youth as avidly as he did Scripture. By the early 1910s Park was screening movies

12. McKinney and Baldwin, *PCC: One Hundred Years,* pp. 95-114. The PCC Archives contains a remarkable 102-page "History of the Tens" that details their organization and many activities; quotation, p. 42.

13. On progressive liberalization, see Van Vulpen, *Faith Journey,* pp. 21-24, and McKinney and Baldwin, *PCC: One Hundred Years,* p. 65. On the new creed and PCC's World War I enthusiasm, see Van Vulpen, *Faith Journey,* pp. 34-35, and the sermons of April and May 1917, in the sermon collections in PCC Archives.

14. McKinney and Baldwin, *PCC: One Hundred Years,* p. 35.

in the sanctuary to overflow crowds to attract youth to its "Pleasant Sunday Afternoons." Charles Merriam (pastor 1916-33) pleaded that the "spiritual ideals of Jesus" be upheld as the only power able to harness the "material and technical" forces which the 1920s had unleashed, but his laity greeted the decade's revolution in manners by forming the Meri-Parkers club for church couples, which featured dance bands Tuesday or Saturday nights in the fellowship hall.[15] By then the church founders' Wednesday night prayer meeting had long since given way to a "church night" filled with a shared supper, hymn sing, book reviews for adults, youth activities in the church gym, and seasonal parties for all. In an attempt to bring the men as deep into church life as women, the Sunday evening service was assigned in the early 1900s to the men's club for topical lectures and musical programs. In February 1904 they sponsored successive talks on "Russia," "How Lincoln [the next week, Washington] Came to Manhood," and "Capital and Labor," between opening hymns like "Abide with Me" and closing ones like "Onward Christian Soldiers."[16] It is difficult to determine how much of this was Protestant Christianity and how much American civil religion. Park Church men perhaps did not sense a difference.

THE SPACE FOR SOCIABILITY at Park Church was a full-service parish hall of the sort American downtown congregations built in the early twentieth century to become a "full-time church" for all ages. Such facilities aimed to shape as much as serve a broader public, to show a responsibility *for* as well as *toward* society, itself a politically salient statement. But how did these gestures in the playful space of socialization match up with rituals in the sacred space of worship? To simplify, the apparently "secularizing" trends toward theological accommodation and relaxed mores begun in J. Morgan Smith's pastorate were paralleled by a steady rise toward high-church liturgy. Park's parish hall was completed in the early 1920s, just after William Alden Smith had left the U.S. Senate; a dramatic remodeling of its main sanctuary to facilitate stately processions began late in the decade, just as Arthur Vandenberg took over the seat.

15. Statement against theater quoted in McKinney and Baldwin, *PCC: One Hundred Years,* p. 114; on Smith and Shakespeare, see Van Vulpen, *Faith Journey,* pp. 13-14; on PCC social activities, McKinney and Baldwin, *PCC: One Hundred Years,* pp. 55, 123, and Van Vulpen, *Faith Journey,* pp. 30-31. For typical sermons of Merriam, see those of March 1925 in the PCC Archives.

16. McKinney and Baldwin, *PCC: One Hundred Years,* p. 53; "Park Has Touched Me," #9. For song and topical titles, see bulletins of February 1904 in PCC Archives.

By then Park Church's worship had been moving up the liturgical ladder for some time. In its pioneer days, a table-top organ pumped by elbow straps provided almost a parody of the plain style. In 1855 Park installed one of Grand Rapids's first pipe organs which, accompanied by a vocal quartet, led services with proper hymnals and regular orders of service. In 1885 both organ and quartet were replaced with much larger versions and a more elaborate musical regime. Church bulletins in 1893, for instance, show almost exclusive choral singing at morning services (Schubert, Mozart, Mendelssohn), while the congregation joined in on evangelical hymns ("Green Hill," "Jesus Savior Pilot Me") in the evening. A decade later, as Sunday evenings were given over to topical lectures, the morning liturgy added responsive readings to high-art performance. With affluent Park members off to cottages and vacation travel, summer services became joint ventures with other downtown churches; the liturgical year thus effectively ended with Mother's Day and school commencement.[17] Increasingly, music supplemented the spoken word: Park introduced Grand Rapids to Easter cantatas, Christmas candlelight services, and Sunday afternoon concerts by its choir, whose seasonal tours gained it a statewide reputation. The decisive pastorate was Edwin Bishop's (1909-15). Precisely as the Wednesday prayer service gave way to "church night," Sunday morning worship became forthrightly high church, and fourteen Tiffany windows were installed in the sanctuary depicting the life of Christ — also demonstrating Park people's aesthetic, and financial, resources.[18]

Still, the design of the sanctuary, with side but no center aisles and a pipe organ blocking the Gothic arch in front, militated against liturgical consistency. The late 1920s remodeling, designed by Ralph Adams Cram, aimed to solve that problem. It installed a broad center aisle, a fifty-stall chancel, main and side altars, a $36,000 four-manual, antiphonal Skinner organ, and elaborately carved lectern and pulpit (given by Senator Vandenberg in memory of his mother). Services could now begin and end with a proper processional and recessional. They proceeded via recitation of collect and Lord's Prayer, sung Amen and Gloria, interspersed with choral anthems and congregational responsive readings. The latter were taken from a volume that Charles Merriam published with the Congregational-

---

17. McKinney and Baldwin, *PCC: One Hundred Years*, pp. 8-9, 40, 51, 81. On musical styles, see bulletins of March and April 1893, PCC Archives.

18. McKinney and Baldwin, *PCC: One Hundred Years*, pp. 51-52, 81-85; Van Vulpen, *Faith Journey*, pp. 30-31.

ists' Pilgrim Press, collecting "the most ancient and beautiful forms . . . and some of the finest prayers from all denominations. . . ." Supporting it all was a massive choral program intended to "train choirs for all ages which would create the correct atmosphere for beautiful worship." Five choirs there would be, numbering 250 voices, the lot of them vested in "purple cassocks, white linen cottas, with purple Canterbury caps for the girls and women," all "imported from England." The Senior Choir now went on to national reputation, winning a competition at Princeton in 1934 and taking the occasion to perform at Radio City Music Hall and on two NBC broadcasts.[19]

Impressions of this regime were mixed. A visiting academic went away lauding Park Church as a veritable "college of religion and culture." On the other hand, a visiting English clergyman found the whole business bizarre. "They have an altar against the wall," he wrote, on which stands "a cross, flanked with candles which are lit just before the service by two acolytes gowned in purple, with white gloves." The side altar came into play not at the Eucharist, however, but following the offering, when the minister walked over with the plates. "As he stands with bowed head before the cross, the congregation sings the Gloria." There followed a moment of silence, punctuated with three bells from the organ, "as at the raising of the Host in a Roman Catholic Mass. During the singing of the Gloria, at the words 'Father, Son, and Holy Ghost,' everybody bows. Just what the 102 souls on the Mayflower would make of it," the visitor concluded, "I am not certain."[20]

Some of Park's pioneers and the contemporaneous Dutch Calvinists at Eastern Avenue Christian Reformed Church would have felt no such uncertainty. Their assessment would be that, as the congregation lost the original formula of plain-style piety — in which worship served as a weekly, personal recommitment to strict doctrine and strict behavior — "mere" external forms had to supply strength instead: practical programming for the men, social service for the ladies, and aesthetic appeal on Sundays for both. Park Church's own ministers gave a more charitable explanation but along similar lines. The church's best service lay in providing sound moral leadership for the larger society, their argument ran. To insist

19. McKinney and Baldwin, *PCC: One Hundred Years*, pp. 63-64, 81-85; Van Vulpen, *Faith Journey*, pp. 41-42. The service of the "Dedication of the Main Altar" on February 19, 1933, set the template for liturgical worship; see bulletin in PCC Archives. Quotations and details on choir composition and performances are from "Park Has Touched Me," #57.

20. Quotations from Van Vulpen, *Faith Journey*, p. 42, and "Park Has Touched Me," #51.

on the "finer points of doctrine," as opposed to the broad and general "truths of Christianity," would fracture the membership and dilute this power to serve. Likewise ascetic mores which, however appropriate to the weak in faith or at a more "primitive" stage of history, became pharisaical among the more civilized and mature. Yet the erosion of strict markers could leave people open to uncertainty, especially under the quickening pace of change to which the modern church had to adapt. This anxiety is palpable throughout Charles Merriam's sermons in the 1920s, as he asserted, over-boldly, that all roads of technological and scientific development really did mark a "progress" that led to the cosmic Christ. The architectural remodeling that he supervised in the same years thus aimed to surround worshipers with the arts and beauty from which, he insisted, so much of faith drew its inspiration.[21] More charitably yet, we may argue that rationality and technique, the marks of doctrinal precision and ethical exercise, had so triumphed in the 1920s, yet in so secular a fashion, that these old measures of faith were themselves co-opted, leaving the elaborate aesthetic that the Puritans had rejected a principal, because fresh, resource for faith.

In any case, Park Church's confidence reached its peak during World War II. If the bulletin for Sunday morning, December 7, 1941, invited the Meri-Parker couples club to a "Tinsel Tangle" Christmas party, the sermon two weeks later showed serenity undisturbed: "I have never come to a Christmas with a greater feeling of confidence in an inevitable and permanent world of peace and cooperation," declared Pastor Edward A. Thompson. "The ultimate futility of force will become more and more clear. We must *now* . . . lay our plans for a new order of permanent peace, freedom, and cooperation in the world. Jesus, nearly two thousand years ago, showed us the way. No other method has proven successful."[22] At war's end Arthur Vandenberg would salute that promise in leading a bipartisan affirmation of the United Nations and Marshall Plan. Yet, the new internationalism could bring conflict along with "cooperation" as evident in Vandenberg's endorsement of a hard line against the Soviet Union. Back home, the senator donated the $10,000 he received as *Collier's* magazine "Man of the Year" in 1949 to help furnish the new chapel Park built next to its parish hall, a major ex-

21. Merriam's theological themes are evident in sermons of March 8 and 15, 1925, in the PCC Archives ("The Great Voyage of Discovery" and "Can Religion and Prosperity Live Together," respectively). His reflections on religion, art, and beauty are laid out in McKinney and Baldwin, *PCC: One Hundred Years*, pp. 63-65.

22. PCC bulletins of December 7 and 21, 1941, PCC Archives.

tension of the orbit of religious beauty. Ironically, public visitation for his funeral in 1951 would be the first event held in the completed facility.[23]

More ominously, the building project did not hide fissures that were emerging at the very foundation of congregational identity. In 1948, a national proposal that Congregational churches merge with the Evangelical and Reformed Synod (of German background) was defeated at Park Church 717 to 54. Nonetheless, the proposal resurfaced in the mid-1950s with the support of Park Church's new clergy. Once again a cohort of church women arose, this time to resist any initiative that would "weaken the power of our influence and leadership." What "we" and "our" meant became clear in the group's repeated invocations of the Pilgrim spirit, the Mayflower Compact, and the Congregationalist heritage of local autonomy. When hundreds of members seceded from Park Church in 1958, the New England tribalism behind these sentiments spoke dramatically in their new building on edge of town, a colossus of Georgian brick ("colonial," locals called it) topped by a weathervane modeled on the Mayflower. Fittingly, that was also the new congregation's name.[24] Far from helping to retain "our power and influence," however, this step effected its loss. On the national scene, Arthur Vandenberg's nephew, Hoyt S. Vandenberg, would become Director of Central Intelligence and Air Force Chief of Staff in the early Cold War, while Harvey Hollister's great-grandson, McGeorge Bundy, would be National Security Advisor during the growth phase of the Vietnam War and director of the Ford Foundation afterward.[25] But back home, neither in the suburbs where Mayflower loomed nor in the decaying center city where Park remained did these congregations play a significant role in local politics.

*   *   *

At the very time that the Park Church dissidents were organizing their departure, the Christian Reformed Church was celebrating its centennial. Al-

---

23. Van Vulpen, *Faith Journey,* p. 44, and program of the dedication of the chapel, PCC Archives.

24. The Mayflower separation is told from the PCC point of view in Van Vulpen, *Faith Journey,* pp. 43-49; from the dissidents' in Susan C. Lovell et al., *Mayflower Congregational Church: The First Twenty-Five Years* (Grand Rapids: Mayflower Congregational Church, 1984), pp. 4-18.

25. On Bundy, see David Halberstam, *The Best and the Brightest* (New York: Random House, 1972), pp. 47-50. Bundy's paternal grandfather and namesake, McGeorge Bundy, was also a PCC member and leader: McKinney and Baldwin, *PCC: One Hundred Years,* p. 27.

though it was the only denomination headquartered in Grand Rapids, its message on the occasion was mostly directed inward, not to the larger public, and bore an insistent tone that bespoke some anxiety as well as pride. In 1957 the CRC was still sectarian Reformed in matters of religion and overwhelmingly of Netherlandic descent (Dutch, Frisian, and border German) in culture and ethnicity. Ecclesiologically, it had been oppositional and segmented even before its formal beginnings in the United States: its founders traced their heritage back to an 1834 "Secession" of local congregations from the national Reformed Church in the Netherlands — and before that to a century and a half of pietist conventicle formation. This pattern, particularly suspicions of laxity in the established church's doctrine and morals, reemerged within a decade of the founding of Dutch immigrant communities in the Midwest. Rejecting the decision by the "kolonie's" clerical leaders to join the venerable, east-coast Reformed Church in America, in 1857 four congregations seceded to "return to the standpoint of the fathers."[26]

The fledgling denomination floundered until the late 1870s, when the flow of Dutch immigration into the United States entered upon its fifteen-year peak phase and when city churches, like the one planted on Grand Rapids's "East Street" boundary in 1879, arose to harvest the tide. Drawing off strong migration chains back to the northern Netherlands, and situated close enough to both garden farmers outside the city limits and factory workers downtown, the church quickly had more than enough to fill its new 1,200-seat structure.[27] There the strict Reformed gospel was deliv-

---

26. James D. Bratt, *Dutch Calvinism in Modern America: A History of a Conservative Subculture* (Grand Rapids: Eerdmans, 1984), pp. 3-13, 37-39, gives a brief overview of these developments. The most detailed history from the CRC side is Henry Beets, *De Christelijke Gereformeede Kerk in Noord Amerika: zestig jaren van strijd en zegen* (Grand Rapids: Grand Rapids Printing Company, 1918); from the RCA side, William O. van Eyck, *Landmarks of the Reformed Fathers; or, What Dr. Van Raalte's People Believed* (Grand Rapids: The Reformed Press, 1922). Robert Swierenga, *Faith and Family: Dutch Immigration and Settlement in the United States, 1820-1920* (New York: Holmes & Meier, 2000), is a recent, comprehensive, and expert quantitative social history of Dutch-American immigration; a thorough, more traditional narrative is Henry S. Lucas, *Netherlanders in America: Dutch Immigration to the United States and Canada, 1789-1950* (Ann Arbor: University of Michigan Press, 1955).

27. *100 Years in the Covenant*, pp. 11-17, 22-25. Swierenga analyzes Dutch-American chain migration in detail in *Faith and Family*. The concentration of immigrant origins was astoundingly dense: twelve percent of Dutch municipalities generated almost three quarters of these immigrants between 1820 and 1880; five percent provided half of them; two percent, one third (p. 76).

ered in the spare old style: no choirs, no hymns, no pageantry, only sung psalms for music alternating with prayers and Scripture reading. All this led to the main course, a lengthy sermon divided between exegesis of the text for the day; detailed theological commentary thereupon, noting differences between the Reformed and other, erring interpretations; and candid practical application to sins within the body. The message in the sanctuary was as tight as the sociology in the neighborhood, and perhaps necessarily so, for these transplanted villagers in a strange new city were not the most orderly lot. A notorious display occurred in 1888 when a thousand of them gathered in front of the church to tear up the new streetcar tracks which threatened the peace of the neighborhood. A few years later the church council had to hire an off-duty policeman to keep order in the balconies during evening service, when — by venerable tradition — the young people got to sit by themselves. Pastor S. B. Sevensma met the challenge by turning evening worship into youth-oriented inquiry sessions, a Dutch Calvinist counterpart to revival meetings and productive of the same end: the weeping penitents who gathered on the front benches were added to the church by the score.[28]

The Reformed tradition contained more than these strains, however, and a revival of its political and social activism back in the Netherlands was soon reverberating at Eastern Avenue as well. Led by the theologian-statesman Abraham Kuyper, "Neo-Calvinism" insisted that *all* of one's life, not just Sunday and the "spiritual," belonged to God, and that believers should organize themselves together to study and then to practically deploy the distinctive "Reformed principles" that held for "every domain of life."[29] Under the pastoral leadership of the dynamic, American-born Johannes Groen (pastor 1900-1919), the congregation was soon swirling with discussions about the Progressive crusades of the day: government health and safety regulations, Prohibition, women's suffrage, and labor organization. Groen gave measured approval to cooperating with outsiders on various of these issues by warrant of Kuyper's emphasis upon the "common grace" that God dispensed in the world. His successor, Herman Hoeksema, could not have disagreed more. Hoeksema emphasized instead

28. *100 Years in the Covenant,* pp. 18-19, 46, 68, 85-86.
29. Bratt, *Dutch Calvinism,* pp. 14-33, surveys Kuyper's work in background to Dutch-American immigration and religious life. James D. Bratt, ed., *Abraham Kuyper: A Centennial Reader* (Grand Rapids: Eerdmans, 1998), provides English translations of his seminal shorter works with introductory commentary. Kuyper's key work in English is *Lectures on Calvinism* (Grand Rapids: Eerdmans, 1931 [1899]).

the "antithesis" which Kuyper insisted lay between the ultimate purposes of Christian and unbeliever, and which made the point of Reformed activism to be the creation of stark alternatives to the products of "the world." In the early '20s these were live issues for the church, since the CRC, with other immigrant denominations, had just run the gauntlet of patriot suspicion during World War I. Commanded to conform, they wondered just how far. The CRC's highest assembly answered in 1924 by rejecting Hoeksema's denial of common grace, but coupled that with official warnings in 1928 against the "worldly amusements" of theater, dancing, and gambling. The first edict cost Eastern Avenue its pastor and eighty percent of its membership, who followed Hoeksema into his new affiliation of Protestant Reformed Churches. The second edict left Eastern, along with other Christian Reformed congregations, minding a pietistic behavioral boundary between church and world.[30]

Over the ensuing decades, Eastern Avenue gradually built back up its membership while reaching out to neighbors via evangelism. They had done so earlier via street missions to Italian and Jewish communities in the core city; after World War II they turned to suburban tracts on the emerging edge of town. All along they sustained the more holistic ministry of the Ladies Industrial Aid society which had grown out of Progressive-era concerns for the many women working in local furniture factories.[31] Economic burdens grew heavier during the 1930s Depression, for besides everyday needs, the Christian Reformed were devoted to maintaining their system of Christian day schools. Mutual sacrifice within the community proved the formula of survival, to the point that the church council discouraged needy members from having recourse to public welfare funds. Indeed, in good times and bad, much of the congregation's energy was devoted to building up a complete associational world within Christian Reformed parameters. Like Park Church, if a generation behind, Eastern Avenue came to offer a society for every age, sex, and marital status — all of which, however, were to cultivate "distinctively Reformed" consciousness. It, too, sponsored money-raising ventures — for three local Christian elementary schools, the city-wide Christian high school, the denomination's Calvin College and Seminary. It encouraged regional assemblies — of Christian Reformed Sunday school teachers and youth groups (Calvinist

---

30. Bratt, *Dutch Calvinism*, pp. 14-33, traces these developments in detail, pp. 76-141. See also *100 Years in the Covenant*, pp. 30-40, 46-47.

31. *100 Years in the Covenant*, pp. 20, 41-42, 61-62.

Cadets and Calvinettes, not Boy and Girl Scouts). It advertised lectures, concerts, and eventually stage plays — typically by Calvin professionals.[32]

Worship services themselves made modest accommodations to the American world. English services were introduced alongside the Dutch only at the end of World War I, and against the will of even the progressive Johannes Groen. The singing of hymns, as opposed to exclusive psalmody, had been a major grievance of the 1834 Secession in the Netherlands, but the practice tended to come along with English services. The CRC's 1914 *Psalter Hymnal* limited hymns to an obscure, heavily didactic Presbyterian collection calibrated to the fifty-two Lord's Days of the Heidelberg Catechism. In 1934 the denomination published a more extensive *Psalter,* including 141 hymns next to 327 Psalm settings, the former selected according to "doctrinal soundness, New Testament character, dignity and depth of devotional spirit, and clearness and beauty of expression." None had the slightest odor of Arminianism. At the same time, leaders tried to impose a uniform order of worship across the denomination, a movement that Eastern Avenue resisted because of the "formalism" of some of the new order's prescriptions: recitation of the Apostles' Creed, reading of the Decalogue, and a service of confession and absolution.[33] The same reform allowed choirs to take part in worship, another "American" gesture that Eastern had long suspected. They did encourage vocal and instrumental ensembles but had these perform after services. The church year was not organized by liturgical seasons but by preaching through the Catechism. Baptisms (once a month) far outnumbered celebrations of the Lord's Supper (once a quarter), but profession of faith — normatively in one's late teens — overshadowed them both. Groen's pastorate averaged two a week.[34]

As for theology, a glimpse at Pastor Christian Huissen's deliverances during World War II reveals the most resolute Calvinism in force, at great odds with the more liberal confidences in play at Park Church. The calls that Vandenberg heard for immediate planning to institute a postwar regime of peace Huissen decried as arrogant folly: unless everyone started to "reckon with the risen Christ . . . the coming peace treaty will be the beginning of the next war." Upon news that one of the eighty-eight youth that

32. *100 Years in the Covenant,* pp. 41-42, 73-76. The church's weekly bulletins provide the best record of its activities and attention; see EACRC Files, CRC Archives, Box 2.

33. James A. DeJong, *Henry J. Kuiper: Shaping the Christian Reformed Church, 1907-1962* (Grand Rapids: Eerdmans, 2007), traces this initiative and the resistance it encountered, pp. 42-46, 77-87; quotation, p. 84.

34. *100 Years in the Covenant,* pp. 68-69, 79-83, 89.

Eastern had sent into the armed forces had died in action, Huissen responded: "The world would say you have given your life so that the world may be a better place to live in. We do not believe that. The world will not be a better place to live in." Rather, the young man had done his duty before earthly powers, enjoining those left behind to exceed mere duty and perform joyful service unto the power that really counted, the eternal Lord. That God exercised as specific and absolute a control over events as any Calvinist could imagine: "every bullet and every bomb goes exactly where he has predestined that it should go," Huissen declared, so that of Eastern's fallen son it could be said, "The time, manner of death, and all the circumstances are exactly as he deemed best."[35] In so anxious a world, Christian Reformed people whether at war or at home were simply to keep their minds daily on God and keep themselves weekly at worship.

The two decades after the war would render such strenuous resignation difficult. On the one hand, if the Cold War brought anxieties, it also bred prosperity and opportunities enough to erode suspicions of the outside world. After all, this was not just "the world" anymore; it was "America." On the other hand, their great northward migration landed a large body of African Americans right in Eastern Avenue's neighborhood. These two forces converged in the mid-'60s when the church received an offer from a local black Baptist congregation to purchase their property, and with it the prospect of following other white churches to the suburbs. Eastern's people defined their future, and altered some of its character, by declining the offer.[36] Immigrant heirs who would not move, they would still serve the neighborhood in which few of them lived. By extension they would come to lead in the city as well.

Their first gesture in this direction was renewed attempts at neighborhood evangelism. To be successful this strategy would have required (as some other core-city Christian Reformed congregations effected) a commitment to bi-racial church leadership and a liturgy radically revised in an African-American direction. Eastern Avenue did neither. Rather, it recov-

35. The mimeographed monthly newsletter, *Presenting Eastern's People* (collected in the EACRC Files, CRC Archives), which was mailed to all of the congregation's service people during World War II, gives a detailed picture of the mood and concerns on both the war- and the home-fronts. Huissen contributed a column to most issues; his perspective is especially forthright in those of April 1944, November 1944, December 1944, July 1945, and April 1946 (quotations from the latter two, p. 1 and p. 12, respectively).

36. *125 Years*, pp. 31-32. See the detailed memos of 1963-64 in EACRC Files, CRC Archives.

ered its neglected Kuyperian past and entered upon a multifaceted program of holistic ministry. First, the council saw to a loan that enabled the would-be purchasers of their property to erect a new building of their own nearby. They helped turn the phased-out neighborhood Christian school into a community social service center. Young adults who had been college students in the '60s started rehabilitating houses on neighboring streets, an enterprise that would grow into a city-wide housing ministry that accumulated $60,000,000 value.[37] The church added a program of selling food wholesalers' surplus to the needy at low cost on Saturday mornings and began offering tutoring assistance to neighborhood youth weekday evenings. To house all this activity the church finished a $2.5 million addition in 2001, moving the venerable parish house thus displaced up the street to serve as an intentional-community venue for Calvin College students.[38]

Just as this expansion of facilities and programming paralleled Park Church's ventures three generations before, so too did Eastern Avenue members' move into political office-holding. The first step came in 1974, simultaneously with the start of the housing ministry and on the heels of the Watergate crisis which so scandalized his Republican sensitivities, when Calvin College physics professor Vernon Ehlers was elected to the Kent County Commission. Eventually working his way up to chairing that body, he subsequently moved on to the state House of Representatives, thence to the state Senate, and finally to Congress. He was followed on to the County Commission and then into the state House by two other Eastern Avenue members, one of whom, Richard Bandstra, was subsequently elected to the state Court of Appeals. Later, a U.S. District Judge, Gordon Quist, joined the church as well. Put another way, for twenty years Eastern Avenue could claim a representative in county government, for eighteen years in state government, for fifteen years (at this writing) on the state or federal bench, and for fourteen years in Congress.[39] This record is unmatched in West Michigan since the death of Arthur Vandenberg and would be difficult to rival elsewhere in the state.

Several factors can be adduced to explain this success. First, all these officeholders have been Republicans, befitting the historic preponderance of that party in the CRC and in the southeastern section of Grand Rapids

37. Personal correspondence to author from Jonathan Bradford, director of Inner City Christian Federation, July 4, 2007.

38. *100 Years in the Covenant*, pp. 50-56, 64-66, 71-72, 113-14; *125 Years*, pp. 22-29, 32-33.

39. *125 Years*, p. 30.

which has served as their base. On the other hand, at least on the level of county and state governments, they have been more progressive than most of their party, on issues of environmental policy in particular and in their muted support of the free-market individualism that has been the party's orthodoxy over the last quarter century. The former stance might be rooted in Dutch habits of cleanliness, the latter in the CRC's strong communalism, on which free enterprise can act as a harsh solvent. Theologically, the classic Calvinist notion of stewardship has supplied a transcendentally suspended counterweight to the calculus of short-term self-interest that has become the operational creed of American politics. Sociologically, by worshiping in one of Grand Rapids's hardest-pressed inner-city neighborhoods while having their voting base toward the more affluent suburbs, Eastern Avenue's politicos have been able to serve as mediators between "blue" and "red" as St. Mark's leaders did between Protestant and Catholic a century before. Too Republican to achieve consistent success in city politics, too "liberal" to pass with the exurbanite Right, they have found a niche where the progressive heritage of their party can live on while it faces extinction in national councils.

The liturgical ambience behind these developments also changed at Eastern Avenue at least as radically as it had at Park Church earlier in the century. The most notable change has been the presence of women in the pulpit, the end result of a twenty-year campaign for women's admission to all church offices which dawned with the rest of the congregation's social activism in the mid-'70s. Eastern Avenue quickly became a leader in this battle across the denomination. First moving to install women as "associate elders," then ordaining them to the office fully despite official bans to the contrary, Eastern Avenue was among the first in the CRC to avail itself of the local-option policy by which the denomination hoped to settle the issue, installing two woman successively as senior pastor (Mary Hulst, 1995-2003, succeeded by Thea Leunk, 2006-present).[40] Since gender issues lie behind much of the polarization in state and national affairs over the past generation, the congregation's progressive posture within a conservative denomination has reinforced its members' mediating stance in politics.

At the same time, changes in the sounds and styles of worship itself have been so dramatic as to render today's service unrecognizable to parishioners from fifty years ago: a set liturgy with written formularies enough to qualify as modestly high church; lay leadership from the pulpit

---

40. *125 Years*, pp. 43-44.

at all cardinal points except the sermon; and a variety of music that is global in reach and resources. The whole evinces careful planning and order, once again a deliberately mediating response amid the worship wars of the latter twentieth century. Originally per council mandate, now by custom, services at Eastern Avenue include both "classic" and "contemporary" music, but the classic drafts far more off continental than off American-revival hymnody, while the contemporary hails much more often from global Christian and Catholic-renewal sources than from megachurch seeker services. Symbolizing the shift is the new *Psalter Hymnal* that the CRC adopted in 1987, featuring 210 Psalm settings but 330 hymns, many of these from the world church. The volume's editor was Eastern Avenue member Emily Brink.

The service dedicating the building addition in October 2001 exemplifies the results. Opening with the Te Deum, the service moved through the Catholic folk-inflected "Sing Your Joy" by David Haas, a litany on Psalm 136 recited by the congregation, the singing of "The Steadfast Love of the Lord" from Maranatha Music of Calvary Chapel roots, a sermon on "Making All Things New," a musical setting of the same from the Iona Community, and Charles Wesley's "Love Divine." With a Telemann offertory and Burghardt postlude on the organ, and brass and guitars joining on the songs, the circle of musical styles and instruments was complete. The prayers offered by leaders representing both sexes, three ethnicities, and four different social-service agencies supported by the church boxed the compass of diversity. Yet the theme of the service sounded as characteristic a Calvinism as had been voiced at the congregation's inaugural a century and a quarter before: divine sovereign grace, obedient human response, and faith as a venture upheld by grace amid uncertainty.[41] Eastern Avenue was now a white enclave in an African-American neighborhood as it had then been a Dutch enclave on the edge of an American town. Genevan psalms had then sounded continuity; ecumenical lyrics now sustained outreach. In one world worship provided the bulwark, in the other a bridge, for a Protestant tribe.

THE "IMMIGRANT" TRIBE succeeded the "settler" tribe in local politics not only because a significant sector of the latter group left the city but because the two churches brought significantly different theological formulas to their work. Park Church operated on the assumption that the community

41. EACRC Bulletin, October 14, 2001, EACRC Files, CRC Archives, Box 2, Folder 7.

could be one only if covered by a single canopy, and as the city (not to mention its own congregants) more and more diversified, that canopy stretched ever thinner until it was indistinguishable from good citizenship in general. By contrast, the Kuyperian tradition behind Eastern Avenue's ventures took modern religious pluralism for granted from the outset; asserted maximal, rather than minimal, confessional claims in that context; and thus yielded a system in which a variety of viewpoints could each take a place at the civic table, none of them pretending to monopolize it. The formula was well suited to the latter third of the twentieth century, when both more, and more forthright, religious voices were heard in American politics than ever before. Descendants of immigrants, rather than of settlers, were better made for that situation, especially since Eastern Avenue's people could pass for evangelicals while still genuinely promoting diversity.

That era might now be closing. On the one hand, Congressman Ehlers's voting record became less and less distinguishable from that of the Religious Right in national affairs, just as Christian Reformed people have increasingly become more evangelical and less Reformed in sensibility. On the other hand, in the 2006 state elections an Eastern Avenue claimant to the local state House seat was defeated in the Republican primary by a Roman Catholic who outdid him on "family values," winning the all-important endorsement of the Michigan Right to Life lobby. A pyrrhic victory, for the general election went to the Democratic candidate for the first time in decades, an African-American clergyman from the Church of God in Christ. Another Eastern Avenue member, running as a Democrat, went down to defeat in the state Senate election to a black Republican incumbent based in a suburban Pentecostal megachurch. These results might augur the rise of a third Protestant tribe in local politics, African Americans rendered safe enough by their religious grounding to mediate the remaining great divide in local, as in national politics, that between races.

Generations: American Catholics since the 1950s

Leslie Woodcock Tentler

Let us begin with the Detroit of my childhood. My non-Catholic childhood, I should add, although our neighborhood was heavily Catholic and I was sometimes taken to Mass by my immigrant grandmother. That Detroit had more than 200 Catholic churches, most of them enormous, and almost as many Catholic schools. It was not unusual in the larger parishes for six or seven Masses to be offered on Sundays — a striking contrast to the 9 and 11 o'clock services featured at just about every Protestant church of my acquaintance. Those Masses were well attended, too, given that roughly 77 percent of Detroit's Catholics in the mid-1950s attended church weekly, or at least claimed to do so.[1] (Mass was always packed in my grandmother's parish church; I can remember growing light-headed from the summer heat and the press of bodies.) Perhaps most remarkable to my childhood self — more than nuns in full habit or the hideous mysteries of the confessional — was Catholics' imperturbable confidence. I had heard from adults I respected that "Catholics couldn't think for themselves"; as an instinctive sociologist — most little girls are such — I knew that they didn't rank at the top of the status hierarchy. And yet my Catholic neighbors clearly saw themselves as God's own tribe. I was resentful. I was also impressed.

By the time I joined that tribe myself, in the mid-1970s, the confidence was gone. So were most of the markers of Catholic identity that had so impressed me as a child: no more nuns in full habit, no Latin Mass, and

---

1. Gerhardt Lenski, *The Religious Factor* (Garden City, N.Y.: Doubleday, 1961), p. 49; Lenski did his Detroit study in 1958. Middle-class Catholics in this study were more likely than working-class Catholics to report weekly church attendance.

hardly anyone in the dreaded confessional. The story of my conversion need not detain us here; suffice it to say that the collapse of Catholic triumphalism helped to make it possible. At the same time, I retained a lively interest in the contours of that earlier Catholic world. What had fueled its communalism, its vitality, and above all its seemingly unshakable confidence? Why had that apparently cohesive world imploded so rapidly? Good questions all — unless I was proceeding on erroneous assumptions. Perhaps my perceptions were clouded by romanticism and wistful memories of my much-loved Irish granny.

In defense of my clear-headedness as an observer, a great deal of evidence attests to the vitality of that now-vanished Catholic sub-culture. In addition to high levels of religious observance, to which we shall return momentarily, was an energetic commitment to institution-building. Catholics were moving to the nation's new suburbs in record numbers by the late 1940s, as their rate of upward mobility began to soar. Once there, they set about church and school building with a zeal reminiscent of the immigrant generation. Although parental standards with regard to education were rising rapidly, the Catholic commitment to parochial schools remained strong; the number of children in Catholic high schools nationally grew by 60 percent over the course of the 1950s, while the numbers in elementary schools increased even more dramatically.[2] (Church leaders in Detroit were distressed that, as of 1958, "only" 56 percent of Catholic children in their archdiocese were enrolled in Catholic schools; given the period's exploding birthrates and the total absence of state aid, that figure represents in retrospect a truly remarkable achievement.)[3] The fifteen years after 1945 also saw vigorous growth in Catholic higher education, with numerous colleges being founded or significantly expanded. Catholic hospitals, social service providers, and recreational associations were proliferating and expanding too, underwritten — as were all Catholic institutions in this most voluntary of worlds — by the contributions of the faithful. American Catholics, in short, did not behave in the 1950s as if they were tired of the Catholic ghetto. They seemed willing, even eager, to replicate that institutionally separate world in their new suburban precincts.[4]

2. Statistics from the *Official Catholic Directory*, quoted in David J. O'Brien, *The Renewal of American Catholicism* (New York: Paulist Press, 1972), p. 139.

3. Msgr. Vincent Horkan to Cardinal Edward Mooney, June 23, 1958, Archives of the Archdiocese of Detroit, Chancery records — Schools Office.

4. For further reading on the texture of Catholic life in the late 1940s and '50s, see Charles R. Morris, *American Catholic: The Saints and Sinners Who Built America's Most Pow-*

Vocations to the priesthood and the religious life in the twenty years following World War II also point to communal vitality. The numbers of women religious in the United States, as in the Archdiocese of Detroit, rose steadily throughout the postwar period, in striking contrast to the situation in not-so-faraway Quebec, where the ranks of women religious grew not at all between 1945 and 1960.[5] Ordinations to the priesthood increased as well, albeit in the context of an incipient priest shortage. Ordinations simply could not keep pace with growth in the Catholic population. But Catholic seminaries in the 1950s were filled to bursting; seminaries opened or expanded in that decade at a rate never before experienced in the United States.[6] (Here was yet another claim on the generosity of the faithful.) The Archdiocese of Detroit reflected national trends when it opened a new major seminary in 1949 — one built to a plan that would make possible a doubling of the building's size without compromising its architectural integrity. Even in 1963, as normally prescient an observer as Andrew Greeley could predict a "coming surplus of priests," for which the nation's bishops — as Greeley saw it — would be wise to plan creatively.[7]

And then there was Catholic family life, truly a marvel to my childhood eyes. I did not imagine that the parents of my Catholic friends got

erful Church (New York: Random House, 1997), pp. 196-281, and Garry Wills, *Bare Ruined Choirs: Doubt, Prophecy, and Radical Religion* (Garden City, N.Y.: Doubleday, 1972), pp. 15-75. For interesting reflections on the inter-relationship of Catholic spirituality, institution-building, and neighborhood rootedness, see Gerald Gamm, *Urban Exodus: Why the Jews Left Boston and the Catholics Stayed* (Cambridge: Harvard University Press, 1999), and John T. McGreevy, *Parish Boundaries: The Catholic Encounter with Race in the Twentieth-Century Urban North* (Chicago: University of Chicago Press, 1996).

5. Melanie M. Morey and John J. Piderit, S.J., *Catholic Higher Education: A Culture in Crisis* (New York: Oxford University Press, 2006), pp. 263-64; on Quebec, see Kevin J. Christiano, "The Trajectory of Catholicism in Twentieth-Century Quebec: Institutional Religion and Elite Politics During an Era of Change," in *The Church Confronts Modernity: Catholicism Since 1950 in the United States, Ireland, and Quebec*, Leslie Woodcock Tentler, ed. (Washington, D.C.: The Catholic University of America Press, 2007).

6. There were 388 Catholic seminaries in the United States in 1950, and 525 a decade later. In this same period, the number of seminarians grew from approximately twenty-six thousand to almost forty thousand. O'Brien, *Renewal of American Catholicism*, p. 139.

7. A. M. G., "The Coming Surplus of Priests," undated but almost certainly 1963, Archives of the Archdiocese of Chicago, Catholic Action Federation papers, box 2, folder 48. Although the author of the document is not otherwise identified, I am quite sure it was Greeley, whose initials are in fact "A. M. G." Greeley was an active member of the group for which the document was written, and it is written in his characteristically brisk, colloquial style.

along any better than my own parents did; in this sense, at least, I was not a romantic. It was the size of most Catholic families I knew that amazed me. On my own block alone were families with nine, ten, even thirteen offspring. The nation's birthrate had been rising steadily since World War II; the total fertility rate for American women exceeded 3.5 when the baby boom peaked in 1957. But religion made a difference: the Catholic birthrate in the postwar years was probably 20 percent higher than that of the nation as a whole. It was highly educated Catholic women, moreover, who were most apt to have the largest families; hence the population explosion in my own affluent neighborhood. A Catholic college education was especially predictive of a woman's obeying her Church's teaching on contraception, which despite its difficulty was remarkably widely observed in the mid-1950s. A national fertility study done in 1955 found only 30 percent of the Catholics sampled admitting to ever having used a means of fertility control other than abstinence or the Church-sanctioned "rhythm method."[8] Bishops and priests might rue these numbers, which did indeed translate into legions of difficult confessions. But given the very young ages at which Americans married in the postwar years, it seems near-astonishing in retrospect that the rate of compliance was so high. It presumably helped that Catholics, for all their upward mobility, still tended overwhelmingly to choose other Catholics as spouses. Despite a marked trend toward Catholic assimilation, there was almost no change in the Archdiocese of Detroit in the rate of religious inter-marriage between 1930 and 1960.[9]

Let us now return to the multiple Sunday Masses and the crowded pews of my childhood memories. Here we find the most compelling evidence of Catholic sub-cultural vitality. The frequency with which American Catholics attended Mass almost certainly reached its zenith in the twenty years following World War II, as did the frequency with which they received the sacrament of penance, or "confession," as it was invariably called. Many immigrant Catholics had been accustomed to confess and receive communion only once or twice a year. Annual confession — the minimum required by Church law of every Catholic — was quite enough for the older male members of his first Detroit parish, according to Father

8. Leslie Woodcock Tentler, *Catholics and Contraception: An American History* (Ithaca, N.Y.: Cornell University Press, 2004), p. 133.

9. Leslie Woodcock Tentler, *Seasons of Grace: A History of the Catholic Archdiocese of Detroit* (Detroit: Wayne State University Press, 1990), p. 476.

Ferdinand DeCneudt, who encountered some less-than-forthcoming penitents as a brand-new priest in 1938. "Some of those old Belgians and Italians," DeCneudt told me, confessed a year's worth of sins with remarkable dispatch: "Same as last year, Father."[10] Their grandchildren, however, were socialized to more exacting norms. The modal Catholic by the 1950s probably received the sacraments monthly, while the more conspicuously devout received communion every Sunday or even daily. Many weekly communicants, like my grandmother, also confessed on a weekly basis, not necessarily because they fell regularly into serious sin — my grandmother's clandestine visits to a neighborhood fortune-teller took place at widely spaced intervals — but because Catholics in the postwar years were routinely encouraged to do so.

Confession and the reception of communion were so intimately linked for most Catholics that it was customary in many parishes for confessions to be heard during Mass. A prospective communicant could slip into the confessional prior to the Consecration and be virtually certain of approaching the altar in a state of grace. Catholics born since the Second Vatican Council (1962-65), accustomed as they are to a liturgy structured around congregational participation, would be astonished by such behavior. But the Tridentine Mass was very much the priest's preserve. He might be a prisoner of its rigid rubrics, which prescribed his every word and gesture. He was nonetheless its central actor: the one who was fluent in liturgical Latin, the one who "said" the Mass — mostly, it should be noted, with his back to the congregation. His hands alone could touch the Host; he alone could consume the consecrated wine. Priests used to speak unselfconsciously of "my Mass," usage that seems to have disappeared over the course of the 1960s. If no one showed up for a priest's daily Mass, he said it anyway. Nobody thought it odd.

What did the faithful gain from such passive involvement in an arguably arcane liturgy? Their numbers suggest that they got something, if only the comfort of having propitiated their God. "When I grew up," the late Bishop Kenneth Untener — a son of Detroit — liked to say, "you had two choices: go to Mass . . . or go to hell. Most of us chose Mass."[11] That so

10. Author interview with Rev. Ferdinand DeCneudt, October 19, 1998, Roseville, Mich. DeCneudt was born in Belgium; his family emigrated to Detroit in 1920.

11. Quoted in Peter Steinfels, *A People Adrift: The Crisis of the Roman Catholic Church in America* (New York: Simon and Schuster, 2005), p. 172, ellipses in original. Bishop Untener said much the same to me when I interviewed him for my *Catholics and Contraception* in December 1998.

much of the Mass belonged to the priest also created a quiet space for prayer and meditation. My grandmother usually said the Rosary during Mass, laying her beads aside only at the Consecration. Younger and better-educated Catholics often used a missal to follow the priest's words and actions, as Catholic youngsters were generally taught to do in school. Following the Mass in this fashion made for properly Christocentric prayer, they were told; it showed appropriate reverence for this summit of the Church's sacramental life. But using a missal was no easy matter: one had to be something of an adept to page through its thickness for the Propers of the day, particularly if the presiding priest tore at breakneck speed through the Latin. Most Catholic youngsters, based on my limited and long-ago observations, neglected their missals for daydreams and covert glances at their contemporaries. Even seemingly devout Catholics of my acquaintance spoke unashamedly of their appreciation for priests — and there were some — who could charge through the Mass in twenty-three minutes flat.

At the same time, there was something undeniably powerful about the experience of the Latin Mass. It didn't typically derive from the majesty of the language or the beauty of the music and setting. A great many Catholic liturgies were badly done — the Latin mumbled or otherwise inaudible, the sermon composed of limping platitudes. Frequently there was no music. The church itself, more often than not, was chock-a-block with appallingly sentimental statues; at so-called "family Masses" — as opposed to those intended, say, for the adult male members of the Holy Name Society or the women of the Altar Guild — the squirming and snuffling of too numerous children could drive one to distraction. But an aura of reverence was still palpable. Perhaps it derived in part from devotional body-language — the genuflecting as parishioners entered their pews, the gestures of blessing at the holy water font. Perhaps it had to do as well with the evident prayerfulness of the more devout members of the congregation, and often enough of the celebrant. Certainly it had to do with the silence that descended at the Consecration. "They are almost motionless as they watch the priest elevate the Sacred Host and the chalice," reported the Jesuit sociologist Joseph Fichter from Mater Dolorosa church in New Orleans, where he did research in the late 1940s. "This is the moment when any observer must be convinced that these people have a deep realization of the central mystery of Catholic worship."[12] So it was in the Detroit

---

12. Joseph H. Fichter, S.J., *Dynamics of a City Church Southern Parish*, vol. 1 (Chicago: University of Chicago Press, 1951), p. 139.

churches of my childhood. Even for one who stood outside the fold, that silence pointed toward something tremendous.

If my grandmother longed for a liturgy that made greater room for congregational participation, she never said so. I doubt that the notion ever occurred to her. The Mass she knew as an old woman was the one she'd known as a child; for Catholics of her generation, the Mass — like the Church — was immune to change. The Mass simply *was;* it had no history. The Mass, moreover, was only one focus of my grandmother's prayer life. Her needs for a more emotive form of liturgical expression were amply met by the many devotions on offer at her own and other churches. Marian piety was what she favored — Rosary devotions in May and October, the school children's crowning of the Blessed Mother's statue on May Day, periodic novenas to Our Lady of Perpetual Help. Presumably she prayed to a number of saints as well. If the cult of the saints was in decline by the 1950s, at least in terms of its public manifestations, there were still rich possibilities locally. Within easy commuting distance of her east-side parish my grandmother could attend novenas and other devotions to St. Anne (a particular favorite in once-French Detroit), St. Anthony, St. Jude, St. Theresa of Lisieux, St. Francis Xavier, and Blessed Martin de Porres. Had she been able to drive, she could also have had the family car blessed and placed under the protection of St. Christopher.[13]

Catholic devotionalism has always been the province of the female. By the 1950s, it was increasingly the terrain as well of the late-middle-aged and old. My grandmother, in other words, was a proto-typical member of a dying tribe. In Detroit, that tribe had flourished most mightily in the 1930s, when economic depression ravaged the city's predominantly Catholic working class. Huge public novenas to Mary and the saints were then the order of the day, as was in fact the case in other American cities. (Devotions to Our Lady of Sorrows, inaugurated by the Servite Fathers in

13. On Marian devotions and the cult of the saints in Detroit in the 1930s, '40s, and '50s, see Tentler, *Seasons of Grace,* pp. 408-13. On Marian devotion, see Paula M. Kane, "Marian Devotion Since 1940: Continuity or Casualty?" in *Habits of Devotion: Catholic Religious Practice in Twentieth-Century America,* James M. O'Toole, ed. (Ithaca, N.Y.: Cornell University Press, 2004), pp. 89-129, and Robert A. Orsi, "The Many Names of the Mother of God," in *Between Heaven and Earth: The Religious Worlds People Make and the Scholars Who Study Them* (Princeton, N.J.: Princeton University Press, 2005), pp. 48-72. On devotion to the Virgin of Guadalupe, popular among Hispanic Catholics, see Timothy Matovina, *Guadalupe and Her Faithful: Latino Catholics in San Antonio, from Colonial Origins to the Present* (Baltimore: Johns Hopkins University Press, 2005).

Chicago in 1937, drew 70,000 people a week to the Servite church there.) Even men were drawn to Depression-era devotions in numbers far larger than usual, particularly when the devotion in question was specifically addressed to relief from unemployment.[14] The devotional world has always had its instrumental side, and Catholics like my grandmother — a middle-aged, stay-at-home wife during the most desperate days of the Depression — were perfectly at home with public prayer "offered up especially to obtain employment, for financial assistance, for help in paying debts and for sale of property," as Detroit's Dominican church advertised a 1935 novena to the Souls in Purgatory.[15] Since my grandfather was a militant trade-unionist who managed to get himself black-listed in the early 1930s, my grandmother had ample need for heavenly helpers as she confronted mounting bills and the growing threat of eviction. She needed spiritual comfort, too, which she presumably found as she sang and prayed in the vernacular — devotions were seldom if ever conducted in Latin — and experienced, in the company of her neighbors, a sense of chosen peoplehood.

The instrumentalism of the devotional world, along with its sentimentality, was a principal cause of its undoing. Highly educated young Catholics in the postwar years, happy products of relative affluence, were often embarrassed by what they saw as the "bargaining" quality of their elders' prayer life. Growing numbers of priests were troubled, too. Detroit's Archbishop, later Cardinal, Edward Mooney cautioned his clergy even in the 1940s against publicizing novenas to the saints and forbade their outdoor celebration. (Marian devotion was acceptable to Mooney, given Mary's intimate association with Christ, but only if it was kept within the bounds of liturgical good taste.)[16] That the laity, and most especially the female laity, could exercise impromptu leadership when it came to devotions particularly bothered the clergy. "At different times we have found in the church mimeographed explanations of the Novena to St. Martha," the pastor at Detroit's St. Rose parish told his congregation in 1956, with reference to a kind of boot-legged devotional exercise. "Now we have nothing against this good and holy woman but I do not think that the emphasis is placed on the prayers but on the days, the lighting of the candle and the leaving of a copy in the church." Such devotions were "not to be recom-

14. Tentler, *Seasons of Grace*, pp. 412-13.
15. Tentler, *Seasons of Grace*, p. 412.
16. Tentler, *Seasons of Grace*, p. 413.

mended," Father Emmet Hannick told his flock. "Let your prayer be more Christocentric."[17]

Father Hannick had obviously been influenced by what is called the liturgical movement, which progressed rapidly after 1945 throughout the United States.[18] Popular mainly among the young and well-educated, the liturgical movement aimed at schooling the laity to a more active participation in the Mass. The "dialogue Mass" — where the congregation recited the Latin responses normally assigned to the altar boys or the choir — was a favored reform. Father Leo Trese, a Detroit priest-author and an ardent proponent of the liturgical movement, thought the dialogue Mass should be introduced into every parish; something of a liturgical radical, he even endorsed a liturgy with all but the Canon in the vernacular. "Even though he use a Missal and follow the English translation," he wrote of the lay man, "he still feels a looker-on, as though a restrictive circle had been drawn around the altar. . . . It was not so in the early Church."[19] Trese's boss, however, was more cautious. When Trese wrote the words just quoted — surprisingly enough, in 1945 — priests in the Archdiocese of Detroit were permitted to offer dialogue Masses on week-days only. Very few did so, at least on a regular basis. It was not until 1951 that Cardinal Mooney allowed a dialogue Mass to be said on Sunday, and then only at six o'clock in the morning. He made this concession, if concession it was, at the request of the Young Ladies Sodality at Sacred Heart parish in suburban Dearborn.[20] Who better to represent the future of the Church?

If reforms like the dialogue Mass made only limited progress in Detroit and many other dioceses in the 1940s and '50s, the logic of the liturgical movement had progressive impact on the thinking of younger Catholics. That logic stood in direct opposition to the devotions my grandmother cherished, even the Eucharistic devotions that were so ubiquitous a part of parish life. Adoring the Blessed Sacrament might be properly Christocentric, but the devotee's role as pious spectator seemed to echo the laity's passive role at Mass. Eucharistic devotions remained popular among Cath-

17. Rev. Emmet Hannick in *St. Rose Messenger*, April 4, 1956, copy in Archives, Archdiocese of Detroit.

18. For an excellent history of this movement, see Keith F. Pecklers, *The Unread Vision: The Liturgical Movement in the United States of America, 1926-1955* (Collegeville, Minn.: Liturgical Press, 1998).

19. Quoted in Tentler, *Seasons of Grace*, p. 415. Trese was writing in a January 1945 issue of *Commonweal.*

20. Tentler, *Seasons of Grace*, p. 414.

olics in the immediate postwar years; indeed they were in many respects more public than ever before. As in many other dioceses, the Holy Name Society in Detroit inaugurated an annual city-wide Holy Hour in the late 1940s that was held at Briggs — later Tiger — Stadium. But as in other dioceses, attendance at these highly public ceremonies began to wane in the late 1950s. Catholics seemed suddenly less hungry for high-profile affirmation of their distinctiveness, less eager to twit Protestant sensibilities with extravagant displays of Catholic liturgical otherness. For many younger Catholics, indeed, some varieties of liturgical otherness may already have come to seem inauthentic. The stadium Holy Hour was quietly discontinued just a few years later.[21]

By the early 1960s, then, Detroit's Catholics were — if unbeknownst to themselves — a people in transition. The devotional Catholicism that sustained my grandmother's generation was in decline, but the reformation heralded by the dialogue Mass was far from full realization. That large numbers continued to attend Mass weekly does suggest that this was not a world in crisis. But a growing chorus of critics, not all of them clergy, was lamenting its spiritual tepidness. I do not mean to suggest that these critics were sociologically acute. Their preternaturally high standards indicate that they dealt with the "ought" and not the "is." "We have a dozen Trappist monasteries and a good number of laity dedicated to the Apostolate," as one Detroit seminarian conceded, "but how do our other 30 million Catholics differ from those without the Faith?"[22] These critics, nearly all of them highly educated, were testimony to the successes of American Catholicism — its disciplined sacramental practice, its moral seriousness when it came to sex, its generous commitment to institution-building. But they were still critics. Like the Catholic academics in these same years who decried their co-religionists' lack of intellectual achievement, they articulated a hunger that was real, if apparently peculiar to themselves. The future, however, belonged to precisely these sorts of people, who were products of a sub-culture more permeable than any of them knew. My grandmother represented the past in more than just her devotional preferences.

The Second Vatican Council, which opened in the fall of 1962, initially

21. Tentler, *Seasons of Grace,* pp. 405, 428; on Eucharistic devotion in the United States more generally, see Margaret M. McGuinness, "Let Us Go to the Altar: American Catholics and the Eucharist, 1926-1976," in O'Toole, ed., *Habits of Devotion,* pp. 187-91, 201-6, 215-20.

22. Edward Farrell to Jerome Fraser, November 15, 1954, Archives of the University of Notre Dame, Jerome R. Fraser papers [CJRF], box 1, folder: "Farrell & I, 1953-57."

seemed a distant event to most American Catholics, who hardly knew what to make of its purposes or its squabbles over agendas. (Although Vatican II was the Church's first truly global council, it had been convened mostly out of concern for the troubles of the Church in Europe — troubles of which few Americans were more than dimly aware.) But since the Council turned early on to reform of the liturgy, it soon affected the life of every Catholic. The Council Fathers authorized a limited use of the vernacular in the Mass, as well as its limited restructuring. The priest now faced the congregation for most of the Mass, the altar was brought closer to the people, and many of the liturgy's more baroque prayers and gestures were eliminated. Scripture assumed a new prominence, as did the sermon. The American bishops quickly agreed to make maximum use of the Council's "vernacular concessions," and on the first Sunday in Advent, 1964, Catholics around the country experienced the Mass in a new way.[23] The change was not easy for priests, even the very young. "We were perfectly trained to serve in a world that disintegrated as soon as we stepped into it," as Baltimore's Joseph Gallagher, ordained in 1957, remembers of liturgical reform, which quickly came to stand in his mind for a host of other changes.[24] Nor was it entirely easy for the laity. "A passer-by couldn't tell us from the Methodists," my grandmother told me in 1965, whether gleefully or in sorrow I couldn't now say. I suspect it was a bit of both. She clearly missed the liturgical habits of a lifetime. But she liked the novelty of hearing English at Mass and the expanded readings from Scripture; she also loved to sing, which Catholics were suddenly encouraged to do. I hadn't the heart to tell her that Methodists, being far more full-throated in their hymn-singing than the vast majority of Catholics, would have sounded quite different to a remotely discerning passer-by.

The reforms introduced in 1964 were just the beginning. A commission that outlived the Council eventually authorized more far-reaching change: permission to say the entire Mass in the vernacular, a further restructuring of the rite, the introduction of new Eucharistic prayers.[25] A totally revised order of the Mass was made mandatory in 1971, by which time liturgical Latin was a thing of the past. Unofficial changes left their mark as

23. Msgr. Vincent Yzermans, ed., *American Participation in the Second Vatican Council* (New York: Sheed and Ward, 1967), p. 146.

24. Author interview with Fr. Joseph Gallagher, February 3, 1999, in Baltimore.

25. Joseph Komonchak, "Interpreting the Council: Catholic Attitudes toward Vatican II," in *Being Right: Conservative Catholics in America,* Mary Jo Weaver and R. Scott Appleby, eds. (Bloomington: Indiana University Press, 1995), p. 18.

well. In the climate of the late 1960s, experimentation sometimes proceeded unchecked in places like university parishes, where practices as alien as liturgical dance or as sensible but still-unauthorized as lay Eucharistic ministers were the order of the day. Certain of these experiments eventually moved into the mainstream. The American bishops in the 1970s gave their blessing not just to lay ministers of the Eucharist but to the laity receiving the Eucharist in their hands.[26] The youngest Catholics often did not know that only a decade earlier the laity had been forbidden to touch the Host or drink the consecrated wine. The latter was a widespread practice in the United States by the early 1970s.

The net effect of the various reforms was a Mass that was essentially "horizontal" — or perhaps "communal" would be a better word, since that is what the liturgical reformers were striving for. The priest now functioned more as a presider than an exclusive conduit of the sacred, sharing the liturgical stage not just with lay lectors and Eucharistic ministers but with a congregation whose active participation was integral to the new rite. The origins of the Mass as a meal were more readily apparent, and Catholics mostly ceased speaking of the Mass as a "holy sacrifice." Was the reformed Mass as a result less suffused with a sense of the sacred? That is not easy to judge. If the moment of the Consecration was somehow less charged than it had previously been, attentiveness to the Word read and preached was clearly greater. If the faithful were less likely to genuflect and bless themselves upon entering a church, they were far more active as liturgical participants. If young Catholics sometimes ambled up to Communion with studied indifference and their hands in their pockets, they were nonetheless receiving Communion more often than the previous generation had done. It takes a bolder historian than this one to presume to know interior dispositions.

Still, it must be conceded that attendance at Mass declined throughout the 1960s, particularly among the young and more rapidly after the advent of liturgical reform. A slight decline was evident as early as 1961, when 71 percent of American Catholics nationally claimed to attend Mass weekly, down from 75 percent just a few years earlier. The figure stood at 65 percent in 1969.[27] Then the downward trend accelerated: 54 percent

---

26. The National Council of Catholic Bishops approved communion in the hand in May 1977, by which time the practice was widespread in many dioceses. They had approved lay Eucharistic ministers several years earlier. See McGuinness, "Let Us Go to the Altar," in O'Toole, ed., *Habits of Devotion*, pp. 225-27.

27. William V. D'Antonio et al., *American Catholics: Gender, Generation, and Commitment* (Walnut Creek, Calif.: Altamira Press, 2001), p. 52.

claimed to attend Mass weekly in 1976, 44 percent in 1987, 37 percent in 1999.[28] At some point in the 1960s, a good many Catholics evidently ceased to regard missing Mass as a mortal sin, although Church teaching in this regard has not been formally changed. (What did change, beginning in the 1960s, was a pronounced de-emphasis in both preaching and catechesis on eternal punishment. The logic of Bishop Untener's childhood simply ceased to resonate.) In every decade since 1960, the young have been least likely to be regulars at Mass — a worrisome portent, given that fewer and fewer seem to return to vigorous practice of the faith once they marry and become parents. Indeed, the rates of religious intermarriage for Catholics have risen steadily since the late 1960s, and with them the likelihood that Catholics in such marriages will eventually turn to another church or fail to raise their children in any religion at all. An equally worrisome portent for the future of the Church is the failure of young Catholics to embrace the priesthood or religious life. Today's priest shortage has less to do with the unprecedented number of clergy who left the active priesthood in the wake of Vatican II — as many as 10 percent of priests in the United States resigned between 1966 and 1975[29] — than with a simultaneous plunge in the numbers of seminarians. Those numbers have not recovered, being lower today — despite dramatic growth in the Catholic population — than they were in 1970; about 20 percent of today's seminarians, moreover, are foreign-born.[30] As for women religious, they are all too clearly a dying breed.

A particularly telling development of the later 1960s was a sharp decline in the frequency of confession. Priests were commenting on that phenomenon as early as 1966; by the mid-1970s, the sacrament was widely conceded to be in a state of collapse. Reform of the Mass may have been partly responsible: Catholics now acknowledged their sinfulness in the vernacular at the opening of the Mass and received assurance of forgiveness; once a Saturday late-afternoon or evening Mass was authorized as

28. D'Antonio et al., *American Catholics*, pp. 52-53.

29. Anthony J. Blasi with Joseph F. Zimmermann, *Transition from Vowed to Lay Ministry in American Catholicism*, Roman Catholic Studies, vol. 20 (Lewiston, N.Y.: Edwin Mellen Press, 2004), pp. 6-7.

30. Howard R. Bleichner, *The View from the Altar: Reflections on the Rapidly Changing Catholic Priesthood* (New York: Crossroad Publishing Company, 2004), p. 40; on foreign-born seminarians, see Mary L. Gauthier, ed., *Catholic Ministry Formation Enrollments: Statistical Overview for 2001-2002* (Washington, D.C.: CARA, Georgetown University, March 2002), p. 2.

fulfilling the Sunday obligation, which happened in the United States in 1969, the classic time for confession in most parishes was severely truncated.[31] But the causes clearly ran deeper. Over the course of the 1960s, American Catholics came to a more psychologized understanding of sin than they had previously possessed. Their disagreement with Church teaching on such matters as contraception, masturbation, and even premarital sex grew apace and went increasingly public. Frequent confession and especially the rapid-fire itemization of one's sins came to seem, for a great many Catholics, both pointless and even dishonest. In 1975, almost 40 percent of Catholics in a national poll said they seldom or never went to Confession, although annual reception of the sacrament had not ceased to be a canonical requirement.[32] An altered perspective on religious authority thus gained ascendance in the later 1960s, particularly but not exclusively among the young. By this logic, one might be a good Catholic and not go regularly to confession or Mass; one might use contraception and still receive the Eucharist; one might experiment sexually prior to marriage and still expect to be married in the Church.

My grandmother died in the winter of 1966. Had she lived much longer, she would have joined the ranks of the liturgically dispossessed. She would not have liked folk Masses or Communion in the hand; she would not have understood public challenges to Church authority. She would also have missed the consolation of familiar devotional practices, since devotions of every variety decreased markedly over the course of the mid- to late 1960s. (They were stigmatized by many religious authorities as immature and unecumenical.) It would have been natural, I suppose, for her to have blamed the reformed liturgy for the chaos that came in its wake. Better to have kept the Latin, she might have said; better a mostly silent congregation than a liturgy where everyday words crowded out contemplation and mystery. She would certainly not have attached herself to the Catholic Traditionalist movement, which was already underway by the time that she died.[33] My grandmother was too conditioned to obedience for that to happen. If the Church Militant had become the People of God, my grandmother was willing to accept it on authority. But had she lived,

31. Tentler, *Catholics and Contraception,* p. 229; James M. O'Toole, "In the Court of Conscience: American Catholics and Confession, 1900-1975," pp. 168-71, 174-75, in O'Toole, ed., *Habits of Devotion.*

32. O'Toole, "In the Court of Conscience," pp. 171-72.

33. William D. Dinges, "'We Are What You Were': Roman Catholic Traditionalism in America," in Weaver and Appleby, eds., *What's Right?* p. 243.

she would have been an alien in the Church that had been her life-long home and the linchpin of her moral universe. Despite my own preference for the reformed liturgy, this conviction still distresses me.

In honor of her memory, then, let me ask the question I think would eventually have been hers: to what extent was liturgical reform a cause of subsequent Catholic disarray?[34] Remembering the late 1960s and especially the excesses of liturgical experimentation, I am in certain moods tempted to give it great weight. Liturgical life in today's Church is not in great shape; one wants someone or something to blame when the Mass is so flat-footed and spiritless in its presentation that it might have been better to remain at home. But then I remember the flat-footed liturgies I sometimes experienced as a child, which even the mysteries of Latin could not disguise. What made those liturgies endurable to the hordes of worshipers typically present? The answer, I think, lies as much outside the sanctuary as within. The liturgy for an earlier generation of Catholics was so rooted in communal experience and values that it can't really be said to have stood alone. That is much less true for today's American Catholics, for whom parish life in the old sense is largely a thing of the past.

My grandmother's parish, named for St. Ambrose, was incongruously located on the border of Detroit and an affluent suburb. The Detroit section of the congregation was primarily working class, with a sprinkling of lower-middle-class households; the Grosse Pointe side embraced a middle- to upper-middle class population. The parish was thus representative of post-war Catholic demographics. If record numbers of young Catholics in the late 1940s and '50s were moving toward affluence, most still had roots in a working-class world which, while shrinking, had by no means disappeared. The cultural climate of the parish was equally representative, coupling great vitality with a pervasive authoritarianism. (St. Ambrose parish supported an elementary school and a high school, as well as an almost dizzying roster of social and devotional organizations.) Married couples at St. Ambrose, for example, could join the Christian Family Move-

---

34. For an intelligent survey of the current state of the intra-Catholic liturgical debate, see Steinfels, *A People Adrift*, pp. 165-202. For a more vigorously opinionated perspective, see Thomas Day, *Why Catholics Can't Sing* (New York: Crossroad, 1990). For an insider's mildly disillusioned perspective, see George Devine, *Liturgical Renewal: An Agonizing Reappraisal* (New York: Alba House, 1973). For thoughtful reflections on liturgical reform and its ultimate impact on priestly morale, see Robert P. Imbelli, "The Priest in America Today," in *Where We Are: American Catholics in the 1980s,* Michael Glazier, ed. (Wilmington, Del.: Michael Glazier, Inc., 1985), pp. 115-18, and Bleichner, *View from the Altar,* pp. 20-27.

ment, something new to American Catholicism as of the late 1940s. CFM couples met in small groups to discuss how best to live their vocation — a vocation which, they were now being told, had as much significance and integrity as that of a priest or a religious. How to understand spousal love in a fully Christian way? How to make the home sufficiently devotional that one's children grew into serious Catholics? But married couples at St. Ambrose also knew — had been taught, indeed, from adolescence — that contraception was always mortally sinful, no matter what a couple's circumstances. So was re-marriage after divorce. Their situation was oddly analogous to that of St. Ambrose's junior clergy. The long-time parish pastor was something of a tyrant, as canon law permitted him to be. He would not allow his assistant priests, one of whom was a man in his forties, to use the rectory living room.[35]

My grandmother was not fond of the pastor, although she was proud of his family connections — he belonged to an old political clan in Detroit — and his status as a monsignor. But she never questioned his right to be brusque with the laity or rude to his assistants. In her experience, authority often worked that way. Her own father was apparently something of a tyrant, demanding that she delay marriage for several years after falling in love, so that she might keep contributing to the family exchequer. Landlords could be tyrants, too, as could employers. (My grandfather's blacklisted status in Depression Detroit should not be forgotten.) Even history could be a kind of tyrant: my grandfather, a British national working in Germany in 1914, was interned there for the duration of the First World War, marooning his wife and two small children back home in the English Midlands. If her husband was not a tyrant — I remember my grandfather as a gentle man — he was still the family's principal decision-maker. Economic stagnation in Britain in the 1920s prompted my grandfather to opt for emigration, first to Canada and then to the United States — not an easy prospect, surely, for a middle-aged wife with no kin in either place. If her story had a happy ending, centered on successful children and grandchildren, it was not a story with autonomy as a central theme or value.

But if my grandmother found St. Ambrose an easy fit, as appreciative of its vitality as she was indifferent to its authoritarianism, she had fellow parishioners for whom this was progressively less true. Consider the couples in CFM, most of them young and well-educated. CFM preached what might be called the gospel of sacralized sex: sex in marriage, couples were

---

35. Author interview with Fr. William Pettit, December 10, 1998, in Livonia, Mich.

told, was a form of prayer — a literal means of grace. Lovemaking meant communication not just with one's spouse but with God. The message had strong appeal, given its tender idealism and the value placed by the culture at large on sexual adjustment in marriage. But these same couples were forbidden by their Church to practice any form of fertility control besides the rhythm method — a method that, in most cases, severely limited the frequency of marital intercourse. My grandmother had been the product of a fundamentally abstinent culture, with which Church teaching had seemed grimly consistent.[36] Not so the young Catholics coming of age in the affluent post-war years, when a popularized neo-Freudianism was the middle-brow cult of the day.

Or consider the professional men who were a sizeable minority in St. Ambrose parish. Unlike their working-class fathers, such men were accustomed to the exercise of authority and the deference of clients and peers. Particularly if they had attended Catholic colleges, moreover, they thought in terms of lay witness in the world — something that necessarily assumed a degree of independence on the laity's part and respect for their competence. Not that they expected the Church to be a democracy; highly educated Catholics were probably more prone than others to romanticize the Church's counter-cultural aspects. But tactlessly wielded clerical authority could still grate. A one-time assistant at St. Ambrose remembers the pastor barging into church on a day when confessions were especially heavy and ordering the more than 200 people waiting there to go home and return at a later time: "The priests gotta eat!" This particular pastor was hardly the norm. "He was always considered a hard assignment," as my priest-informant said.[37] But urban parishes were very large, priests seldom knew all their parishioners, and the laity had no rights in canon law beyond access to the sacraments. A certain amount of clerical high-handedness was almost inevitable, and it could happen inside the confessional just as easily as on the street.

So there were fissures in the Catholic population by the 1950s and related rumblings of discontent. These were not easy to hear at the time, given the continued vitality of Catholic communal life. To a contemporary observer, a place like St. Ambrose seemed mainly a hive of activity — all of it voluntary, lest we forget. But in retrospect, one can discern, especially af-

36. On the concept of a "culture of abstinence," see Simon Szreter, *Fertility, Class and Gender in Britain, 1860-1940* (Cambridge: Cambridge University Press, 1996), pp. 389-424.
37. Author interview with Fr. William Pettit.

ter the mid-1950s, such potentially explosive developments as accelerating tensions around contraception, a new resistance to the cruder manifestations of eschatological consciousness, a growing incidence of attrition among seminarians, and evident alienation on the part of younger Catholics from traditional devotions. Even the liturgical movement, which showed unprecedented vigor in the later 1950s, could be read as a sign of discontent. None of this is surprising, given the extent to which younger Catholics in the post-war years were socially mobile. Joseph Chinnici, a historian whose work I greatly admire, once told me that suburban Catholics in the 1950s had "the rhetoric of subculture" but not its substance.[38] I don't entirely agree with him: the post-war Catholic baby boom, a primarily suburban phenomenon, suggests serious engagement with what were by then decidedly sub-cultural values. He is right, however, in a general sense. Affluent suburban Catholics in the post-war years had at least one foot in the secular world that had been so good to them. They admired its openness, its seeming fairness, the breadth of experience it could provide. They wanted these things for their children.

The Catholic debate over contraception, as it unfolded in the United States, provides a revealing case study. Compliance with Church teaching in this country was remarkably high as of 1955 — higher, in all probability, than had been true in the previous generation. But 1955 was also the year when lay dissent from that teaching made its first significant appearance in Catholic periodicals. Perhaps the dissent wasn't new; perhaps the priest-editors of these periodicals simply decided in the mid-1950s to permit it to appear in print. That would suggest, however, that the priest-editors thought it was pastorally prudent to do so. Did they sense a restiveness on the part of the obedient? A dangerous alienation among those forced, as they undoubtedly saw it, into sin? (Nearly every priest knew that birth control kept numerous Catholic couples, especially those in their 30s and early 40s, away from the sacraments. The fact was routinely acknowledged in pastorally oriented literature.) Whatever the explanation, the first public stirrings of dissent were immensely important. The effect was to legitimize the private grievances of many Catholics and ultimately to embolden that growing population whose families were rapidly becoming too large. Too large, that is, for parents determined to put their children through college and who worried, with

---

38. Author conversation with Joseph Chinnici, O.F.M., at the meetings of the American Catholic Historical Association, January 7, 2007, in Atlanta.

other thoughtful Americans, about the consequences of an exploding global population.[39]

Lay dissent grew, if modestly, into the early 1960s, by which time significantly more Catholics than in the mid-1950s had turned to forbidden modes of fertility control. It exploded early in 1964, when the lay-edited *Jubilee* magazine devoted several issues to the subject of contraception. The *Jubilee* letter-writers, most of whom doubted or opposed Church teaching, raised hard and theologically informed questions. If generous sexual communion was essential to marriage, as young Catholics were now being taught by their Church, how was one to make moral sense of the lengthy abstinence normally required by rhythm? Could a penitent honestly claim in confession to have "a firm purposes of amendment" — essential to receiving valid absolution — if she knew in her heart that she would return to contraceptive practice? What if a penitent did not believe that contraception was wrong? Were there not patent weaknesses in the natural law argument against contraception — precisely the argument that Catholic authorities most frequently deployed?[40] Questions like these sparked a larger debate among the laity, in the secular as well as the Catholic media — a debate that soon involved the clergy. "The issue ranks number one in the problem category of confessional work," a Baltimore priest reported in 1966, "and as of late, thanks to the openness of our people, in conversations on the street and in the office."[41]

By 1966, more than half of all Catholic women of child-bearing age were using a means of contraception forbidden by their Church. Most had elected to do so on their own initiative, presumably in concert with their spouses. Even in 1966, few confessors would give an explicit blessing to the Pill, even for desperate penitents. (The Pill was the contraceptive most frequently used by Catholic women in the later 1960s and one that many theologians argued was exempt from the logic traditionally applied to barrier methods.) Deciding in conscience to commit what their Church still defined as mortal sin thrust Catholics like these into moral autonomy — a new place for Catholics, if not for most other Americans. In 1966, many of these same Catholics were staying away from Communion in what might be read as symbolic deference to ecclesial authority. Such behavior was rare

39. Tentler, *Catholics and Contraception*, pp. 199-203, 135, 136-37.

40. Tentler, *Catholics and Contraception*, pp. 212-18.

41. Fr. N.N. to Cardinal Lawrence Shehan, May 19, 1966, Archives of the Archdiocese of Baltimore, Lawrence Shehan papers, uncatalogued. Given the recentness of the letter and its still-controversial subject, I have not used the writer's name.

after 1968, when Pope Paul VI reaffirmed the Church's traditional teaching. Some Catholics left the Church in response to *Humanae Vitae*. The great majority, however, stayed — but on their own terms. By the mid-1970s, Catholic contraceptive practice differed hardly at all from that of other Americans, once one adjusted for education and income. When those same Catholics attended church, they received Communion more frequently than ever before.[42]

Liturgical reform was thus effected in something close to a turbulent context. The Catholic sub-culture in the United States, rooted as it was in the ethnic working class, was in the final stages of disintegration. (This reality came home with particular vividness in the later 1960s as parochial schools began to close.) Tensions over sexual teaching were coming to a head. American society, moreover, was passing through a period of profound cultural upheaval, which spawned a more intense and pervasive individualism than the nation had ever known. Without the institutional and psychic protections of a now imploding subculture, Catholics were as vulnerable to the new individualism as most other Americans. The Berrigan brothers, anti-war priests on the run at one point from the FBI, were both a sign of altered times and of full Catholic assimilation.

One could argue that the reformed liturgy, centered on the congregation and governed in practice by far looser rubrics than the old rite, was oddly congruent with the altered times. The alienation of Catholics like my grandmother, by this logic, was a relatively small price to pay for a liturgy that was relevant to the rising generation. But the new liturgy often lacked the aesthetic and moral power to compensate for a suddenly eroded sense of community. In part this had to do with the clumsiness of top-down reform: the awkwardly worded vernacular texts (long since revised), the failure of many priests to explain to their people the theological underpinnings of the new rite.[43] It did not help that American Catholics, suddenly ordered to sing in the vernacular, had no rich store of hymnody. Once priests had to say Mass facing the congregation, moreover, many proved wanting in liturgical presence. "In the years immediately after Vatican II, presiding (the grace, appropriateness, and effectiveness of the priest and other worship leaders in their physical gestures and speech) was a disaster zone," as Peter Steinfels remembers it.[44] Even the rise of professional

---

42. Tentler, *Catholics and Contraception*, pp. 137, 220, 228-32, 236-37.
43. See Devine, *Liturgical Renewal*, pp. 48-50.
44. Steinfels, *A People Adrift*, p. 184.

liturgists hampered the development of communal liturgical ownership. Liturgy, it seemed, was still the property of an ecclesial elite — no matter that many liturgists are members of the laity. At its best, the new liturgy was warmer than the old, more energetic and inclusive. But as in most endeavors, excellence was only intermittently achieved.[45] Uninspiring liturgies in neighborhood churches caused many Catholics to shop around for more satisfying alternatives, which further undermined the sense of local community. (In my grandmother's day, Catholics were forbidden to attach themselves to other than their neighborhood parish.)[46] Growing numbers of liturgically undernourished Catholics simply stayed home.

Irony abounds, as is generally the case when human beings meddle with rituals of long standing. Striving for a more communal experience of worship, liturgical reformers inadvertently accelerated an already intensifying process of subcultural collapse. Wanting to make Catholics more mature in their moral deliberation, they unwittingly facilitated an individualism that sometimes seems to have no room for traditional moral prohibitions. But this simply means that today's Catholics inhabit the same circumstances as the vast majority of Americans — circumstances at once dismaying and yet rich with the possibilities of responsible choice. Few of us live any longer amid cohesive communities of faith; almost none of us can guarantee that our children will ultimately embrace the tradition in which they were raised. Even my grandmother failed in the latter regard, very likely because of her then-unusual marriage to a non-Catholic who refused to convert. Both of her surviving children left the Catholic Church as adults.

My grandmother would have been delighted by my eventual conversion, even seen it as a kind of redemption of the mongrel family over which she presided. What she would have made of my children's Catholicism is another story. All three, young adults now, call themselves Catholics. But they seldom go to Mass. My children are not mad at the Church; I'm not sure that their youthful religious experience, which included Mass every Sunday, was sufficiently vivid to have generated such strong emo-

45. See Steinfels, *A People Adrift,* pp. 178-88, for a thoughtful discussion of the quality of contemporary liturgy.

46. I should modify this statement by noting the existence of so-called "ethnic" parishes, which had originally been established for non-English-speaking immigrants. One might licitly travel outside one's immediate neighborhood to attend an ethnic parish. Few new ethnic parishes were founded in the 1950s, when existing ethnic parishes were typically losing members.

tion. They certainly do not belong to a tribe, as my grandmother did, although their self-identification as Catholics bespeaks a hunger for peoplehood. My children are quintessential Americans — free to create their own identities, they are quick to dismiss the notion that any tradition has a prior claim on their allegiance. My grandmother, could she have known them, would find them in this regard almost impossible to understand. But she would have loved them and, in her instinctive Christian charity, appreciated their moral seriousness.

COMMENTARIES

Recovering the Spiritual
in American Religious History

George M. Marsden

The essays in this volume are designed in a most helpful way to get at the often elusive topic of the meanings of religious experience for ordinary parishioners. The topic is elusive simply because we have so few sources relative to the huge numbers of people involved in religious practices over the course of American history. For instance, we know that tens of millions of Americans worshiped at Protestant or Catholic services every Sunday in the nineteenth century, but we know almost nothing of the particulars of what those activities meant for the overwhelming majority of these people. Even regarding the few who left some record, we seldom find more than fragmentary evidence. Usually we can do little more than just to assume that those who followed a particular religious leader or the formal practices of a church or denomination did so because they were in essential agreement with the teachings and practices that the leadership taught. So often the best we can do is to concentrate on religious leaders or church records and publications.

The present essays do not overcome this limitation entirely, but they make the most of it by focusing on worship, something that we know all practicing Christians do, and by asking how their various forms of worship intersected with other dimensions of their lives, work, and worldviews. Furthermore they illustrate nicely how such intersections of life and worship are always two-way. By exploring these themes in an intriguing variety of ways, these essays should successfully impress upon their readers that Christian worship, far from taking place in the abstract or operating in an isolated sphere of "spiritual exercises," both shapes and is shaped by the social, cultural, and personal experiences of those who worship.

These essays examine the broader meanings of worship by a sufficient variety of methods to raise consciousness about looking at worship in this broader scope, rather than concentrating simply on what goes on in formal services or in private devotions. The examples are taken from four centuries, several Protestant and Roman Catholic traditions, rural and urban settings, rich, poor, and middling social classes, and several ethnic and racial locations. The only shortcoming is that in American history this handful of examples can hardly provide a *representative* sampling of the enormous diversity of types of Christian worship throughout American history. Some major traditions are inevitably left out, such as Eastern Orthodoxy, white Southern Baptists, or the immense phenomena of popular evangelical worship of recent decades, to name only a few. Nevertheless, the major point is well made, and probably more effectively so by not piling up examples. As it is, the collection is sufficiently brief that it might actually be read and assigned.

The major comparison these essays invites is between low-church Protestants (Puritan, frontier Methodism, African-American, Congregationalist, and Christian Reformed) and Roman Catholics (also in several varieties). Perhaps what is most striking in reflecting on this comparison is that, despite strongly contrasting theories and practices regarding formal worship, the interactions of worship and other dimensions of life have much in common. Puritans, for instance, were wary of designating special sacred spaces and sacred times, excepting the Sabbath, in part because they wished to emphasize that one could encounter the sacred anywhere. God was everywhere present and the faithful should be responding to God's presence in all that they did, in their family lives and their vocations, however humble. Their formal worship was by Catholic standards austere, since they attempted to restrict themselves to what was explicitly mandated in Scripture and to eliminate what they considered to be subsequent human inventions. Yet, for example, in their grave celebrations of the sacrament of Communion, for which they prepared their hearts for days, the "real presence" of Christ was as central to their worship as it was in the transubstantiation of a Catholic Mass, even though the two understandings of what was most essentially involved were so far apart. And if we turn to Catholic examples from very different times and places, we find twentieth-century liturgical reformers attempting to make the Mass more meaningful for rural laborers and thus to encourage a sacramental view of all of life and work. Puritans could easily have related to these ideals, such as "cooking for Christ." And, despite the fact Puritans would have been appalled by the pre-Vatican style of formal priest-dominated liturgy, they would have shared with mid-twentieth-century American Catholics a sort of sacramental view of all of life including, for instance, that lovemaking should be an act of worship.

Among the themes that these essays underscore most prominently is how much social position affects the interactions of worship and life. James Bratt's analysis of two urban churches in Grand Rapids, Michigan, and Leslie Tentler's reflections on changes in Catholicism in twentieth-century Detroit, Michigan, are particularly illuminating in this regard. Bratt's examples are especially helpful since he offers a direct comparison and also traces change over a longer time than do any of the other essays. Grand Rapids's First Congregational Church, founded in 1838, was heir to the Puritan tradition that in two centuries had already lost much of its austerity. Yet in 1838 it was still recognizably Reformed. During the succeeding hundred years, however, many of the dominant forces transforming its outlook were related to the social prestige and political leadership of the leading members of the church community. By the early twentieth century not only had the distinctive teachings of Reformed theology disappeared but, says Bratt, it was becoming difficult to distinguish the congregation's Protestant Christianity from American civil religion. One positive dimension of this transformation was that it supported an ideal of elite service to the community as a dimension of its leadership. The corresponding transformations in formal worship were in the direction of signaling refinement. The church was steadily "moving up the liturgical ladder," as Bratt puts it, but the eclectic mix of processions, choirs, candles, and altars with vestiges of the Reformed heritage could look overdone to those with fixed ideas as to proper formalities. The final irony, in Bratt's telling, is the move to the suburbs in 1958 and the adoption of the name Mayflower Congregational Church at a point when the church's Puritan heritage no longer functioned except as a pedigree.

Though it started on a somewhat lower rung, Eastern Avenue Christian Reformed Church likewise steadily moved up the liturgical ladder from its founding in 1879 until the present, paralleling its move up the social ladder. A crucial difference, however, was that the Dutch immigrants and their descendents always thought of themselves as something of social and religious outsiders in this American setting. So even during the past forty years when its political influence began to rival that of the Congregationalists in their heyday, the congregation retained relatively more of its Reformed identity (though more conservative Dutch Reformed would say that, in its zeal to keep up with the times, it had slipped irretrievably off the ladder of biblically mandated worship by ordaining women). In any case, it remained an essentially Dutch-American outpost in an urban area that had become predominantly African American. Bratt helpfully suggests that the differences in the respective transformations of the two congregations can be better understood if we recognize that the Congregationalists were predominantly a culturally dominant group who assumed that the community should "be covered by a single canopy," while the Christian Reformed never entirely lost their Dutch-American sense of being one sub-community in a pluralistic setting.

These Protestant examples invite comparisons with the transition among Catholics in Detroit during the latter half of the twentieth century. In that case liturgical change was not something that arose in the context of changes in local social position, but rather it was imposed from abroad by outsiders who had the explicit intention of making formal liturgies more relevant to the rest of life. The result, as Leslie Tentler points out in her engaging account, was riddled with ironies. The liturgical reforms corresponded with an apparent weakening of the local church communities, of parishioners' loyalties to the Church, and of practices and attitudes that carry worship beyond what happens in the sanctuary. The lesson here seems to be that liturgical reform is not best undertaken apart from careful attention to particular social contexts, a lesson that the present volume seems intended to underscore.

Tentler nonetheless helpfully raises the question of whether the apparent disarray of American Catholicism in the decades that followed the reforms of Vatican II was in any substantial way *caused* by the liturgical reforms. More likely, she suggests, by the end of the 1950s the cracks were already in the walls of the tight-knit observant Catholicism that had been so strong at mid-century and the collapse would have happened with or without liturgical renewal. In any event, we are left to wonder how this Catholic case might fit into Bratt's analysis. In the 1950s many Catholics had a sense of being ethno-religious outsiders in America, almost as much as did the Christian Reformed. Yet American Catholics seem, as a general rule, to have had greater difficulty in retaining a strong identity than have the Christian Reformed. That is so even though they have encountered many very similar cultural forces, such as population shifts to the suburbs and dramatically changing mores, that eroded ethno-religious identities. Though there are many differences to take into account (especially those of the size and homogeneity of the populations in question) perhaps one significant factor is that while most ethno-Catholics have been American cultural outsiders, they have also been, by virtue of being "catholic," shaped by the longstanding ideal that there should be a single canopy for all. As a result, many contemporary Catholics feel deeply ambivalent as to what their mission to the culture should be as their communities have come of age in a pluralistic American setting. The Christian Reformed, appropriating the tradition of Abraham Kuyper, by way of contrast, have long been operating with theories about how particular religious communities should accommodate cultural pluralism and how mainstream culture should accommodate particular religious communities.

Another dimension of the relationship between forms of worship and social position, suggested in several of the essays, is worship's functions in relation to social-political betterment. In the current discourse concerning African-American religion, that is *the* preeminent question and Paul Harvey addresses it with nuance and subtlety. As he points out, much debate regarding African-American religion centers on whether its overtly otherworldly dimensions and its functions as "communal solace in a harsh world" undercut its potential power as social protest. During the Jim Crow era, African-American leaders debated concerning which was more beneficial: more ecstatic worship forms drawn from slave culture and African precedents or more "respectable" forms following models in white churches and often associated with social uplift. Either one, as Harvey shows, could be interpreted as a form of accommodation to oppression. Yet in the light of the subsequent civil rights movement these interpretations need to be revised. Harvey follows David Chappell's very important *A Stone of Hope: Prophetic Religion and the Death of Jim Crow* (2004) in arguing that the African-American revivalist tradition provided the necessary base on which the civil rights movement could be built.

Timothy Matovina and Ruth Alden Doan each consider the impact of worship forms on the status of women. For Tejana women in Texas the Guadalupe celebrations provided rare opportunities for women's leadership, but that did not extend to changing their role in society. For early Methodist women in the early American republic, by contrast, the more fluid social setting meant that even as intense revivalist religion could redefine sacred space, so it was also connected with reconceptualizing women's space and renegotiations of authority. What is cause and what is effect in such settings is difficult to distinguish, but there is no doubt that new religious forms helped open the way for new social forms.

My one observation regarding these important and illuminating topics is that in contemporary scholarship there is some tendency to engage such questions regarding social position and power in a way that preempts consideration of all other aspects of lived religion. The result can be reductionistic. That is, religion comes to be understood solely in terms of the social forces that shape it and is evaluated in terms of its social functions. Such approaches typically reflect far more the concerns of contemporary historians than they reflect the leading concerns the vast majority of their subjects. So, for instance, it has been popular in recent decades to point out that women are the majority in virtually every religious group and hence to argue, at least rhetorically, "Women's history *is* American religious history."[1] All too often, however, the next step in the scholarship is to ignore the primarily spiritual concerns of most religious women and to concentrate on the historians' own concerns regarding the extent to which religion functioned to perpetuate oppression or was used by women to fight oppression and establish their own power and independence.

The present volume, while highlighting many of these social dimensions and functions of worship, avoids such reductionism since it is still first of all about *worship,* which has an irreducibly spiritual element and is, after all, most essentially about people's relationships to God. Consistent with this approach, I would suggest that the corollary to the above rhetoric might be, if we truly are concerned about majorities, "women's [or men's for that matter] religious history *is* the history of their spirituality." Religious history is, of course, about lots of things in addition to spirituality. Yet when we are considering those many other intriguing dimensions of how religion operates in its personal, communal, institutional, and cultural settings we should not lose sight of its core spiritual dimension.

Happily this volume makes that clear. The great preponderance of the religious activity of Tejanos, for instance, concerned their relationship to God in the midst of a very precarious world. Much the same would hold of the spirituality of Leslie Tentler's grandmother and her generation,

---

1. Ann Braude, "Women's History *Is* American Religious History," in *Retelling American Religious History,* Thomas A. Tweed, ed. (Berkeley: University of California Press, 1997), pp. 87-107. R. Marie Griffith, who provides an exception to such reductionistic tendencies in "Female Suffering and Religious Devotion in American Pentecostalism," in *Women in Twentieth-Century Protestantism,* Margaret Lambert Bendroth and Virginia Lieson Brereton, eds. (Champaign: University of Illinois Press), pp. 184-208, observes that most historians of women and religion seem "both embarrassed and nonplussed by the devotional lives of their subjects . . . and to sweep women's prayers and testimonies under a grand historical rug" (p. 184).

whether women or men, even though they lived in a twentieth-century urban setting. That is also transparently central for early Methodist women
and men who were crying out in distress and prayers for mercy at meetings, experiencing fires of ecstasy and the glory of spiritual wholeness,
"swallowed up in God" or "bountifully filled with God." These experiences
were all more about dependence than about independence, even if they involved important elements of self-fulfillment and led to the liberations of
self-discipline. Even among the socially elite or those with less demonstrative forms of worship one can presume many equivalents, even if they
would be less likely to leave a record of their spiritual lives. Presumably
most of the people involved in each of the groups here considered saw
their religious life as first of all about a relationship to God, worshiped and
prayed as acts of dependence on God in a precarious world, found community in these common spiritual concerns, and sought in some ways to
discipline their lives to serve others as a service to God. These spiritual experiences were not the only things going on in their religious lives, as this
volume also makes clear, but when we are talking about "lived religion" it
is essential to keep in mind that these were the main things.

History — about Worship, or for the Sake of Worship? Reflections from Practical Theology

Dorothy C. Bass

The worship committee of a Presbyterian congregation in a changing Seattle neighborhood is planning for the coming year. As so often happens, music becomes the focus of discussion. Members of the committee have been entreated by various factions in the congregation: Include more praise songs! Make sure our singing reflects the diversity of global Christianity and of Seattle itself! Give us the classic hymns that enable us to sing our lives to God in rich, familiar words and tunes! What should the committee recommend, and why?

In a small town in North Carolina long torn by racial animosities, a community garden has been planted. Among the gardeners are landless farmers — some born nearby, others displaced from the Mexican countryside — as well as folks who have never before worked the soil. They are black, white, and brown, Protestant, Catholic, and unchurched, economically privileged and immersed in poverty. After working together one Saturday morning, they gather for a meal. They pause before eating, feeling that something needs to be said over this food and this plot of land, which is becoming for them a sacred place of nourishment and reconciliation. Eyes turn to the local Methodist pastor. What words will she offer that are fitting to this time, this place, this people? If she were absent, what might one of the others speak as prayer?

Two professors at a Lutheran seminary in the Midwest are planning a course on the rites of baptism, wedding, healing, and funeral. Keenly aware that their class time is limited, they wrestle with the course design. How much reading and classroom time should be given to biblical material, to the history of each rite, to Lutheran theological interpretations, and to contemporary debates about the meaning of the life stages with which the rites are associated? Through what activities might these future pastors be required to speak and embody these rites in the classroom, rehearsing for their future roles as presiders? How can this class, in combination with wisdom gained over time and the help of the Holy Spirit, prepare these students to convey God's grace to people at crucial life transitions, in ways that also extend beyond the rite and contribute to the well-being of the world?[1]

What Is Practical Theology?

The people in each of these scenes are doing practical theology.[2] Undertaken in concrete situations both within the church and beyond it, practi-

1. James R. Nieman, "Liturgy and Life: An Account of Teaching Ritual Practices," in *For Life Abundant: Practical Theology, Theological Education, and Christian Ministry,* Dorothy C. Bass and Craig Dykstra, eds. (Grand Rapids: Eerdmans, 2008).

2. During the past generation, practical theology has undergone a period of renewal and self-definition. An excellent overview of the academic discipline, ministerial capacity, and Christian discernment that together comprise this field is Kathleen Cahalan and James R. Nieman, "Mapping the Field of Practical Theology," in Bass and Dykstra, eds., *For Life Abundant.* A major new reference work that provides insight into the methods and concerns of this field is Bonnie Miller-McLemore, ed., *The Wiley-Blackwell Companion to Practical Theology* (London: Wiley-Blackwell, 2011). My summary here necessarily simplifies this complex and developing field. What I hope readers will especially note in my account is the emphasis on the telos of practical theology rather than on its method; this is the approach taken in *For Life Abundant.* Obviously, not everything that self-affirming practical theologians designate as "practical theology" goes by that name in its own context; actual participants might call what they are doing, for example, "attending the worship committee meeting." One of the most influential approaches to practical theology written during the recent period of renewal and self-definition is Don S. Browning, *A Fundamental Practical Theology* (Minneapolis: Fortress, 1991), which sets forth a method that includes movements of descriptive theology, historical theology, systematic theology, and strategic practical theology, undertaken in response to urgent contemporary concerns. For almost twenty years, Browning and his colleagues have been addressing the crisis in the contemporary family through dozens of books and articles written by excellent scholars in a wide range of disciplines. For Browning, "historical theology" includes Scripture as well as tradition and is undertaken in large part to clarify the normative claims operative on the community engaged in discerning faithful action. "Historical theology asks, what do the normative texts that are already part of our effective history *really*

cal theology is the thinking by which Christians discern the contours of a faithful, life-giving way of life and ask how they might shape and partici- pate in practices that help them to embrace such a way of life in and for the world. Such discernment is an intrinsic part of Christian existence amid the ongoing challenges and changes that comprise human history, and thoughtful Christians have engaged in it in one way or another in count- less settings over the span of many centuries and cultures. In this primary sense, practical theology is a form of reflection engaged in by a wide range of persons and communities, whether schooled or unschooled, lay or or- dained. Sometimes such thinking happens purposefully, but often it emerges within the informal negotiations of ecclesial and social life.

Among the many who engage in practical theology in this sense, a small number also pursue practical theology's concerns through teaching and research in the academy, where they typically have special responsibil- ity for preparing students to perform the practices of ministry, practices intended to guide persons and communities into life-giving ways of life.[3] These are the persons most likely to call themselves "practical theologians," though most are more likely to identify more fully with one of that field's subdisciplines, such as pastoral care, homiletics, Christian education, or worship.[4] Such distinctions can foster fragmentation and incoherence, to

---

imply for our praxis when they are confronted as honestly as possible?" (*A Fundamental Prac- tical Theology*, p. 49). Browning urges historians in the theological academy to bring rigorous hermeneutical expertise to the exploration of practical concerns, while also noting that simi- lar moves take place in congregations, especially when they return to classic texts in times of crisis. Practical theology as I understand it includes a turn to classic texts, but it also attends to the actual practices of embodied communities.

3. Cahalan and Nieman, "Mapping the Field," pp. 64, 66, consider theological educa- tion and scholarship, ministry, and discipleship as related and mutually influential dimen- sions of practical theology.

4. The chapters in this book are especially related to one of these subdisciplines, of course. The study of worship is a well-established academic specialization that engages scholars who also bring further specialization in biblical, historical, theological, and social scientific approaches. As such, it has a great deal to say *about* worship. When undertaken as a quest for knowledge alone, I would not call such scholarship "practical theology" but, rather, "liturgical studies." However, all of this knowledge can be pursued and presented for the purpose of deepening the capacity of contemporary Christians to worship God actively, in- telligently, and faithfully, within communities that seek the well-being of the world God loves (it often is pursued and presented in this way, even by some of those who call them- selves "liturgical scholars"). *This* is practical theology. John Witvliet demonstrates this dif- ference by asking, "How would the teaching of Christian worship change if it were more firmly rooted in a theologically robust understanding of Christian practice? That is, if vital

be sure — segregating the academy from the church, practical theology from other theological disciplines, and subdisciplines within the practical field from one another — and this has worried seminary and divinity school faculties for decades.[5] At the same time, however, the guiding questions and purposes of practical theology give it great potential as a locus of integration.[6] Practical theology at its best operates in close proximity to the actual lives of persons and communities, learning from and about them even while serving them and, arguably, doing more than the other theological disciplines to bridge the gap between the church and the academy.[7] Further, practical theology's orientation to a telos of faithful living enables it to engage normative perspectives in ways that are crucial to ministry but often discouraged in the historical and biblical fields.[8] Practical

---

Christianity is truly about participating in practices that comprise a life-giving way of life in and for the world, then how should teachers of worship present and probe Christian worship?" Witvliet argues for incorporating rigorous engagement with historical and other scholarship *within* teaching that "forms students in the constellation of knowledge, wisdom, skills, and capacities needed for faithful practice." Teaching at the Ph. D. level, Witvliet notes, rightly takes an approach that is less directly aimed at this purpose. See his "Teaching Worship as a Christian Practice," in Bass and Dykstra, *For Life Abundant;* quotations, p. 118. Another collection of historical essays that explores the focus of another subdiscipline, religious formation, is *Educating and Forming People of Faith,* ed. John H. Van Engen (Grand Rapids: Eerdmans, 2003).

5. Edward Farley's argument that theological education in modernity is hampered by the fragmentation of the curriculum and the lack of a unifying habitus and purpose has been widely influential. See *Theologia: The Fragmentation and Unity of Theological Education* (Philadelphia: Fortress Press, 1983).

6. Kathleen A. Cahalan addresses the problem of integrating all the theological disciplines for the sake of ministry and describes how her capstone course attempts this in "Introducing Ministry and Fostering Integration: Teaching the Bookends of the Masters of Divinity Program," in Bass and Dykstra, eds., *For Life Abundant.*

7. Typically, practical theologians are expected to be very good at the practices they teach. Thus those in pastoral care often have clinical practices, homileticians preach in congregations and denominational gatherings, and so on. Moreover, many are involved in or responsible for contextual and continuing education. Bonnie J. Miller-McLemore explores these and others ways in which practical theologians bridge the gap between church and academy in "Practical Theology and Pedagogy: Embodying Theological Know-How," in Bass and Dykstra, eds., *For Life Abundant.*

8. There are good methodological reasons for historians and biblical scholars to try to avoid normative judgments in their research, of course, and historically this restraint was significant in establishing their academic freedom and making available new insights into the past. It is unfortunate, however, when the embrace of *Wissenschaft* engenders disdain for the different, but highly complex and difficult, work done by those who study practices in

theology draws heavily on these fields, as well as on systematic theology, ethics, and the social sciences; such breadth and collaboration are essential to comprehending the complex situations that practical theology addresses. Most important, all this happens not as an exercise in methodological collaboration but for the sake of faithful living: practical theology moves toward action, in the hope of furthering healing, transformation, reconciliation, and abundant life. Its practitioners — academic, ministerial, and lay — respond to human needs, often focusing on those that are urgent and nearby but also attempting to build up life-giving ways of life over the long term.[9]

Histories of Practical Theologians at Work

The contemporary scenes sketched at the start of this essay are probably quite similar to scenes that actually occurred within the historical movements described in this book. Here, too, practical theologians were at work. For example, debates about what kind of music should be sung in worshiping congregations appear again and again on the pages of this volume. In his chapter, Paul Harvey analyzes the struggle of African-American religious leaders in the Jim Crow era to discern ways of incorporating into church life both European American hymnody and the ecstatic African-born sounds that these leaders associated with the legacy of slavery. At stake in this debate — which was also played out in preaching and other elements of worship — were relationships between the black elite and those with less wealth and education, as well as competing approaches to improving the status of the African-American community as a whole. Later, as shown by Leslie Woodcock Teutler, the reforms of Vatican II placed new emphasis on

---

which they also engage. The value of a range of ways of knowing is a matter theological educators are beginning to explore; see Bonnie J. Miller-McLemore, "The 'Clerical Paradigm': A Fallacy of Misplaced Concreteness?" *International Journal of Practical Theology* 11, no. 1 (June 2007): 19-38.

9. The Religion, Culture and Family Project of the University of Chicago, directed by the eminent practical theologian Don S. Browning, provides an example. Browning's sense that the contemporary family is in crisis prompted the project, but one of its purposes was to build resources and shape policies that would enable religious communities to support families over the long term. Scholars from several disciplines contributed books and articles, which often began as original scholarly work but later emerged as handbooks and magazine articles for pastors and lay people. The team worked in the hope of contributing to transformation, healing, and abundant life.

worshipers' active participation in the Mass, which meant that a new set of songs was suddenly needed; in the absence of an existing repertoire, simple and ultimately unsatisfying music was rushed onto the lips of a puzzled laity. And most recently, as shown in James Bratt's essay, demographic change in Western Michigan combined with a received tradition of psalmody and fresh appreciation for the diversity of global Christianity to engender new musical expressions at Eastern Avenue Christian Reformed Church in Grand Rapids, as well as beyond that congregation through the new denominational hymnal edited by one of its members. The Puritan and early Methodist movements that are described in other chapters also crafted musical practices that embodied ways of worshiping God that fostered each group's distinctive worldview. At some point in the development of each movement, choices about what to sing or what to include in a new hymnal such as *Gospel Pearls* (the National Baptist Convention, 1921) must have been as intense as the conversations taking place today.

Throughout this book, then, we see leaders and communities at work, crafting worship practices they believe will address urgent needs that have arisen in specific cultural settings in ways that will foster a faithful way of life. These practitioners knew — whether in their bones or in well-articulated theories like those developed in the twentieth-century liturgical movement described by Michael Woods — that the shape and content of the embodied life they shared when they gathered to worship God would have an impact on them and their vision of the world, not only while they were worshiping but in other realms of life as well.[10] And so they worked to discern the shape of faithful worship in relation to their hope for faithful living. Such work can occur, these chapters show, at many levels of church and society — in a national assembly of learned divines who design a worship manual for Puritan ministers (Harry Stout's essay), for example, as well as in local communities whose liturgical knowledge is funded primarily by communal memory. Drawing on such memory and the vibrant im-

---

10. How worship forms persons and communities for a way of life is a topic frequently explored by theologians; see, for example, Don E. Saliers, *Worship and Theology: Foretaste of Glory Divine* (Nashville: Abingdon, 1994), especially chapter 11; Christian Scharen, *Public Worship and Public Work* (Collegeville, Minn.: Liturgical Press, 2004); and Leanne Van Dyk, ed., *A More Profound Alleluia: Theology and Worship in Harmony* (Grand Rapids: Eerdmans, 2005), especially the final chapter by David Stubbs. While these and most other scholars agree that participating in worship can have profound effects on a person's way of seeing and living in the world, they also rightly insist that Christians do not worship for that purpose, but rather to serve and glorify God.

ages and objects that distilled it, we learn from Timothy Matovina, nineteenth-century Tejanos crafted rituals in the storied streets and buildings of San Antonio, thereby sustaining deep connections to a sacred tradition in the midst of overwhelming demographic and political volatility.

Michael Woods's account of the National Catholic Rural Life Conference provides an especially clear (and, to me, stirring and impressive) example of the relationship between worship and a way of life — and the creative, integrative, and richly theological efforts of thoughtful leaders to strengthen that relationship for the sake of both. The NCRLC was initially not a program of worship renewal but rather a social mission to farmers facing economic threats and social marginalization. However, an alliance with the liturgical movement then astir among American and European theologians imbued NCRLC with "a thoroughly 'catholic' approach to ministering to rural Catholics, attending to their religious, educational, cultural, and socioeconomic well-being" (p. 139) as integrally related to one another. This was done in a thoroughly *Catholic* way as well, as Masses and devotions located parishioners' daily work in a sacramental world where "a crop's growth, as well as the Christian's, was of the *one* salvific narrative" (p. 121). In Woods's portrayal of Fr. Edwin O'Hara, Fr. Paul Brinker, and others, we see pastoral leaders discerning the contours of a faithful, life-giving way of life and shaping practices that helped Christians to embrace such a way of life in and for the world. O'Hara drew on "his farm experience and seminary formation" (p. 106); Brinker attended closely to the details of Kentucky tobacco culture; and devotional materials "put forward an easily understood theology of rural life, expressed in a manner that was at once cosmic and quotidian, universal and folksy" (p. 123).[11]

---

11. The final comment comes from Woods's assessment of a 1947 publication, *A Day of Christian Rural Living.* NCRLC leaders, and perhaps Woods as well, would probably not call these priests' work "practical theology," which emerged historically from the Protestant academy, but rather "pastoral theology," a term more often used by Roman Catholics that points toward the sacramental character of personal and communal formation and transformation. Yet the language of both Woods and NCRLC leaders resonates with a statement Craig Dykstra and I (both Protestants) recently published: "Through thoughtful engagement with and within situations of personal, ecclesial, and societal existence, practical theology seeks to clarify the contours of a way of life that reflects God's active presence and responds to human beings' fundamental needs. It also seeks to guide and strengthen persons and communities to embody this way of life. Thus practical theology requires stereoscopic attention to both the specific moves of personal and communal living and the all-encompassing horizon of faith. It is undertaken in hope for the well-being of persons, communities of faith, and all creation." *For Life Abundant,* p. 13. See also two articles by Kath-

And yet this chapter does not tell, and lacking sources cannot tell, what difference this movement made.[12] We hear little from the farmers themselves, apart from the grateful memories of one woman near the end of the chapter. Influence on lives like hers is of great value; I do not mean to diminish this in noting, in addition, that not long after the end of Woods's story many of the parishes whose land had been farmed by observant Catholic families were rapidly losing population and communal coherence. This did not happen because NCRLC failed to encourage the children to follow the vocation of farming (it did encourage them) or failed to address the social and economic forces that were already beginning to transform the American countryside (it did address them, passionately and well). Instead, in a process parallel to what happened in the Detroit urban parishes described by Leslie Woodcock Tentler, social changes outside the scope and control of the Church undermined the tight culture of Catholic family and parish life that NCRLC's program of renewal pursued, and on which it relied.

Like the work of NCRLC, all good on-the-ground ministry has been and is closely attuned to settings that are always on the verge of change. Even as creative leaders strive to foster faithful living in a distinctive context, the ground is shifting. This is a truism when noted from a distance — but a wrenching actuality for those living within the time and place concerned, as Tentler's account of the swift demise of the apparently thriving urban Catholic communal life of the 1950s demonstrates. Adaptive change is sometimes possible, as Matovina demonstrates in recounting how San Antonio Tejanos transformed devotion to the Virgin of Guadalupe from an agricultural to an urban practice. But unintended consequences often result as well: as Harry Stout argues, the Puritans were not secular moderns, but the shape of their worship opened the way to both modernity and secularism when the religious fervor of their descendents waned.

The Christians portrayed in this book — and also those who today

---

leen A. Cahalan, "Pastoral Theology or Practical Theology? Limits and Possibilities," in *Keeping Faith in Practice: Aspects of Catholic Pastoral Theology*, James Seeney, Gemma Simmonds, and David Lonsdale, eds. (London: SCM Press, 2010), pp. 99-116; and "Beyond Pastoral Theology: Why Catholics Should Embrace Practical Theology," in *Secularization Theories, Religious Identity and Practical Theology*, Wilhelm Gräb and Lars Charbonniere, eds. (Zurich: Lit Verlag GmbH & Co., 2009), pp. 392-97.

12. Some other chapters in this volume do argue that their subjects had specific and lasting consequences that reached into the political and cultural life of the United States, most notably Stout, Harvey, and Bratt.

serve on worship committees, teach in seminaries, start community gardens, and otherwise try to discern and foster life-giving ways of life — are immersed in changes that historians later describe from a distance. Unlike historians, they operate without the benefit of hindsight, and their work is always open-ended. Like historians, however, they care deeply about noticing the actual details of community life and the thick texture of social reality and asking what difference these make. Among the disciplines typically represented in theological education, these two may have the strongest commitments to seeing things as they are or were. Both ask "what is going on here?" and both are aware of the risk of not seeing reality because they have become caught up in dominant narratives.[13] Both groups have what David Daniels, a historian, and Ted Smith, a homiletician, call "a sense of the glorious untidiness of the world as it actually exists."[14] Yet historians can, with care, see connections that are invisible from within the flow of history itself. In making these connections and placing distinct movements in the history of worship into the frame of American history, the authors of this book prompt those who today embody the contemporary history of Christian worship to place their own efforts on a larger stage.

What Does History Offer to Practical Theology?

Both Daniels and Smith, professors in a seminary and a university divinity school, respectively, are practical theologians in the sense I have been describing. Recently they articulated the "critical and constructive hopes" that shape how and why each, in his distinct curricular location, teaches toward the telos of ministry that will build up a life-giving way of life in and for the world.

---

13. On history: Ruth Alden Doan notes that the history of women in early American Methodism is invisible unless historians look beyond the themes established by the dominant historiographical narrative; see her "Worship, Experience, and the Creation of Methodist Place," pp. 55-59 in this volume. On practical theology, see Cahalan and Nieman, "Mapping the Field," p. 82. This commitment fuels the frequent use of ethnography and social sciences in practical theology. Edward Farley offered an influential theological argument that rigorous description of a situation is the first task of practical theology in "Interpreting Situations," republished in his *Practicing Gospel* (Louisville: Westminster John Knox, 2003). The second task, interestingly, is to interpret a situation in relation to its past.

14. David D. Daniels III and Ted A. Smith, "History, Practice, and Theological Education," in Bass and Dykstra, eds., *For Life Abundant*, p. 215.

Histories of church practices are of more than antiquarian interest. They have the power to demystify practices that have become second nature, and so beyond conscious reflection. By retrieving the historical and social process by which a practice came to be established, we hope to open up critical and faithful conversation. By recalling the reasons given for establishing a practice, we hope to give students vocabulary for sharing in that conversation. And by remembering suppressed alternatives — the losers of historical struggles — we hope to stock the imaginations of pastors with lost treasures. Rummaging through the past can yield historical resources for charting new directions in ministry. But the resources of the past are not endlessly fungible goods that we can use in whatever ways we wish. We believe that the goods of the past also make claims on us. And good histories listen for ways the past addresses the church today.[15]

Historical teaching of this kind is more possible now than it was before the expansion in recent decades of scholarly interest in practices.[16] Although many, perhaps most, courses in the "practical" area of theological education have long included at least some history, attention to practices themselves heightens historians' contributions to this area by undermining simple narratives of progress or decline in favor of textured portraits that explore the importance of context, intention, and craft in the work of religious leaders. Another professor of homiletics, James Nieman, has contrasted the history of preaching he studied in seminary to the messier, contextualized history a practical theological teacher really needs. Yngve Brilioth's *A Brief History of Preaching* was a slim volume that assessed every epoch of preaching with reference to Jesus' first sermon as recounted in Luke 4; today, Nieman yearns for a history that would "instead carefully explore many actual practices, how-

15. Daniels and Smith, "History, Practice, and Theological Education," p. 215. In this excellent exploration of issues quite relevant to the present volume, Smith explains why his courses on practice (e.g., preaching) always explore the history of the practice, and Daniels explains why and how he foregrounds practices of ministry in his survey of American Christianity.

16. The scholarship on worship practices in the present volume exemplifies this interest. Daniels and Smith cite, in addition, David D. Hall, ed., *Lived Religion in America* (Princeton: Princeton University Press, 1997); Laurie F. Maffly-Kipp, Leigh E. Schmidt, and Mark Valeri, eds., *Practicing Protestants: Histories of Christian Life in America, 1630-1965* (Baltimore: Johns Hopkins University Press, 2006); O. C. Edwards, *A History of Preaching* (Nashville: Abingdon Press, 2004); and Beverly A. Zink-Sawyer, *From Preachers to Suffragists: Woman's Rights and Religious Convictions in the Lives of Three Nineteenth-Century American Clergywomen* (Louisville: Westminster/John Knox Press, 2003).

ever flawed."[17] In this collection of histories of worship, it is possible that readers may learn as much from flaws as from successes — for example, from how Tejano rituals confirmed class divisions even while bridging competing cultures, or from strategies that first asserted and then diminished the influence of mainline Congregationalists in Grand Rapids.

In some cases, history sheds light directly on an issue that is of deep contemporary concern. For example, the detachment of the spiritual fervor of early American Methodism from brick-and-mortar structures, portrayed by Ruth Alden Doan, could challenge the priorities and prompt the renewal of contemporary Methodists obsessed by a crumbling building that has become a burden. In addition, conversations about contemporary concerns could be enriched by two chapters that treat twentieth-century subjects. Tensions between relatively restrained worship styles derived from European American Protestantism and ecstatic worship practices growing from African roots are far from resolved; indeed, these tensions have become more complex since the emergence of black elites eager to embrace their African heritage and the rise of Pentecostalism among black, white, and Latino/a Christians. Conversation about how creative leaders such as Henry McNeal Turner, Henry Hugh Proctor, and Thomas A. Dorsey embodied and interpreted a range of possible resolutions would enrich conversations in seminary classrooms, ministerial gatherings, and local congregations. Similarly, Tentler's account of what caused the weakening of Catholic life and piety after Vatican II could be invaluable in crafting liturgical and educational strategies of renewal, if only because of what Tentler argues was *not* the problem: "To what extent was liturgical reform a cause of subsequent Catholic disarray? . . . the answer, I think, lies as much outside the sanctuary as within" (p. 169).

At other times, history's contribution is analogical.[18] Amid today's urgent concern about the relationship between human communities, land, and food, I am eager to share Woods's account of how NCRLC crafted prayer and worship that treasured the well-being of soil and water and air with the Methodist pastor whose parish includes the community garden, and also with a Lutheran pastor and teacher I know, whose passion is to

---

17. Nieman, "Liturgy and Life," p. 150.

18. In her capstone course for Master of Divinity students, Kathleen Cahalan requires her students to draw on all the disciplines of theological study to develop a response to a situation they are likely to face in ministry. One of her guiding questions is "Are there historical analogies to this situation? What can be learned from other Christian communities who have faced similar situations, in the past and today?" Cahalan, "Introducing Ministry," p. 106.

proclaim God's promise of healing for creation through the liturgy. Neither will be able to use the unaltered language of mid-century Catholicism, but both will be delighted and inspired by these ancestors in faith. Similar delight and inspiration may have moved the Latino Catholic leaders of San Antonio who in recent decades have renewed the San Fernando Cathedral and made that building and the streets of San Antonio the scene of highly visible processions and gatherings that once again shape the public life of that multicultural city. Guided in part by the nineteenth-century practices that Matovina describes, processions now visit again "the arenas where residents' homes and persons had been violated, asserting a truth about God's accompaniment larger than the sum of their collective anguish and symbolically consecrating anew the defiled places of daily life" (p. 78).

While historical antecedents can inspire, they can also foster salutary forms of humility. John Witvliet, who teaches courses on worship to both college and seminary students, is conscious when designing courses that "the teaching of worship always happens mid-stream, within traditions that embody complex historical trajectories and to students who are already engaging, with varying levels of commitment, worship practices." Thus teaching in this area always functions as "commentary on existing and evolving practices, even as we participate in them." Those who have a personal and professional stake in renewing worship "best begin not with the hubris that assumes that we can figure it all out on our own, but rather with a profound sense of privilege for joining a centuries-old, global conversation." Historical study undertaken in this spirit, Witvliet notes, can yield both appreciation for traditional practices and a platform for constructive criticism.[19] Ted Smith's account of a classroom exchange provides an example. After studying the historical emergence of different kinds of worship spaces, the students who favored "traditional" spaces and those who wanted spaces more geared to efficiency were finally able to have a good conversation that was both critical and constructive. The class session, Smith recalls, moved "from a surface-level conversation about 'likes' and 'dislikes' to a much deeper conversation about the meaning of community, the purpose of worship, and the ways those meanings and purposes could be sought in the arrangements of space." While differences remained, most participants changed their minds in some way.[20]

---

19. Witvliet, "Teaching Worship as a Christian Practice," p. 126.

20. Daniels and Smith, "History, Practice, and Theological Education," p. 222. Smith's students had just read Anne C. Loveland and Otis B. Wheeler, *From Meetinghouse to Megachurch: A Material and Cultural History* (Columbia: University of Missouri Press, 2003).

Dorothy C. Bass

What Does Practical Theology Offer to History?

Constructive purposes such as those pursued by Witvliet and Smith might sit uneasily with certain academic historians, who are trained to keep their distance from the people and situations they study. However, these and other practical theologians would be quick to insist that they appreciate, indeed demand, the most rigorous historical investigations possible. Idealized portraits of the past will do little to impel immersion in the volatile messiness of contemporary religious life. (To the contrary, as Witvliet notes, his students take courage from the fact that worshipers in Calvin's Geneva sometimes did not understand the great reformer's preaching.)[21] For Smith, ironic interplays of disjunction and continuity are more instructive than simplistic accounts could ever be. Even when practices persist, as the nineteenth-century preaching styles about which Smith writes have done, discovering that these practices are historical rather than natural can ease the cold grip of the taken-for-granted on contemporary practitioners, awakening the critical consciousness and the constructive imagination of those who preach today.[22]

One of the contributions of practical theology to academic history, then, is to provide an audience of readers who are eager to receive the books and articles historians write. This audience will respond most readily, of course, to histories that explore issues that matter to them. Historians are thus wise to listen for the questions that are currently arising in church and society — something most have always done as a matter of course, as they bring interests shaped by their own social locations to the study of the past. Deliberate consultation with practical theologians provides one more means of discerning what topics to explore. Indeed, the present volume originated in this way, when a practical and theological project that aims to renew Christian worship as part of a faithful way of life commissioned a group of historians to provide accounts of worship in the American past. It is important that these accounts and others with similar purposes be intellectually independent, of course, and that research arising from elsewhere in the historical profession also be given the opportunity to surprise and instruct.

21. Witvliet, "Teaching Worship as a Christian Practice," p. 130.
22. Smith's book on preaching both tells a history of practices and reflects theologically on historical method and meaning. See Ted A. Smith, *The New Measures: A Theological History of Democratic Practice* (New York: Cambridge University Press, 2007).

As this volume demonstrates, the historical exploration of topics suggested by contemporary endeavors in practical theology can also lead historians to discoveries they might not otherwise have made, expanding knowledge of the past — a good thing in itself, by the lights of that profession. Questions that might lead to pathbreaking historical work might emerge from any field, of course. And yet as interest in practices increases in both history and theological education, similar commitments to viewing human communities in context, in all their messy particularity, make natural allies of the two disciplines under consideration here.

And so let us consider another scene of contemporary practice, parallel to the three sketched at the beginning of this chapter:

> A new assistant professor in a theological school is planning a course that will survey the development of Christianity in the United States. Her doctoral studies at a major research university gave her a strong command of the literature in this field, but now she is puzzled. How can she present this material in a way that not only interests the future pastors who will be in the course but also helps them to lead Christian communities and to encourage Christian discipleship in daily life?

David Daniels, a historian who has responded to this question in his teaching for two decades, makes the practice of ministry one of the featured themes running through his survey courses.[23] Other historians respond by coteaching courses with colleagues in theology, ethics, or one of the subdisciplines of practical theology, endeavors that often cause both parties to ask new questions of familiar sources.

When historians embrace such opportunities, they add their discipline's critical eye, contextual sensitivity, and stock of stories to the ongoing process of discerning the contours of a life-giving way of life in and for the world. Their contributions need not be direct, and they cannot be directive. In this service, however, some find a vocation, and with it the conviction that their work truly matters to the well-being of persons, communities, and the life of the world.

---

23. Daniels and Smith, "History, Practice, and Theological Education," pp. 228-37.

Liturgy's Passions and Polarities

Joyce Ann Zimmerman, C.PP.S.

Medieval people "conducted their communal lives on the unspoken assumption that the sins of one were the business of all," astutely penned historian Jonathan Sumption.[1] They lived in small, homogeneous, closed societies where everyone knew everyone else — generally true of nobility and peasant alike. In a postmodern age of suburbanization, globalization, and ecumenism, perhaps an accurate rephrasing of Sumption might be that people "conduct their lives on the unspoken assumption that the liturgy of one is the business of none." Liturgy for some has become one more privatized commodity, often being directed to individual needs and satisfaction. We can surely notice a huge historical shift from how and where worship took place in years gone by to our present experience in the seven case studies presented in this volume.

That religion (and worship) played a major role in the settlement of North America can hardly be disputed. Immigrants sometimes came to this country to escape oppressive governments or economic problems back home, and sought here freedom of religious expression and new economic opportunities. It is no surprise, then, that when they came to this wide-open land they tended to settle with their own kind, replicating to a great extent the society, home life, and religious familiarity of the land they left. The story is told locally in Ohio how immigrants riding barges northward up the Miami-Erie Canal into the rich farmlands would have an-

---

1. Jonathan Sumption, *Pilgrimage: An Image of Mediaeval Religion* (Totowa, N.J.: Rowman & Littlefield, 1975), p. 12.

nounced to them as they passed by a settlement, "Catholic" or "Protestant," and would disembark accordingly.[2]

While polls point otherwise, we still consider ourselves a religious nation. But times have changed. No longer is the local church or meeting house the center of both religious and social life. Small, intimate gatherings in some instances have been replaced by mega-churches with seating capacities rivaling sports facilities. A limited number of musical instruments (or none at all) and hymnals have now mushroomed into the use of every conceivable music-maker, complex amplification systems, and elimination of the need for hymnals altogether, with dominating screens and projected stage backdrops replacing apse frescos.

Would the seventeenth-century Pilgrim discerning the meaning of Scripture, eighteenth-century Methodist worshiping in a small praise house, or nineteenth-century Tejanos erecting shrines to the Lady of Guadalupe find themselves comfortable with this new religious and worship landscape? Have worshiping communities today fared any better with handling prejudice than during the Jim Crow pre–civil rights era? Has worship connected individuals with life, society, and the political arena in such a way as to shape decisions with values, laws with concern-for-others justice, and the economy in terms of an equitable sharing of goods so that no one is in need? As we encroach on more and more farmland to support suburban sprawl, are we still able to be touched by the beauty and simplicity of creation in such a way as to be moved by the sacramentality and holiness of all things? Have we so lost our devotional lives that religion and worship are relegated to a sparse bit of time once in a while (no longer even weekly)? Such are the issues and questions these case studies invite us to reflect on and challenge us to address.

Too often today liturgy involves congregants in polarities that play out in various games of tug of war — only much more is at stake than one side being strong enough to pull the other side into a mud pit and get a good laugh over it. Polarities become evident historically as we compare different eras, liturgically as we compare different traditions and service styles, and pastorally as we compare different ways liturgy has or has not borne fruit in the everyday lives of worshipers. What is at stake in these polarities now is the prospect of worship that is strong enough to pull people not into tug-of-war mud pits but into the clear waters of new religious self-understanding, into blood-red passion about covenantal fidelity, into the

---

2. To this day particular farming communities in central Ohio have a noticeably higher than average percentage of one religion over any other.

sweet peace of salvation already realized but not yet fulfilled. What is at stake is remaining faithful to our country's deep religious roots and renewing ourselves so that we renew the face of the earth. And in all this, what is most at stake is keeping God the focus and center of our lives, our worship, our society. Truly, there is much at stake.

These seven case studies describing the history of differing worship communities in the United States are written from the purview of historians, not liturgical theologians or pastoral ministers. This provides fresh insight for regarding worship. My commentary on these case studies comes from my purview as a liturgical theologian. I have chosen to align myself with a current thrust of ecumenical dialogue, namely, to consider what is passionately shared in common about worship by the communities represented in this book. To this end, I comment on seven major themes that are essential for good liturgy in our contemporary churches, themes which I state here as foundational principles. Thus, rather than looking at denominational differences (or even polarities of worship purpose and styles within denominations), I want to consider what we are all passionately struggling with and why. I encourage the reader to apply these principles to the seven case studies in this volume to see how they worked, or where and with what consequences they were limited. In a concluding section I show how together we can make these passions and polarities work for us to promote authentic liturgy.

1. All Liturgy Is Directed to Praise and Thanksgiving of God

While this seems an obvious principle, sometimes there may be a real tug of war going on between whether liturgy focuses on God or on the individual worshiper or on the gathered community. Three case studies suggest that liturgy is about the individual's and community's heightened emotional expression, and to some extent this is true. But for all three of these groups, the personal experience served the larger community.[3]

Eighteenth-century New World Methodists, for example, created themselves as community through sound and voice, and the community in turn created the sacred space where God could be encountered. Although venting individual emotion, the "shout" expressed more than individual joy — "the spiritual crossed or erased the boundaries of flesh and of

---

3. On Methodist worship experience by Doan, on Tejanos devotions by Matovina, and on African-American ecstatic worship by Harvey, all in this volume.

individuality." The Tejanos' devotion, especially to Our Lady of Guadalupe and the saints, is highly personal at the same time it reaches its climax in festivals that are necessarily communal. In both devotion and festival are meshed cathedral, piety, daily life, and an ability to cope with dire social conditions. This latter point — ability to cope — also is at the heart of African-American worship where oppressed blacks could envision a different future (if only in eternity) and voice their fears and frustrations in worship. Worship gave these people courage to see themselves as good and whole, lovable in God's sight, and as God's children endowed with dignity and honor. During worship they were what God intended them to be and could praise their God for being made in the divine image.

Much of present-day worship still unfolds with a great emphasis on personal experience and passion. Sometimes, though, the worship experience is severed from small and supporting communities, often taking place in mega-churches. A diminished sense of community risks passion staying within the individual rather than helping the individual transcend time and place to reach out to others. Moreover, many worshipers today are bored with worship because they "don't get anything out of it." All too often seekers look more for a supportive, caring community than for faith; emergent churches shape worship to satisfy the disenfranchised or increase membership rather than to praise God; and music and rhetoric carry the day rather than that sort of worship which calls congregants to surrender to deeper covenantal relationship.

2. All Liturgy Is Communal

"Communal" can suggest one clarifying differentiation between worship and liturgy. Individuals might worship God through private devotions, pilgrimages to holy sites, various ways of praying, intercessions, sacred dances or ecstatic utterances, wonderment at creation, hearts turned to gratitude. While some of these worship expressions might also be communal, liturgy, on the other hand, is always communal. It has as its purpose to make visible the gift of salvation God offers to and within the community and the promise of eternal new life to those who are faithful. The work of the people[4] is to surrender to God's saving presence and promise. It is in

---

4. "Liturgy" comes from two Greek words, *laós* (people) and *érgon* (work); hence, the etymological meaning of the word "liturgy" is "the work of the people."

the very surrender that praise and thanksgiving are offered to God because in that surrender we more perfectly conform ourselves to God's will and purpose for us. In the surrender is expressed our covenantal fidelity.

Each of these seven case studies describes inherently communal worshiping groups. Here, however, "communal" is to be understood as more than people simply coming together for the common goal of worship. True, in all these cases people come together. But in the very act of worship (liturgy) the community is both constituted and transformed through meaning (Puritans), liminal experience (Methodists), fiestas advancing religious and cultural hegemony (Tejanos), "evangelical culture emphasizing spiritual liberation" (black church life in Jim Crow Georgia), "recommitment to strict doctrine and strict behavior" (two Protestant congregations in Grand Rapids), deeper entry into and convergence of the rhythms of nature and the liturgical seasons (rural Catholicism), and shared aesthetic and moral power evoked by a sense of mystery and awe at a transcendent and immanent God (1950s Catholicism).

In their own ways, each of these communities is striving to enter more deeply into their baptismal identity as the Body of Christ. This shared, common identity cuts across denominational boundaries.[5] Further, liturgy is an expression of our share in the common priesthood of Christ our high priest.[6] The surrender of ourselves to liturgical action is a giving over of ourselves to become more than we are, to intercede for all of humanity, and to mediate for each other God's care and presence.

3. All Liturgy Is of the People

One of the greatest criticisms of highly ritualized — "high church" — liturgy is that it is impersonal, nonexpressive of people's lives. Sometimes ritual might be exactly this, especially when it is mechanical and performed in perfunctory ways. We ought not give God praise and thanksgiving out of vacuums, but out of the very stuff of our daily lives expressed in vibrant, vital, passionate ways. Liturgy is both personal expression and commitment of people and their lives. Three corollaries

---

5. It is not insignificant that most Christian congregations recognize each other's baptisms — that sacrament which conforms us to Christ and from which we receive our Christian identity.

6. See Heb. 5–10; Rev. 1:6; 5:9-10; 1 Pet. 2:5, 9.

derive from this principle and are embedded in the very fabric of the communities in these case studies.

First, all liturgy is inculturated; that is, it is expressed in actions and words, music and symbols that are culture-bound. Culture is a sine qua non context for doing good liturgy. Indeed, all of these case studies describe people who are clearly culture-bound: Puritans, woodlands Methodists, Catholic Mexican Americans, African Americans, Dutch immigrant Protestants, rural Catholics, pre–Vatican II Catholics. If the liturgy itself becomes non-expressive of a particular culture (as, for example, with the Tejanos in independent or U.S.-annexed Texas), then popular piety steps in and supplies.

Second corollary: in authentic liturgy social boundaries are erased. This is particularly evident in the Methodist biracial praise house liturgy where slavery was called into question. It is equally true in Tejanos festivals where everyone is invited to attend (or people just wander in, since these festivals are so public). Sometimes, though, social boundaries are made more trenchant through a de facto hierarchy of persons; for example, those who paid for the Tejanos festivals had places of honor, blacks and whites have been segregated in churches as aggressively as in other public places, women preachers and ordained ministers have been resisted in more than Reformed churches, the sharp line between hierarchy and laity is still very evident in Catholicism. In these cases of social prejudice, we must raise the question about how liturgy is truly of the people.

Third corollary: liturgy must always give expression to people's hopes and aspirations, pain and loss. This may be realized by the choice of readings, the prayers of intercession, extemporaneous testimony, or any number of other ritual elements. It is telling that almost half of the psalms are a lament genre which give voice to individual's or community's cries of pain and loss. It is equally telling that most of these laments, after remembering God's faithful and saving deeds on behalf of God's holy people, end with praise and express hope. In this way liturgy is real, encompassing and expressing the grace and sinfulness of our lives.

4. All Liturgy Changes according to Times and Contexts

Each of these case studies describes liturgical practice that grew organically out of previous practice in response to changed times and a different social context. For example, the praise houses, camp meetings, and circuit preachers of early-national Methodism all reflect the vast spaces and sparse population of westward expansion. The integration of the African tradition of ecstatic utterances, drum rhythms, and dance into mainline Protestant worship structures reflects the displacement of black slaves into an entirely different social situation. The liturgical movement of the late nineteenth and first half of the twentieth century, described so well by Michael Woods in the case study on rural Catholicism, is a reminder that liturgy renews and grows with pastoral need, historical and liturgical scholarship, and theological insight. Indeed, the very discipline of liturgy as a recognized branch of theology (unheard of before the liturgical movement) is witness to new times and contexts and a new and more comprehensive understanding of worship.

What is perhaps most telling about the liturgical movement is that, while it began as a Catholic phenomenon, it quickly was taken up by many Protestant congregations. The very first document promulgated by the bishops at the Roman Catholic Second Vatican Council (1962-65) was *Sacrosanctum Concilium* (the Constitution on the Sacred Liturgy; December 4, 1963) which reflects the fruits of 150 years of study and pastoral practice. Moreover, this document has not only served as a guiding light for Catholic liturgical renewal but for the renewal of much Protestant worship as well. When beloved Pope John XXIII opened up the Vatican windows and called for *aggiornamento* — fresh air to be let in — this symbolic gesture affected not only the Catholic Church but many other churches as well. This has ushered in an unprecedented spate of ecumenical endeavors: shared worship services, national and international dialogues, pulpit exchanges, shared sacraments, to name some. For perhaps the first time in over five centuries we are looking more to what we have in common than to what divides us Christians. Prayer and worship together have brought about healing and a new hope and passion for unity. To be sure, differences and polarities remain: intercommunion, ordination validity, infant or believer baptism, to name just three fractious issues. But for the first time in half a millennium we Christians are putting our passion for unity ahead of our penchant for polarities.

5. All Liturgy Unfolds as Rhythms

Liturgy is never static; it always reflects the dynamism of the divine and human spirits. The rhythms of liturgy include that between fixed texts and extemporaneous prayer; sound and silence; calendar and feasts; dialogue between the worshipers and God, between minister/preacher and worship, and among the worshipers themselves. Of all these, perhaps the most difficult is between fixed texts and extemporaneous prayer. One of the reforms of the Puritans, for example, was to eliminate ritual altogether and rely on Scripture alone, there seeking out meaning for life and doctrine for faith. Even Catholicism, with its two thousand-year history of fixed ritual, now allows for greater use of Scripture; more flexibility in prayers (for example, in the prayers of the faithful that conclude the Liturgy of the Word); and a more hospitable, warm, and welcoming atmosphere (for example, churches are no longer absolutely silent, the sign of peace has been introduced).

"Fixed texts" used to be an *anathema* for many Protestant denominations. Emergent churches tout "contemporary" and spontaneous services pitched more to the needs of the people. At the same time, some Baptists and house churches are adopting a lectionary practice of fixed readings, the Triduum liturgies are being introduced into evangelical congregations, and the Lord's Supper is becoming the usual Sunday celebration for many Protestant congregations. The natural rhythms of liturgy have the potential to be creative tensions challenging us to spiritual growth, or they can precipitate divisive polarities.

Perhaps the real problem here is not so much whether liturgy uses fixed texts and rituals, but whether these are used and done with the fullness the signs and symbols might invite. *Sacrosanctum Concilium* called for full, conscious, and active participation in the liturgy by all the people.[7] Subsequent pastoral liturgical catechesis has focused on the richness of symbols and gestures used during the liturgy. In other words, aspersion baptism with only a shell full of water is surely not so powerful a gesture as immersion (or submersion) using a large quantity of water. Perhaps the problem with fixed texts and ritual has to do less with the ritual actions and words than with how well we do and say them so their power is truly appropriated by congregants. Let me illustrate further. This commentary is being written while I am still basking in the glory and power of the Easter Triduum liturgies. An example from each of the three ritual actions illustrates my point about the power of ritual to engage and elicit passion.[8]

7. See nos. 14, 30, 48.

8. Holy Thursday, Good Friday, and the Easter Vigil are actually all one liturgy in Catholicism. To bring this home, there is a proper introductory rite only on Holy Thursday and a proper dismissal rite only at the conclusion of the Easter Vigil. Unfortunately, this unity is lost on many Catholics, especially if they do not participate in all the ritual actions.

Four-year-old Jillian was in line on Holy (Maundy) Thursday to have her feet washed in the ritual optionally prescribed for after the homily. When she was next, and close enough to see the ritual action of the person in line ahead of her, she was totally riveted on what was happening, her eyes fairly popping out of her head. No doubt her parents had washed her feet many times before, but never in church. When it was her turn, she jumped onto the chair and had her shoes kicked off before her mom could even kneel down beside her to help. She watched in silent and rapt awe as the water was poured and the towel caressed dry her little feet. Not a word was spoken, nor was one needed for this little girl to grasp that this was a holy act and Jesus himself was loving her through this humble act of service. Her four-year-old body wriggled with infectious joy.

A severely mentally and physically challenged woman hobbled unsteadily up the center aisle for the Good Friday procession during the veneration of the cross. When it was her turn, she seemed totally to forget the limitations her infirmities placed on her: with great but assiduous effort she knelt down and with all her body embraced the cross. With even greater effort she unsteadily stood up. As she turned from the cross her face had been transformed by a glow of absolute joy; she had embraced her Savior.

Three-year-old Aaron was lifted by his father into the baptismal pool at the Holy Saturday Easter Vigil. He was so small that even this shallow pool came up high on his chest. Yes, the water was deep. As an abundance of water was poured over his head and shoulders in the name of the Trinity, he laughed out loud in glee and beamed forth for the whole community the joy of new life that was pouring over him and within him. As he was lifted out of the pool and wrapped in a white garment, his gleaming face drew the community into a new fervor about their own baptism as they enthusiastically and warmly applauded their welcome of this new member.

Rituals done well — with beautiful and purposeful gestures, full and rich symbols, appropriate and good quality music, insightful and moving proclamation and preaching, and active and conscious participation by all present — are powerful, indeed, and effect what they signify. When rituals engage, they draw us into liminal experiences that elicit from us a response of wholehearted praise and thanksgiving, commitment and fidelity. Good ritual awakens our passions as we encounter God in ever new and unpredictable ways. We only need to surrender ourselves to the action.

6. All Liturgy Releases the Power of Consequences

Grace for too many of us has been an empty intellectual concept. All liturgy confers grace, but rather than some thing to possess, grace is descriptive of God's life within us and relationships to live. Liturgy deepens, first of all, our relationship with the divine Trinity, drawing us into their loving *perichoresis,* a divine dance of unity and new life.

Another set of relationships these case studies remind us of is that authentic liturgy always sends us forth to care for others. Liturgy has social consequences, and when we accept the responsibility of those consequences there is power in the community (the Spirit) to effect change not only in ourselves, but in our whole world.

The history of worship has evidenced a tension between care within the community limited to itself and an evangelical thrust. While evangelicalism popularly has been about gaining converts, its etymological root — the *Evangel,* the Gospel — suggests that the Great Commission to baptize and teach all nations (Matt. 28:19-20) cannot be separated from deep social concern. Liturgy reminds us it is not enough to baptize and teach; we must care for the whole person, help the least to become first and share equitably in the goods of the earth, witness to the unity and identity we share as the one Body of Christ. Without this kind of evangelical thrust — being signs in our world of the Good News of the Gospel — liturgy is empty and our worship is merely a "noisy gong or a clanging cymbal" (1 Cor. 13:1).

The most forceful power of liturgy and its consequences is transformation of ourselves into more perfect disciples who love as the Master loved. Liturgy makes tremendous demands on us. It shatters our solipsism and leaves us connected to one another and all creation in new and ever more life-giving ways. It makes us responsible for each other's well being.

7. All Liturgy Has a Discernable Style That Serves a Deeper Purpose

These historical glimpses into denominational case studies of worship all reveal that worship style wars have been around for a long, long time. They have caused schisms and hurt. They have splintered the one Body. We are working diligently to heal these divisions wrought by various polarities played out in many different games of tug of war. Perhaps one way to approach the inevitable conflicts over style is to admit just that: there will necessarily be different styles because there are different communities of people (and this even within the same congregations). The polarities occur when we stop at style and make that the end of our worship. Healing occurs when we come to understand that differing styles — ecstatic and spontaneous vs. fixed and ritualized; traditional music vs. contemporary music; French baroque cavernous edifices vs. plain praise house; quiet and reserved vs. exuberant and lively; hierarchical vs. in the round; etc. — must lead to the same deeper purpose: praise and thanksgiving of God, transformation of self and society, communities of generosity and compassion.

Authentic liturgy makes present the life, death, and resurrection of Jesus Christ. We are a paschal people — the Body of Christ called to die to self for the good of others so God can raise us all to new life. Clinging to what satisfies me, what I want, what I think worship should be clouds the whole community's vision of a new heavens and a new earth. Stylistic changes and challenges are good — they keep the community growing in their depth of liturgical prayer. But when stylistic preferences become divisive, then we no longer have a worshiping Body of Christ but a "noisy gong or a clanging cymbal" (1 Cor. 13:1).

Passions and Polarities of Good Liturgy

For too long we have tended to pit passions and polarities against each other in a liturgical tug of war. Some congregations judge the quality of their worship by the good feelings or good experiences they have at worship. Other congregations judge the quality of their worship by the quantity of social outreach. Neither in itself is adequate for authentic liturgy. Together they teach us that liturgy is about experiencing passionate relationships with God and others as well as being missioned to reflect in our daily living the Gospel challenge of Word and Table.

Liturgy's inevitable passions and polarities are evident in these case studies. They serve to ensure that liturgy grows with the ever changing insights and lives of worshipers. They serve to challenge our set ways that can ignore a need for organic change that adjusts worship for new social situations and differing contexts. Passions and polarities help us express new ideas about what liturgy is and how it is our work rendered unto God. Passions, however, are destructive when they make *us* the end of worship. Polarities are destructive when they become our own agendas for power and self-satisfaction, when they become subtle ways we change liturgy into that which entertains and pleases rather than that which brings us to self-

surrender before the goodness and majesty, transcendence and immanence of our divine Lover.

Liturgy is a privileged expression of our stance before God. It is cooperating with God to continue to establish the divine reign in this redeemed
world of ours. It is doing what we know best because we are created in the
divine image: opening ourselves to God's faithful presence, surrendering
to the divine will for the betterment of ourselves and our world, loving
God and others with passion that re-creates and renews all life. Liturgy
transforms us to make God's mark on the world — a cross that reaches to
the Divine and that stretches us out to embrace all humanity in justice and
peace.

The Psalms describe liturgy well: "Let everything that breathes praise
the LORD!" (Ps. 150:6) and "Happy are those who observe justice, who do
righteousness at all times" (Ps. 106:3). And to this, let the peoples say,
Amen!

About the Contributors

DOROTHY C. BASS is director of the Valparaiso Project on the Education and Formation of People in Faith at Valparaiso University in Valparaiso, Indiana. Among her publications is *For Life Abundant: Practical Theology, Theological Education, and Christian Ministry* (Eerdmans, 2008).

JAMES D. BRATT is professor of history at Calvin College in Grand Rapids, Michigan. Among his publications is *Gathered at the River: Grand Rapids, Michigan, and its People of Faith* (Eerdmans, 1993).

RUTH ALDEN DOAN is professor of history at Hollins University in Roanoke, Virginia. Among her publications is *The Miller Heresy, Millennialism, and American Culture* (Temple University Press, 1987).

PAUL HARVEY is professor of history at the University of Colorado at Colorado Springs. Among his publications is *Freedom's Coming: Religious Culture and the Shaping of the South from the Civil War through the Civil Rights Era* (University of North Carolina Press, 2005).

GEORGE M. MARSDEN is Francis A. McAnaney Professor of History Emeritus at the University of Notre Dame. Among his publications is *Jonathan Edwards: A Life* (Yale University Press, 2003).

TIMOTHY MATOVINA is professor of theology and the William and Anna Jean Cushwa Director of the Cushwa Center for the Study of American Catholicism at the University of Notre Dame. Among the many books he has written is *Guadalupe and Her Faithful: Latino Catholics in San Antonio, from Colonial Origins to the Present* (Johns Hopkins University Press, 2005).

HARRY S. STOUT is Jonathan Edwards Professor of American Religious History at Yale University. Among his publications is *The New England Soul: Preaching and Religious Culture in Colonial New England* (Oxford University Press, 1986).

LESLIE WOODCOCK TENTLER is professor of history at Catholic University of America in Washington, D.C. Among her publications is *Seasons of Grace: A History of the Catholic Archdiocese of Detroit* (Wayne State University Press, 1990).

MICHAEL WOODS, S.J., is assistant professor of liturgical and sacramental theology at the Pontifical Gregorian University in Rome. He is the author of *Cultivating Soil and Soul: Twentieth-Century Catholic Agrarians Embrace the Liturgical Movement* (Liturgical Press, 2010).

JOYCE ANN ZIMMERMAN, C.PP.S., is director of the Institute for Liturgical Ministry in Dayton, Ohio. Among her publications is *Liturgy and Hermeneutics* (Liturgical Press, 1999).